Are You Present in Your Body with Your Money?

Body-Based Money Relationship Basics
to Reclaim Your Financial Life

By Dana Stovern

To seekers of authentic money relationship
for a healthier financial life.

Somatic Money in Definition

The word somatic means body. When you co-mingle money with somatic you experience your money relationship through your body. How is your body connective with your money relationship? It's time to find out.

Author's Note

Identities of People in Money Stories. Throughout this work, I have judiciously drawn on examples from clients in my Somatic Money programs and workshops. To protect participants' privacy and ensure confidentiality, I have changed the names and identifying factors of the people appearing in money stories to protect their identities. Money stories are told for example purposes only, with the greatest clarity and accuracy, to the best of my memory, notes and knowledge.

Disclaimer. Any income claims shared by my students, friends or clients are understood to be true and accurate but are not verified in any way. Always do your due diligence and use your own judgment when making buying decisions and investments in your business and personal life. Concepts and strategies shared in this book, on my website and in any of my email communications from Dana Stovern, LLC, are ideas that have worked for members of our team, students, clients and friends. They are not specific financial advice for your personal life or business. Always use your own judgment and/or get the advice of specific professionals to find the right strategies for your personal finances and business. Dana Stovern is not a financial advisor, financial planner or certified accountant and does not give financial advice. Instead, this work is for receiving a greater experience and knowledge concerning the inner workings of your inter-personal money relationship. How you apply this work is up to you. Specific results are not guaranteed.

Table of Contents

Acknowledgments 11

Preface
About Healing the Cultural Financial Split 15

Your Introductory Reading Guide to Somatic Money
Somatic Money Hiding in Plain Sight 25

Part One: Setting the Stage

Chapter One: Conscious Financial Mythmaking
My Spontaneous Financial Intervention 39

Chapter Two: If It's Not About the Money, Then What's It About?
Initiating Your Somatic Money Map 53

Part Two: Somatic Money Practices

Chapter Three: Are You Present in Your Body with Your Money?
Presence as the Sacred Power in Your Financial Exchange Space 95

**Chapter Four: About Gentling Wild Mustangs
and Your Biology of Money**
*Unpack Your Somatic Money Triggers
to Reveal Your Authentic Money Relationship* 127

Chapter Five: Make Friends with the Elephant in Your Living Room
Vulnerability as the Heart of Heroine's Journey
with Your Money Relationship 167

Chapter Six: Clearing Your Way Out of the Weeds
Strategies for Cultivating Your Authentic Money Blueprint 207

Chapter Seven: Rearrange Your Somatic Money Furniture
Break Through Financial Compartmentalization
and Toxic Money Environments 229

Part Three: Excavating Your Financial Anthropology

Chapter Eight: Your Big Dig
The Financial Power of Voicing Your Money Stories 267

Chapter Nine: Money Languaging
What Are You Really Saying About Your Money? 305

Chapter Ten: Aligned Money Intent
Unmask Your Real Money Truth 323

Chapter Eleven: A New Money Paradigm
The Three Dimensional (3D) to Five Dimensional (5D)
Money Shift 333

Resources 338

Bibliography and Notes 346

Acknowledgments

This book and *The Magic of Somatic Money* platform that birthed it would not be possible without the people who encouraged and held presence with me through such a dynamic process.

First and foremost, deep thanks to my husband, Bob, for enduring the storms and celebrating the successes with me during the creation and development of this work. Your presence is a gift; your insight and humor unparalleled and your skills as a graphic and web artist are superb. Thanks for helping make the cover for *Are You Present in Your Body with Your Money* and *The Magic of Somatic Money* not only possible, but also look good.

At the outset, Rita Marsh at Davi Nikent's Center for Human Flourishing in Carbondale, Colorado sponsored the seed of my work and publicly believed in its potential, recognizing the spark of brilliance. Thank you for helping me bring the platform of Somatic Money and it's first book to life.

Thanks to the first clients who bravely listened to my story about the Spontaneous Financial Intervention (Chapter One) and were courageous enough to take our extracted tools, put them to work and create miracles in your own lives. You made me enough of a believer in Somatic Money's transformational value to continue delivering to others.

Thanks to Kathie Fingerson, Healers of the Valley in Grand Junction, Colorado; Conscious Business Connections in Fort Collins, Colorado; NAWBO in Sedona, Arizona; The WholeExpo in Durango, Colorado; Colorado Business Women's Luncheon in Aspen, Colorado; and all the others who took a risk and allowed me to speak with your groups about such a new concept. Your platforms gave me the opportunity to air these ideas for the first time.

Thanks to New Renaissance Bookshop in Portland, Oregon and For Heaven's Sake, metaphysical book, events and gift store in Denver, Colorado for regularly hosting my Somatic Money presentations as the work developed over the years. Working in your commercial spaces gave me the confidence that Somatic Money has wide appeal.

Thanks to my many clients who invested your time, money and energy in the concepts, practices and experiences of Somatic Money. We learned together, creating the raw data that ultimately became this book and *The Magic of Somatic Money*. We are the collective think tank. Your experiments and successes were beyond my wildest imagination and they created momentum. I am so happy and proud for you.

Thanks to Wendy Stine, Mary Alyce Cross, Gwendolyn Hill, Deirdre Karger, Jennifer Sanchez, Temani Aldine, Jamee Smith, Scott Dean, Jessica Mills, the Borman sisters and so many others for the hours and hours we spent on the phone combing over the vast and intricate landscape of Somatic Money. Our conversations brought this work to life in ways I never anticipated.

Thank you to my two business coaches, Michael Tertes of University of Superheroes, and Daniel Gutierrez, mindful awareness expert and corporate speaker. I know I was an eager and intense student, pushing limits. Your presence and encouragement helped me face my demons, bring me out of my closet and return to the world with revolutionary ideas to help others with their personal money relationship.

Thank you to the spontaneous mentorships of Linda Lightfoot and John Vandenberg. Linda, the synchronicity of our meeting and your basic consciousness and spiritual teachings during the times of 9/11 are still alive and found here in these pages. Although you are no longer with us on this side of the veil, your spirit, your teachings, your love endures.

Thank you, John, for sharing your life's work of The Wrap-Around Program and Open Table during conversations while our dogs ran and played together. The wisdom you gave helped me envision that the idea and practice of Somatic Money, once seeded, has the potential to become a global wave of peace work through the vehicle of money.

Thank you, Jennifer Jas, my editor, whose calm and consistent editing allowed me to see my writing through new frameworks. Your editing gifts made me a better writer. Your presence in witnessing these words gave me courage to voice and bring them to light.

Thank you, Alyssa Ohnmacht with Light of the Moon Book Publishing, for your book consulting prowess to help me deliver this book across the finish line. You punctuated endless tasks into a clean and finished product.

Thank you to my volunteer content readers who gave this information a spin around the block for the first time. Jill Austin, Anna Rude, Jill Warner, Jessica Mills, your insights for clarity, flow and understandability is exactly what I needed to see this work through fresh eyes.

Most of all, thank you to my Money Guides, and my Divine Financial Light Team. Your enduring energy, guidance and presence helped give me fortitude when I wanted to quit, love when I couldn't love myself, golden nuggets when I needed them the most to illuminate and connect the dots.

Preface

About Healing the Cultural Financial Split

I am frequently asked, "Dana, how did you start doing this Somatic Money (body-based money relationship) thing? Where did this come from? Who taught you?" In a nutshell, Somatic Money chose me after life wrangled my attention through deep trauma and loss. Even then, it took me awhile to decipher and tease Somatic Money out from behind the veil of cultural taboos where the cross-section of the financial community and the consciousness/spiritual community do not meet, but should. It's here where the obvious and profound answers of Somatic Money can be had, but are hushed and hidden, blocking many of us from our empowered financial answers in life.

This paradox of Somatic Money, the hidden obvious that challenges our cultural belief systems about money, makes it even more compelling and powerful. What could be so wild and weird as money relationship experienced through the body?! Who thinks of that? Yet, once you learn how the emotional logic of Somatic Money tools can give you leverage, it's like what so many of my audience members and clients say: "Why didn't I think of this?!" That's just it. We don't think of Somatic Money, body-based money relationship, because we're not trained to. The business/money community does not encourage us to look outside the box of linear, strategized, mental money, and the consciousness/spiritual/denominational communities do not encourage us to look beyond the box of faith-based money. We're especially not encouraged to look through either of these viewfinders in an integrated fashion connecting both of them in a body-based perspective. Yet, that is exactly where the next step of the money relationship landscape begins, uncurls and touches.

For me, it took a lot of loss, pain and falling through the compartmentalized cracks of our financial culture to finally notice the paradox of body-based money relationship. Through the angst of my maddeningly amazing journey, Somatic Money courted me, haunted me and finally hunted me down until I couldn't ignore what was staring me in the face: *that there is a powerful, interactive relation between the money thoughts in our minds that create the reactive emotional, energetic and physiological tide flowing through our bodies, that then re-informs our brains and causes us to act. Our bodies inform our money relationship!* ***And, when we become present in our core bodies with this Somatic Money dynamic, our money relationships improve.***

When I finally absorbed this clarity about the mental, emotional, energetic and physiological Somatic Money loop, along with effective presence work, it became the launchpad that has thoroughly engaged me and my attention since autumn of 2011. That's the turning point when I experienced my rock bottom alongside a spectacular Spontaneous Financial Intervention (as told in Chapter One). The proverbial surrender within breakdowns creates the catharsis of breakthroughs, and that's exactly what happened for me at the "Y" in my road. At the depth of my woundedness where nothing made sense in the middle of heart-rending loss, pain, grief, fear, fatigue and questions about faith, I had to surrender. That's when Somatic Money chose me. It initiated and made me an envoy as a likely and appropriate candidate, even though that wasn't apparent to me at the time. You could say in my greatest trial that my soul put together the heart math of two plus two and came up with Somatic Money as one of my most unexpected yet most needed answers.

Although I kept my intervention experience a secret at the time, telling only two trusted souls, within weeks, clients in my existing coaching practice began arriving on my doorstep with pressing financial issues. The new secret tools I'd just learned appeared to be universal and it was clearly important to share them. The intuitive life coaching foundation I'd developed since 2006 became a rich bed to cultivate and launch this idea of money relationship as experienced through the mind, body, spirit and emotion connection.

Through my comeback since 2011, I've diligently mapped, researched, channeled, intuited, tested and collected data, stories, concepts, practices and a brilliant landscape with my clients, consultees and audience members. Everything I've learned was re-plugged into the work to learn more, pushing the limits to see how far we could go. This is the brilliance of Somatic Money. Once you learn the basics, it's a very intuitive and continual self-teaching system that can be applied to any micro or macro financial event, partnership or agreement. It is an incredible personal financial tool for insight, growth, healing and effectiveness.

Even though this perpetually exciting and inspirational engine of Somatic Money is such an honor to work with, delivering illumination into our lives, it's not the only reason I'm here with body-based money relationship. The carrot of this work is obvious: providing illuminating money relationship solutions where they may not have existed before. It is a great and strikingly beautiful rabbit that I absolutely love to pull out of the hat. Yet, I am also aware of the shadow, the stick, standing perpetually beside me, reminding me that the knowledge I share came at a high personal price. To truly make these teachings worthwhile is to seed the idea of systemic change in revealing how, through centuries of cultural financial assumption and conditioning, we are creating the financial environment that so many of us suffer and fail in. And to learn, with a few consciousness changes, how to improve our financial landscapes personally and collectively.

Once I experienced my financial intervention and initiation, arriving into the gifted illumination of Somatic Money, I began to see how and why I fell through the cracks in our system. I began to see how others are suffering and also falling through the cracks. What did I see? A cultural financial polarity that we are all playing out daily in our collective psyche. This polarity is creating a chasm-like split in our culture and inside ourselves. Miraculously, within this split is the very solution of awakening to a greater and higher center of an integrated financial whole. We just need a nudge to see what is staring us in the face.

Let me paint the picture with these broad and somewhat exaggerated brush strokes demarking the two polarities and then the integration. This information comes from my initial perceptions after my awakening, and then subsequent data collection and research since 2011. During this description and throughout this book I regularly refer to the terms IQ and EQ in relationship with money. The term IQ, intelligence quotient, is meant here as a representation of the logical, left-brained, reasoning processes with money. (The IQ test was developed by French researchers Alfred Binet and Theodore Simon in 1904 for The French Ministry of Education.) The term EQ, emotional quotient, is meant here as a representation of emotional intelligence, empathy, heart connection and intuition with money. (The concept of emotional intelligence, EQ, was developed by John Mayer and Peter Salovey in the early 1990's, as personified in Daniel Goleman's 1995 book *Emotional Intelligence*.)

One of these polarity positions is held by the traditional business community, or what I call the home of Masculine Money IQ (left brain), where money is a mental intelligence process that is primarily professional, rational, logical, logistical and analytical. This is the school of thought where applying budgets, financial strategies and financial planning to personal money management is the financially responsible thing to do for success. It's a place where t's are crossed, i's are dotted and the facts about money and finance are the focus with little attention to emotion, intuition, or openings of higher consciousness. Being irrational in this space is taboo. In other words, it's not a place to express emotion or a gut instinct or intuition or anything out of the ordinary. (Yes, I'm exaggerating in black and white to make my point.)

The mirroring polarity position is held by the communities of non-religious consciousness and spirituality, therapy services and the religious community. It's what I call the home of Feminine Money EQ (right brain), where emotional intelligence, intuition, knowingness, belief in deeper ideological philosophies, self-development, healing and faith practices are the softer-sided state of being and process. This is a place where boundaries are blurred, people are hugged and held, and communications of heart-opening with inner and higher consciousness are shared. It's the place in the consciousness community where tools of abundance, manifestation, Law of Attraction, visioning and mantras are commonly taught and supported when it comes to living a better life with money. Yet frequently, this space has little to no room for matters of direct conversations about personal finance. Instead, in many of these places, money is seen as "a necessary evil" that is impure and gets in the way of a purity of faith and connection to God. (Yes, I'm still exaggerating in black and white to make my point.)

Here's how the cultural physics of this polarized mirror plays out from the collective to the individual. In the financial community, the logic of Masculine Money IQ (left brain) is deified, and money is a god, while the Feminine Money EQ (right brain) is demonized. In the soft-sided EQ community, the expression of emotional intelligence (right brain) is deified, along with God and faith, while the logistical IQ of money is often ignored or even demonized. And the result? We are reflecting this collective left-brain, right-brain cultural split with money right into our personal lives, where we create an internal magnetic push-pull of financial friction that triggers uncertainty through the body. This confusing split of our cultural left-brain money IQ and right-brain money EQ teeters back and forth between whether what we think about our money or what we feel about our money is more important – when *both* should be equal. *Both Money IQ and Money EQ are needed for instrumental mental and emotional processing and integration through the body as we experience the money events and issues of our lives to create our best money relationships.* Instead, many of us get stuck with our money issues through the silence of our compartmentalized lack of internal process, unmoving, frozen in this unconscious fracture, that usually results in greater triggers with fear, scarcity, argument and even war within ourselves and one another. This compartmentalized and fractured model is not creating financial peace. It's creating financial unrest, isolation and pain for so many people who are financially hurting in their private lives.

Let me frame it to you like this: *Where do we go, what do we do, who do we talk to when we have deep emotional, mental and personal questions, especially in our bodies, about our financial lives?* Since the financial culture discourages displays of irrationality and emotion about money, we're not truly encouraged to open up with our emotional intelligence in our spaces of budget building or financial strategizing. Since our EQ-based communities largely discourage direct conversations about money and money relationship, we're not able to be open here either. To boot, our culture carries epidemic levels of discouraging personal money talk because "it's not right or polite" and it's easier and seems better to practice cultural codes of financial silence. So, I ask again. *Where are the safe and sacred spaces in our culture where we have the emotional support to openly talk about and safely explore the deeper meanings, emotions, vulnerabilities and irrationalities of our money relationship, even financial line items, that we're experiencing in our bodies?*

Bridging this gap is about defining the distance between the financial professionals who are helping us with our money lives, but are not able to have authentic EQ money conversations with us – and the EQ professionals in our lives, our spiritual and consciousness practitioners, therapists and church leaders who don't know how to have private money conversations with us. It's this distance between the two points of cultural polarity where we are missing essential aspects of our money relationship that ultimately can create a healthy and whole money relationship picture.

What is the change I am talking about here? A shift in ideology to create movement into *cultural financial integration, blending Money IQ and Money EQ for healthier money relationships.* The first ideological shift is to recognize that contrary to popular opinion, money is not only a logical and rational means of exchange in our lives. Money is also one of the most personal, intimate, vulnerable, emotional and sometimes highly charged vehicles of expression that we experience through our entire body. This ideological shift is the integrated action of Masculine Money recognizing, embracing and honoring Feminine Money. The second ideological shift is to recognize that money is not evil or dirty. Money, held and used in constructive intent, is our friend, our accomplice in healing, our financial advocate. It's time to make peace with it. This is the integrated action of Feminine Money recognizing, embracing and honoring Masculine Money. The third ideological shift is to recognize that this integration is not only happening through left and right-brain mental function, it's occurring through emotional and physiological space in the body – integrated body-based money relationship.

As one example, when shifts like this occur, it means that people who are terrified of budgets (Masculine Money IQ) and avoid them begin to find the emotional support (Feminine Money EQ) to work out their money demons, so they may be present (Body-Based Money) with the financial line items in their monthly game plan. They are able to breathe, ground and center in their bodies with the empowerment of claimed money relationship. This is Feminine Money providing emotional support in the body to work with Masculine Money logistics. As another example, when shifts like this occur, it means that when you're working with an EQ Law of Attraction tool and can't get the financial leverage you're seeking, you could have a direct and specific money conversation with a money-based practitioner, therapist or EQ-based financial advisor. The resulting conversation can be about how the line items in your financial picture are triggering in your body to learn what it means and how to heal for better financial functionality. This opens the door to options for direct healing work with the numbers in your financial spreadsheets, creating an inside-out money shift. These direct EQ actions with money replace the typical dance-of-avoidance around critical financial topics using vague spiritual terms. This is about the specificity of a Masculine Money conversation being allowed in the Feminine Money consciousness space. Both examples show how our Masculine Money and Feminine Money may work *with* one another in integrated action instead of against one another in polarization.

The good news is that we're already bridging this polarized gap with a framework of amazing professionals who are already somewhat aware of this issue and are providing tools, options, ideas and resources. These are money therapists, money coaches and money practitioners who can have a soft-sided EQ money conversation with you about your specific financial logistics. These are accountants and financial advisors who can walk you through money strategy *and also* hold space with you as you're open about your EQ money life. Also, financial support groups within communities and online are emerging, where you may visit with others about your personal money journey in life. And of course, there are breakthrough books and works, including Lynne Twist's *The Soul of Money*, Bari Tessler's *The Art of Money*, Kessel and Sherman's *The Money and Spirit Workshop*, Suze Orman's work connecting money psychology with life issues, Esther and Jerry Hicks' *Law of Attraction*, Dr. Joe Vitale and Dr. Hew Len's *Zero Limits*, and more.

Given all this, now, more than ever, we are ripe and ready for the paradigm-busting concepts of Somatic Money, body-based money relationship, to help us continue to bridge the polarized financial gaps in our culture and inside ourselves. Somatic Money is not a "different" anomaly "out there" existing as a radical idea on its own. We've already paved the way to Somatic Money, and it's sitting smack dab in the middle of our landscapes, ready for powerful and healthy implementation. That's why *Are You Present in Your Body with Your Money?* is the breakthrough book delivering the revolutionary idea that being present in your body with your money relationship can positively transform your money life, connecting your Money IQ with your Money EQ through your body in a healthy financial dance.

The tools, practices, concepts and stories featured here provide essential information to connect the dots in the landscape between the polarized financial gaps in our culture. Whether you know it or not, or believe it or not, your body is already and always informing your financial life. Your body is money relationship smart. Your Somatic Money is already choosing you! Wouldn't you like to be present at the helm of your ship to know what that is and how to work with your Somatic Money self?

So, whether you're looking for a financial breakthrough, a money relationship solution, debt dissolution, a shift in your perceptual money filters or overall money relationship improvement, you will find insights here to illuminate the corners of your money questions. Ultimately, I believe money relationship is one of the deepest, most complex, beautiful and most cathartic modalities we have available to us for our greatest healing and growth.

My hope is that you find the nuggets of truth about your relationship with money to give you hope, peace and ultimately the type of self-defined financial money success you want to create in your life.

Dana Stovern
Founder and Coach
The Magic of Somatic Money
February 2021

Your Introductory Reading Guide to Somatic Money

Somatic Money Hiding in Plain Sight

When the numbers in our money picture don't stick the way we want them to, even with a solid budget or a money management plan, something else is amiss in our money relationship. We might believe we can solve our financial messes through the house of our Masculine Money IQ (logic, strategy, rationale), and sometimes we drive ourselves crazy trying to find those answers in our logical mind. But the truth is that this truncated view of money, in the Somatic Money model, is only about 25 to 30 percent of the money picture! We can also drive ourselves just as crazy while we wish, hope, pray, psychologically wrestle or work our faith-based Feminine Money EQ relationship principles into submission while trying to get the numbers to work. In the Somatic Money model, this is also about 25 to 30 percent of our money picture, which leaves anywhere from 40 to 50 percent of the money relationship picture up for grabs.

No wonder we're driving ourselves bananas trying to solve our money issues with only portions of our financial tools, our financial picture. Where is the rest of our Somatic Money picture hiding? It's hiding in plain sight where few have trained us to look. I regularly refer to this dynamic as our missing money links.

Our cultural Money Story hiding these obvious missing money links is a lot like the Wyoming Easter Egg Hunt I experienced as an eight-year-old when our family traveled from northeastern Colorado up into the wild lands of Wyoming. My father paired his business trip with our family holiday so we could all spend time together. I remember him completing safety-engineering inspections on job sites for his insurance company that had offices based out of Denver, Colorado.

Because I was a kid, I didn't care nor understand about safety inspections. I was more concerned about the Easter Egg Hunt. How was the Easter Bunny going to find us in Wyoming? Where were the painted eggs? How was this going to work out? Somehow, the Easter Bunny did find us in Wyoming (Mom secretly packed Easter goodies in the trunk) and we had an Easter Egg Hunt in the Wyoming countryside outside our hotel room.

It's funny what you remember from childhood – freeze-framing certain details of life while forgetting others. As an adult, I wonder less about the colored eggs and more about the venomous rattlesnakes in the Wyoming scrub brush and prairie grass. Yet, my child self was adamantly focused on one detail of that egg hunt. This detail had to do with finding all the eggs except the last one. During the end of this egg hunt, my dad kept saying to my brother and me, "The Easter Bunny left one more egg. Where is it?" The game went on and on. We searched under and over every rock, crevice and bush, but for the life of us, we could not find that one last egg. It was a mystery. Finally, we gave up.

We flopped down on the only large carpet-sized swath of the hotel's green grass beside our baskets, giddily tired from the hunt. Then, my dad casually walked over to an unfinished hotel fence where an uncapped chain link fence pipe stuck out of the ground, and he plucked a cheery, bright-colored egg off the top of the pipe. This egg was balancing in plain view during the entire hunt.

I still remember the shocked feeling that coursed through my childhood body, and the questions that repeatedly played in my mind, "How could we not find an egg that was sitting in plain sight? How did we not see it?" My world cracked open a little bit in that moment, much like an egg. The memory of this experience occasionally revisits me in adulthood, and I wonder about the anomaly of searching diligently for something you want to find, not see it, while it's completely obvious, coming out of hiding from the envelope of the magical blind spot.

Somatic Money is the Wyoming Easter Egg hiding in plain view with available answers to what's been missing in your money relationship. For you to see your egg, for you to reconnect your missing money links, for you to have any kind of significant change and improvement in your money life, you're going to need to stop scrounging around and scraping yourself in the Wyoming scrub bush. It's time for you to entertain new frameworks, new perceptual viewfinders, and try new things with your money relationship that might seem different, radical, taboo or uncomfortable. We might even have to sacrifice a few traditional financial sacred cows to get where we need to go. We're going to break with convention so that you may find your Wyoming Easter Egg sitting on top of your financial fence pipe, right in plain view.

To prepare you for locating your hidden money eggs in our body-based money relationship journey through this book, and to prepare you for reconnecting your missing money links, I'd like to introduce you to a few basic ideas.

What's Your Somatic Money Type?

First and foremost, Somatic Money is for those who are curious about it. I work with people from the poverty line to millionaire status, and what each person has in common is a sense of curiosity about how Somatic Money may constructively impact their money life.

As for defining personal money types, this is where savers, spenders and other types of money personalities are usually depicted in other money books. I have a different scale of money personalities to share with you, and this scale runs a continuum from the most logical and least intuitive people in our culture to the least logical and most intuitive people. These money types are very similar to the research reflected in Elaine Aron's *The Highly Sensitive Person* about the non-sensitive to sensitive scale of people in our culture.

How does this work? In working with several thousand people, I have found that individuals either lean logical thinking with their money or lean intuitive feeling with their money, with a vast majority living in the middle – a sort of cultural financial soup of these two polarities – displaying a mix of these two characteristics.

On one end of the continuum, the logical money thinkers are our "spreadsheet, budget, line item, clockwork, put-money-in-a-box" people. These are the folks who don't know that emotion or intuition could come into play with money. (What financial gut instinct?) Our money system is primarily geared toward this money type, unless the numbers aren't sticking the way they should or personal relationships are on the fritz. That's where Somatic Money can lend insights for retuning and rebalancing, as well as open a new way to look through the money viewfinder.

On the other end of the continuum, the intuitive money feelers are our "floaty, trust-in-the-Universe, the-money-always-magically-shows-up-just-at-the-last-minute, fly-by-the-seat-of-their-pants, no-budget-in-sight (what budget?)" people. Our money system is not really geared for this money type, yet somehow, these individuals magically find ways to make their money work out. These are the people who land on my doorstep, with frustrated attitudes about our money system, ready for breakthroughs because they just can't live by the seat of their pants anymore. If you're this person, Somatic Money is tailor-made for you. If you really want a change with your money life, it's time for you to float in on your angel wings and sit your tushy down next to me in your safe and sacred space. It's okay.

It's time to talk money, numbers, in a way you understand so that you may learn the principles of Somatic Money to augment and improve your money life.

And the majority of people in the middle? You are the ones who fiddle with your numbers, and that's helped, but it's not exactly worked out for you the way you need. Or you're working with faith-based money practices, and that's helped, but it also has not fully helped you. Or you're intermittently working with both your numbers and faith-based money work. Sometimes, something begins to click, but all the pieces of the puzzle are not coming together yet. If you find yourself having tried one, the other or both, and you're tired of burnout on the hamster wheel, saying things like, "I can't do this anymore! I have to have a breakthrough! Something better has to work for me!" – then Somatic Money is utterly for you. Why? You are showing me that you're seeking and trying solutions beyond the limited scope of the tools you've been given. That you're ripe and ready to plug in what you've already learned with a handful of new tools! Yay! You're here!

And me? As the author of this book and Somatic Money founder, what money type am I in this context? I'm a lot like my mentor, Linda, who was one of those rare people working by day as an accountant, taking satisfied happiness in lining up all her numbers and then unfurling at night as a joyous closet psychic. Once I healed the trauma of money and numbers in my body, I learned that I absolutely love numbers too – calculating them, working their puzzles, letting numbers tell me their Money Story. I am also an intuitive, facilitating my abilities through my work with clients as a powerfully gifted empath, channel, shaman and healer. I combine these two elements, the numbers and the intuitive, to help people heal with their numbers through their bodies. Truth be told, in my core work, I've named the rare combination of all my gifts as Angelic Financial Shamanism, the ability to teach people how to heal the cellular coding of their money through their bodies to improve their financial lives. Yes, our money relationship runs that deep.

Take Your Time and Trust in the Process.

I can still hear her voice ringing in my ears, "In time and on time, Dana! In time and on time!" That is one of the primary basics that Linda, my mentor, used to say to me. She'd say, "Dana, we are ready when we're ready and don't push the process."

Linda's belief about the process is one of the primary cornerstones of my work that I now share with you. The basics that I'm giving you in this book might seem simple and surface-level, but don't let appearances fool you. As you work with these tools, sometimes what seems to be basic might affect you deeply; therefore, it's important to give your body and psyche time to sort things out in your unconscious space. *Sometimes sorting things out might take an hour, a day, a week, a month, a year.* I have some people take to this method like a fish to water and process through the work rapidly. I also have some people who slog their way through, set the work down and months or a year later reconnect and experience total ignition. *So, please give your body and psyche the time that you truly need to allow the work to unfold in the way that is right for you.* I cannot emphasize this enough. Remember, as you work the Somatic Money process, if it feels like you're trying and "nothing is happening," rest assured that it is. Deep down, where you can't see it, changes are happening. You're going to need to take your time and trust the process.

On that note, newcomers arriving to Somatic Money who expect specific financial results right away are usually disappointed. Remember, as you apply a qualitative process to a quantitative system, the path and quantifiable results might not always be clear. Yet, when individuals check their expectations at the door, lean into the practices and processes, and allow a natural emergence to occur, they frequently experience the Universe delivering outcomes beyond what they first imagined. The concepts and practices I provide here are powerful through the use of process. If you are looking for specific money results from Somatic Money, more than likely, you will not receive them. In this disappointment, while looking the other way, you will probably miss the positive aspects occurring for you. If you are willing to live, like physicist, Fred Alan Wolf says in the movie *What the Bleep Do We Know*, more in "the mystery" of this process instead of "the know," then you will more than likely enjoy the surprising fruits of your labors.

Cross-Training to Strengthen Unknown Money Muscles.

Regularly, when my husband, Bob, and I are hiking in the Colorado mountains, he'll encourage us to turn 180 degrees and look at what is behind us, no matter how spectacular the views might be in front of us. This 180-degree turn has amplified our outdoor experiences, giving us fields of mountain flowers, wildlife and other views that we might have missed. During our time together with Somatic Money, I'm regularly going to ask you to look at your money relationship with fresh eyes, and maybe even look 180 degrees behind you, to reframe your money life in ways you hadn't imagined.

We'll also regularly pair Masculine Money IQ tools with Feminine Money EQ tools creating a cross-training synthesis in this work. These unexpected pairings will help you shift out of financial compartmentalization which creates toxicity and adversarial stances with your money and harness them into greater synergy. It's time to train your mind, your spirit and your body to work *with* one another in your money relationship. Here are a few examples of what this new landscape might look like for you: Conscious breathing during a money exchange, calling in your favorite higher power to be with you at a specific financial line item in your spreadsheet, or embracing your triggered emotion during a financial money thought. I'm going to ask you to regularly strengthen your Masculine Money IQ muscles across the divide with your Feminine Money EQ muscles in your body. These elements are rarely identified in our lives and even more rarely paired to work together, especially with money relationship.

At first, these ideas, practices and tools might seem awkward or strange for you, but eventually, you'll find that they will help rewire your brain, your psyche and your body into new pathways that will open up new options in your life.

The Empowerment of Identity Inclusion within Money Management Books.

Most personal money management books are written in neutral tones and lean towards the Masculine Money identity. We're not going to do that. We're going to break cultural financial protocol and create greater diversity inclusion in the context of our money conversations. That means I will write from a foundation of neutral tones and then lean towards Feminine Money identity with masculine inclusion, greater racial diversity inclusion and inclusion of gender identity (She/He/They) and sexual orientation with LGBTQ.

Please note, if I offend anyone in my first attempts to create greater inclusion in a money book, I apologize. I totally understand that we're all more than labels. Each one of us is a very uniquely designed human being who embodies our own blend of experiences, ages, hereditary lineages, body types and sizes and colors, ethnic and cultural tones. Our expressions of life run the continuum of a very lively and colorful bandwidth.

My hope is that you find inspiration from these pages to claim your very precious and unique identity of who you are with your money relationship. Why? I have found, through my work in Somatic Money, that identity matters for value and empowerment with your personal money relationship. Which means it's *very* important that you be able to locate your unique blend of personal identity in your own money management practices. In that spirit, feel free to mark this text as you read for your best matched personal identity — I'll give you a few reminder prompts along the way. You'll see at junctures in the following chapters where I entertain identity choices. Use that spark to identify your best Somatic Money match. This is your Best Quest — name it!

Emotion and Energy as a Financial Tracking Device.

If you accidentally put your hand on your stove burner when it's on, would you ignore the feeling of your skin burning? No. You'd yank your hand off the burner to keep from getting burned even more!

Here's the funny thing we've done with money and feeling in our culture. We've unhooked our feeling sensation from our bodies about the money events in our lives and labeled them as "bad." I've heard it, and I'm sure you've heard it too, that "mixing money with emotion is bad!" We should only and always make our money decisions from sound logic. Well, I call bullshit. This is an outdated and warped belief system that is not true. Let's clarify. Making a financial decision in the heat of *emotionalism* is not a good idea, but don't banish emotion entirely from your money relationship framework.

Your emotion, your energy and your feeling sensations about your money, especially through your body, are some of your most important tracking devices, telling you what you need to know about your money life. Furthermore, even though money is physical (the Masculine Money aspect), it is also energy (the Feminine Money aspect). The energy of money is as powerful and maybe even more so than the physical nature of money. Don't you want to know how the energy and emotion of your money are affecting your money life? Then it's time to stop unplugging and stop insulating yourself from your Feminine Money EQ feeling sensations. Stop letting your hand burn on the stove! It's time to tune in to how you are feeling about any given money exchange, line item, partnership or agreement in your life. This is you, beginning to develop your Feminine Money EQ tracking ability, while you collect your emotional and energetic data about your money life so you may make better financial decisions.

Money Patterning from the Inside Out.

Our cultural popular belief system practices a concept that life happens to us and at us from the outside in, especially with money. We're taught how we are disconnected from the seemingly random financial events of our lives without having an ability to be in control. The more I've studied the body, mind and spirit connections of money in my life and my clients' lives, the more I believe that this is not true. We're actually creating our money lives from the inside out through a deeply woven tapestry of patterns that is connective with a greater Universal whole. Money is not separate from you, happening to you and at you from the outside world. You are part of an integrated whole where you are able to create from your inside out. We have the power to be aware and connected to our internal money patterning where we may create better choices to improve our financial lives. The tools and concepts in this book are geared toward awakening and positioning you into the center of your money relationship patterning so that you may consciously co-create your money life into new patterns that better serve you.

Select Your Money Relationship Journal Now.

It goes without saying, but I'm going to say it anyway: be sure to select your designated money relationship journal now. You'll need it to track and notate your process. My hope is that you're already noticing, even in this Introduction, that you'll be working diverse and new landscape with your money relationship. Regularly, I'll be asking you to review information that you begin developing at the front of this book for steps later in this book. Your journal will bear witness to your evolution, stories, thoughts, emotions and personal illuminated moments, becoming a trusted friend and confidant.

Laugh as You Work the Cyclical Somatic Money Process.

Do you know why I like to laugh when I'm working in the trenches with clients on particularly sticky money relationship issues? I like to laugh because it breaks up the old, heavy, dark patterning of money. I'm not laughing to make fun of my clients. I'm laughing with them to lighten up what might be entrenched money anchors keeping them from their authentic money empowerment.

Yes, we've all been taught that money is *serious*. It's heavy. It's survival. It's no joking matter. Don't mess around with it. But I don't buy that this attitude is helping us. This is the old, heavy, fear-based energy that's nonverbally put the fear of God in people about their money lives — quite literally. This fear is triggering more of the heavy fear-scarcity cycles. It's time to shatter these cycles.

You may begin this process by finding ways to lighten your emotional load with money, and one of those ways is to notice what's humorous about your money life. You might notice aspects of financial comic releif popping up. Take time out to have a "Funny ha-ha" moment with your money, even if it's tinged with dark humor. Laugh at the money shadow that scares you. Laugh and begin to break it up.

What you'll notice as you lighten things up, working your Somatic Money steps, is that old and heavy layers will peel back from your money life. In unison, you'll find yourself in gentle cycles, moving in the upward direction. You'll read this book in linear fashion from the front cover to the back cover and receive gems from the first few layers of your play and practice. Then, as you're ready, return to the front of the book and lightly repeat. Treat the informative works here like a connective circle spiraling up. Every time you move around the Somatic Money wheel, you'll glean new insights and new developments from inside your money relationship. The process is interconnective, so the more you learn and experience, the more your money relationship will rise in the spiral of your life to a more balanced, holistic, less emotionally charged, more peacefully understood space.

Remember, newly defining and co-creating your personal Somatic Money relationship with the Universe is up to you! So, I will say what no one has probably said to you about your money life:

Have fun with your money creation!
Laugh!

Part One:
Setting the Stage

Money As More Than a Budget
or a Financial Strategy

CHAPTER ONE

Conscious Financial Mythmaking

My Spontaneous Financial Intervention

The fortune of the Magic of Somatic Money began from a place of deep misfortune. It's a place I hope never to journey through again. Yet, this most unfortunate place birthed experiences, concepts and tools that are the gifts I've successfully financially used, and so have many others.

It all began when I lost my son.

It was the spring of 2010 in Durango, Colorado, and I was six months pregnant with my son. This was a miracle pregnancy near my fortieth birthday, and it was likely our only chance to have a family. My husband, Bob, and I were living in a cabin overlooking the rapturous Animas River Valley in Colorado.

But then, six months into the pregnancy, early one morning, I experienced a rapid onset of severe pre-eclampsia, spiking my blood pressure at 275 over 175, creating seizures and threatening my life and our son's life. I remember little from that morning. Only momentary memory clips return to me. First, carefully stepping down the stairs while speaking in garbled language to Bob. Then, trying to sit upright in our truck while Bob rushed me to the hospital. There was the fog around me while I sat in a hospital chair before it all went blank. That's when I seized again and the doctors and hospital staff rushed me into an emergency C-section and delivered our son.

I was sustained on life support for thirty-six hours while initially the hospital team tried to resuscitate Kenyan, our son. His heart did not hold the precious beats of life, and the Flight For Life helicopter en route from Denver to pick him up was sent back. When I miraculously returned to consciousness from my near-death, I found myself alive, yet facing my son's funeral. Our chance at having a family was gone.

In the wake of the shock, the numbness, the loss, I thought things could not become worse, but my life continued to unravel for the next eighteen months. By autumn of 2011, I was physically broken, emotionally broken, financially broken and my faith was broken. My intuitive life coaching practice was limping along, and I was barely making it.

I reached rock bottom in a financial "rolling-dimes-for-gas" broken state, feeling emotionally and financially desperate, well beyond the desperation I'd experienced in my twenties. By 2011, I felt that for all the progress I'd made in my life, I was still living in a terrible *Groundhog Day*, where I was always dumped back at the horrible beginning of a financial pattern that haunted my life, always playing out with the ground financially falling out from beneath me.

Also, during this time of 2010-11, I did not know the loss of my son was a symptom of my traumatic family history that had not been revealed or diagnosed. For the purpose of this story, succinctly put, I eventually learned that I am an incest survivor, with that history traveling from my maternal grandfather, to my mother, to me. I am an adult child survivor of a dry-drunk home and a mother with undiagnosed and untreated trauma, and likely a narcissistic personality disorder. My father is the enabler and my brother, the unawakened bystander. By 2010, I'd already lived through a toxic and emotionally abusive marriage, which I left in divorce; a toxic job, from which I resigned; and the toxic hold of my home of origin, from which I was finally able to release myself, understanding partial family truths. I was living as independent a life as I could claim during the unfoldings of my psychic awakening that had begun nearly ten years earlier in 2001.

By 2011, I had pieced together much of my personal trauma and healing puzzle, but not all of it. Losing Kenyan, my son, became an ignition of sorts, sparking me to sort through the rest of my personal truths. I rumbled around at the rock bottom of life with the helpless sense that I could not escape the traumatic cycles of my life. The grief of losing my son amplified my fear, disorientation and distraught state.

What I did not know is that my life was about ready to crack wide open, revealing great revelations that would lead to the fantastical recovery I have made today. That's when my close friend Mary Alyce, in the autumn of 2011, invited me to stay at the hotel where she was attending a water yoga class at the hot springs in Pagosa Springs, Colorado. It was a heaven of a place, these hot springs buried at the base of the San Juan Mountain Range. Although she didn't know my distress level, she intuitively knew I was having difficulties, and it prompted her to extend the invitation. I almost didn't go, even though I had said yes. During the drive from Durango to Pagosa Springs, I experienced a panic attack and nearly turned around. Yet, I knew I had to get there.

I arrived at the hotel, slung my bag over my shoulder, retrieved a key from the front desk and located the room. Even though Mary Alyce was at water yoga class, her skill at creating sacred space was incredibly present. When I opened the door, I found she'd transformed the room from a regular hotel room into a spacious sanctuary with unlit candles, crystals, aromatherapy and figurines sprinkled throughout. It felt wonderful.

I relaxed for the first time in a long time. My entire body and psyche surrendered as I collapsed on one of the beds and released a deluge of tears. I'd been fighting to stay alive and be okay ever since the loss of my son. I had fought to keep it together in front of our community. I had fought to keep my business going to contribute cash flow to our household income. I had fought to keep a steady face so my husband wouldn't worry about me. I had fought to recover quickly, and just months after the loss, I strapped on my backpack to prove I was healthy and alive: Bob and I trail-climbed to eleven thousand feet above Silverton, Colorado, in the mountains of the Mary's Lake region. I had been fighting for normalcy because I was just so terrified of what would happen if I stopped.

Some part of me knew the good fight wasn't working, and the moment I stepped into the hotel room I finally let down my guard and surrendered. After my cry, in the quiet of that room, I felt a glowing light growing stronger at the side of my bed. Gradually, this glowing light became so strong, I felt it vibrate through my body. What I did not know then is that I was at the threshold of a massive turning point in my life. This turning-point experience is what I now call my Spontaneous Financial Intervention.

When I intuitively tuned in to the glow near my bedside, as it was now flowing through my body, I was astonished to find how strong it was, how powerful the light felt. Even though I'm intuitive and familiar with vibrational energies, I'd never experienced a light so strong, deep or profound. This light filled the room with a deluge of love, depth, patience, forgiveness and mercy – effusively filling me, glowing throughout my body with an effervescence of calm healing. As I experienced this interaction, I tuned in to a sense of, "Who is this working with me?" What returned through me was the powerful energy and knowledge that Sananda was present in me. (Sananda is the consciousness community's name for Jesus.) Let me be very clear that though my traditional roots include being brought up in the Methodist church, I do not consider myself religious, especially because of the church's defensive and shunning stances against female psychics and healers. To me, Sananda's appearance had a much more shamanic and healing context than a religious one. Also, it bears mentioning that even though Sananda appeared to me as White Jesus, he appears to all of us in the form that we most identify with including as Black Jesus, Latino Jesus or the Jesus that works for you. I encourage you to see the Jesus that appears for you as you read about this experience.

The humorous thread in the moment of this monumental experience is that my human self freaked out, thinking, "Oh, my God, Jesus is here! You're 'talking' with Jesus. Girl, remember everything he tells you!" Even though I later found that my memory databanks were wiped clean of that conversation, the energy imprint of the experience will stay with me forever.

Through my healing visit with Sananda, my spirits lifted for the first time in a long time. During this spontaneous healing, I felt the energies rearranged within me in a good way. When he eventually left and his lighted-glow dissipated, I became aware of the physicality of the four walls, floor and ceiling of the hotel room again. I felt more whole, full and calm than ever before.

That's where I paused, knowing I was alone and wondering what had just happened. Breathing deeply, I thought that was it, the end of the experience. But as I recovered, I heard a voice.

A male voice, resonating in the air around me, described a single instructive phrase. He said, "Call in your Money Guide now!" The sound boomed profoundly in the empty space. It was such a surprising and extraordinary command after my profound deep healing in the light.

I froze for a moment. Shocked. First, I registered how clearly and loudly I heard this voice and wondered who was saying the words. My next reaction was nearly comical, wondering, "I have a what?! A Money Guide?!" Even with all my intuitive training and work, I'd never heard of Money Guides. My last reaction was incredulity that I had permission to do such a thing. It sounded sacrilegious, irreverent to allow money and such a profound energy of the light event to commingle. I thought, "I'm allowed to do that?! To call her/him in?" I heard the voice again, repeating the same command: "Call in your Money Guide NOW!"

I decided to follow the instructions and call in my Money Guide.

I gathered myself upright on the bed, crossed my legs in lotus position, placed my hands with palms upraised on my knees. I breathed in and out several times, and with all the will in my body, I boomed out the request, "I call in my Money Guide now!"

I waited and waited, and my Money Guide did not appear. No flicker. Not a speck. Nothing.

This baffled me because I was used to having different vibrational energies appear when I called and asked for help. So, when my Money Guide did not materialize energetically, I was disappointed, thinking, "Wow, if I was instructed to call in my Money Guide and she/he didn't appear, I must really be financially screwed. No wonder I'm having such a hard time with my money." It made sense. How could I do well financially if I didn't have support and guidance?

Yet, when I boomed the request, instead of my Money Guide appearing, it seemed to trigger something else. There was a shift in the air with movement through me that powerfully opened energies to my right side. Rapidly, I was connected into three consecutive deep vision journeys. These journeys felt like conscious dreams, where I experienced a Charles-Dickens-Christmas-Carol version of experiences. I witnessed lifetime after lifetime of my past root lives over past centuries. I was shown the horrific conditions under which I'd practiced my intuitive gifts. There was torture with threat of death. There was little to no pay for voluminous work. There were hostage and even enslavement situations. These experiential pictures rode as energy waves through my body, showing me the horrendous realities of my past lifetime Money Stories that I felt, in the present moment, in very real ways. With the deep threads of my vulnerable Money Story on full display to me, I began to intuitively understand why I was having such financial trouble in this lifetime. The intrinsic connection of drama, trauma and low vibrational finances was alive and pulsing down the centuries to my life in the here and now.

Keep in mind that even as I had this experience, I was well aware of the taboo in the consciousness and spiritual community of mixing healing, shamanic or energy work with money. It crossed all kinds of barriers. Culturally, money is seen as "dirty" and "impure" in many areas of the consciousness and Christian community. To keep consciousness, spirituality, faith and healing practices pure, with as pure a connection as possible to Source, God or the Universe, it's considered important to leave the (dirty) money out of it. Yet, what I found later, and what you'll read about here in this book, is that the internal money mechanism lives in the second chakra. This second chakra in the body (just below the navel) is where the partnership, agreement and exchange of money-making, making love, procreation and sex are all mixed together as natural aspects of life. Partnership, exchange and agreements, the very nature of second chakra energies, and the spirit of money, are connected to the Divine, the Universe, God or Source. To disconnect these precious connections is to keep yourself and others trapped in old financial hostage situations. To cultivate the connection in healthy ways is to create redemption. This Spontaneous Financial Intervention that I was experiencing in this hotel room was my first lesson in connecting these dots without shame or guilt.

As my journey unfolded in that hotel room, my past lifetimes laid out before me, I finally understood why, in this lifetime, I constantly felt like I was "in the fight of my life" and "practicing under the threat of death" while running my intuitive life coaching business – because energetically, I was. Those codes and programs from many lifetimes ago were still alive in the here and now in my body. In some respects, the more I practiced my gift professionally, the more I triggered those financially life-threatening, hostage and enslavement situations.

It was clear to me that try as I might, through all my conscious efforts, I had not been able to financially break through in this lifetime because I was shackled to low vibrational money energies in other lifetimes: energies that mimicked and even felt connected to the underlying emotional codes of the home I grew up in. The coding in my DNA from past lives was imprinted and playing out in real-life scenarios in my present lifetime.

No wonder money left me in sheer panic with little to no breath. No wonder I felt completely unarmed and helpless when it came to my finances. No wonder my money did not show up when I needed it the most. No wonder I felt someone was going to kill me financially. No wonder I regularly felt like I was in cycles of anxiety and emotional collapse with my money. Those money agreements from past lives were literally living and breathing through my body in this lifetime.

As I saw myself drowning in the weight of this abyss so clearly, something began to shift inside. When one of the Guiding Angels in these shaman journeys energetically asked me, "Do you want to change this?" I said, "Yes! Absolutely!" but I still wondered if that was possible because the old story felt so entrenched in my body – so real.

Gradually, in journey after journey that evening, floating above each scene like an out-of-body experience, I was repeatedly asked if I wanted to change the code, the story, from those lifetimes. When I felt my body and psyche shift in the affirmative of "yes" for change, new and dynamic energy steps arrived, completing the transformation. I learned how to rewrite the old lifetime agreements into new lines. *I felt the change as the information in my body shifted.*

All told, I took three journeys that evening, out and back, and each time I returned, the Spirit World of Archangels and Ascended Masters encouraged me to call in my Money Guide. Each time I hailed my Money Guide she/he did not appear. After the third journey, I was tired, yet a calm quietness settled in me. Once again, the voice requested that I hail my Money Guide. This time, instead of the request being met with silence and then a swirling jerk into another journey, the energies ruffled in the air around me in a new way. Wonderfully. Unfolding in magic, the energy of my Money Guide materialized in midair in front of me. He was so calm and so clear.

He energetically showed himself as a middle-aged accountant from the 1940s, dressed in a complete three-piece tweed suit with vest, tie and round spectacles. He pulled a pocket watch from his breast pocket, revealing the chain across his front. There was also a sense of handwritten ledgers and an abacus hanging in the air around him. Even though he held the air of a meticulous accountant, I felt great love and patience flowing through him to me. It was the first time in my life I felt the combination of love in numbers and money and me. Without a shadow of a doubt, I knew this being was, and still is, my Money Guide. His first appearance to me was perfect. Calm. Grounded. Methodical. Kind. And gentle about the numbers and the money.

It was the first time in my life I did not feel intimidated by my money, my numbers. I felt like I was forgiven for any inadequacies I might have in relationship with finances, because, for the first time, I had an ally. This was someone who understood me before I had to understand my money. What a relief.

From that day forward, this Spontaneous Financial Intervention ignited my daily presence practices of communing with my Money Guide for money tools and messages of empowerment and healing. Eventually, I attracted and gathered other members of my Divine Financial Team who also help me with money, money relationship and numbers. *What has gradually emerged is how deeply the experience and vibration of the numbers and money resonate as a profound reflection in our lives, especially through our bodies.* So, it was through this radical, unexplainable experience, born out of deep trauma, that my money relationship was illuminated to me in a brand-new way.

The Birth of the Magic of Somatic Money.

What did I do after this magnificent event? First, I told the story that evening to my trusted friend Mary Alyce in the beautifully lit night pools at the Pagosa Hot Springs. We sifted through the contents of my experience as we floated through the waters under starlit skies, surrounded by the incredible San Juan Mountains next to the river by the same name. The next day, I returned home and shared this amazing experience with my husband, Bob. Even though this event was a huge relief in the abyss of the grief and pain in my life, I told absolutely no one else. I did not want to dilute how powerful and special my experience was. I also knew the event was radical, and rationally, I wondered if I was crazy.

For a while, even though the journey was positive, I did not want to reveal to anyone else this connection I was experiencing between the intuitive and energy work with money and money relationship. A looming feeling that my experience was not acceptable in the consciousness and spiritual community hung in the air around me. I was having difficulty understanding how something so positive and so powerful that was starting to unfold into constructive steps in my life, could seem so unacceptable in my community. I did not know how to publicly progress.

Gradually, day by day, week by week and month by month, my money relationship and finances began to improve. This shift, along with my daily presence practice with my Money Guide and a continued cultivation of tools lifted my emotional state. All of these contributed to further improvements in my financial situation. My anxiety alleviated, my attitude and faith improved, and I became interested in how emotion, energy and the body worked together with money relationship. In a more relaxed state, I watched my monthly income bump within thirty days, first by $100 and then by several hundred more. That was substantial as, at the time, my income was at the poverty line. That gave me the confidence to keep the connection and practices alive.

Then it happened. Several months after my Spontaneous Financial Intervention, I visited a friend's home, and partway through our visit, I felt the guidance come through for me to tell her my crazy Money Story. My Spirit Team seemed to think that my story would help her. I resisted. After several intuitive promptings from the Universe, I felt the nudge turn into a cosmic elbow jab and then a gentle shove: "You need to tell her your story!"

So, I segued from our visit and mentioned to her that my Spirit Team wanted me to share something. I asked her if she wanted to hear a crazy Money Story. Her eyebrows shot up and she nodded, so I veered into describing what had happened just months before. As I told her the story, her eyes opened wider and wider until she wasn't blinking. She didn't interrupt once. She took it all in like a sponge.

I completed my story and stopped talking, asking her if she understood what I was telling her. I mentioned that my money relationship had improved despite my concern that I sounded crazy and that this paradigm did not fit with the practices in the consciousness community. She blew by my concerns about craziness or community taboo and spilled out a story of her own, telling me this was exactly the help she needed to solve her near-financial crisis. A crisis she had not divulged earlier.

I learned that she was the oldest of three siblings responsible for her father's care, as he was in the early stages of Alzheimer's and living in an assisted living facility an hour away from her. The problem was that her father's estate was tied up out of state with an old girlfriend, and my friend was in a financial crisis trying to cut through the red tape so she could pay the assisted living facility for her father's expenses. She was living daily with the drama of her siblings, the drama of the old girlfriend, the other state's red tape, and regular threats from the assisted living facility that they were going to kick her dad out if she didn't pay. My friend was scared she was going to have to take her father into her own home and provide for his care – while she and her husband were already raising their own kids. There was no physical or financial room in the home to be able to add her father to their household.

She was at her wit's end and did not know what to do about the situation. She was in the depths of intensely praying for help. Somehow, I showed up on her doorstep with my story. Was this an answer to her prayers? She thought so and she soaked up every thread of my tale.

After I finished my story and she finished hers, we rapidly put together what was at stake and what needed to be done. We understood there were elements in my experience that were holding precious and powerful tools for us to extract. We identified the tools from my story so she could clearly focus on the internal money relationship work she needed to do with herself to untangle the financial noodle-bowl of her situation. I realized that if money relationship is truly held as code in our bodies, then it was important to provide those tools to her.

Once we were finished, we said our goodbyes and I drove away, hoping that my story and the identified tools would help. Three days later, I received a phone call. My friend was breathless on the other end of the line as she told me what happened after our discussion. After I had left that afternoon, she locked herself in her office for twenty-four hours straight and practiced the energy work with the tools we'd identified. Even though her kids and husband came knocking, she asked them to take care of themselves for the evening so she could go into deep internal space. She did all the work we identified, and then she released it.

Two days later, she received a cordial phone call from her father's assisted living facility. The facility representative told her, "Don't worry about your dad. The board met, and we've decided that we'll help you handle the estate and the other state's red tape in this situation. If we need you to testify in court on behalf of your dad, we'll fly you there on our dime." Shortly after, her dad's girlfriend, who had been so testy, relaxed and began working with my friend instead of against her. The siblings in the situation toned it down a notch and her dad stayed in the assisted living facility. All the finances worked out, and peace was kept in her home without the pressure of having to house and care for her father.

When I hung up the phone from this phone call, I sat in stunned silence. I could not explain what was happening. First, I experienced the positive results I was having with my money relationship after my unexplainable financial intervention. And now, we applied extracted money tools from that experience to someone else's money crisis, which created a dynamic, unexpected and rapid solution. This defied logic, but it was real. In those quiet moments, the phone still in my hand, I realized my crazy secret wasn't supposed to stay a secret. I was sitting in the middle of positive and constructive universal information that needed to be shared with others. I was getting the green light from the Universe to break through taboo and pair holistic, energy and consciousness practices with money and money relationship.

In those moments, my first platform with money work was born as Money Magic. Nearly immediately, clients who appeared in my practice in random and synchronistic ways came to me for one reason, but we found out why they were really there – to learn about my new form of money practice to help them with their money relationship issues. Instinctively, I used every interaction to teach and coach, but also to collect data, track patterns, research, document and learn. This investment in research and development has literally paid off for my clients and me.

In my own life, I rapidly moved out of my own terrible financial state into greater stability and later into a thriving practice where I regularly travel around the country, speaking about Somatic Money. I improved and recovered my credit score, negotiated for and purchased my first vehicle on my own. My husband and I paid off our debt and we became homeowners for the first time. Somatic Money has given me a foundation to continue to improve my financial life and the relationship I have with it.

In my business, my clients, through focusing on the emotional and energetic dynamics of their money relationship through their bodies at the financial exchange space are achieving greater peace and a higher quality of life with their money relationship. Some of the unplanned financial results we've seen include glass ceiling breakthroughs for 20 to 30 percent annual bumps in income, successful negotiations at work for better benefits and working conditions. Some of my clients have successfully shifted their careers with this work, and sometimes done the shift across country. Some of my clients have healed and grown from being barely financially functional to regularly and competently working with their money. Several have rescued themselves from the edge of bankruptcy with this work. And I have single moms who use this process to get off the poverty line, into their careers as well as open the can of whoop-ass on claiming child support. Some of my clients have successfully used this work in multi-million dollar real estate deals or with growing their high end interior design clientele or with growing their retail business. Some of my clients are experiencing debt reduction or complete debt dissolution. Clients have successfully applied this work to the sale and purchase of their homes, while others have untangled a lifetime of complex money issues and put them to rest. Offshoots of the work also include better relationships with family and even attracting better partnerships. These are just a few examples. My own financial journey and sharing this work with clients for their improved financial journey is so rewarding!

What we've all learned in regularly working with Somatic Money is that it applies to micro-cosmic money work and macro-cosmic money work – from a twenty-dollar purchase to a million-dollar deal. Somatic Money also crosses the socio-economic spectrum, providing support to help financially hurting individuals move into a more greatly supported and stable financial position in their lives; while it also gives insight into helping already successful individuals take their money life to a whole new level. And Somatic Money crosses the compartmentalized gap between the consciousness community and the business world, showing that money relationship works best when the masculine and feminine of these worlds are integrated.

CHAPTER TWO

If It's Not About the Money, Then What's It About?

*Your Financial Heroine's Journey
and Initiating Your Somatic Money Map*

How often do we hear the phrase from successful money people, money gurus, who say: "It's not about the money!" Then they go on to fuzzily explain the mysteries of how, if you hold yourself just right, tweak your left ear, twitch your right knee, and do just the right thing mixed with a little luck, you can be a multimillionaire just like them. I heard it often enough that I began to respond with eye-rolls, coughs and under-the-breath expletives.

For the longest time, I wanted just one of these persons to give me something tangible in the form of, "Since it's not about the money, *this* is what it's about." Then, one day, in the trenches of data results from Somatic Money, it gradually occurred to me that I was surrounded by one solid, non-money answer after another. What I felt through my bones on that day was, "Oh, my God, it's true. They're right. It's not about the money!"

At the risk of sounding like an ear-tugging, knee-twitching money commentator, I concur. It isn't all about the money. And yet, that is exactly what our cultural money conditioning has booby-trapped us into doing and thinking. Daily, we are trying to put Band-Aids on our money issues with varying litanies of, "If I only had more money… then…" or "If I could only strategize in certain ways with my money… then…" We are constantly looking to "the money" as the solution that will be able to give us the fruition to the dream. This cycle has us chasing our tails between our money dreams and our money nightmares (or difficulties) in a closed loop circuit. Insanity!

Here's the key: The place where we create our money issues, solve them and create our money dreams is different from the place where we calculate and financially strategize our ability to do so. The first is our soft-sided emotional intelligence with money, our Feminine Money EQ, while the second is our Masculine Money IQ, our logistical brain-based money logic. What we're culturally conditioned to do is to try and create, solve, dream, calculate and strategize all of our money lives in our Masculine Money IQ room. That means we've overloaded our Money IQ with too many tasks, some of which it's not skilled at handling. Now is the time to divvy up the workload and share some of those tasks with our Money EQ department.

Let me show you what I mean about these two different money rooms. We're going to walk through our standard cultural Money Story with the example of debt. This scenario could also apply to glass-ceiling breakthroughs, solving the noodle bowl of money issues, or creating money dreams. Here we go with the debt picture. Please humor me with a little latitude in this process.

Let's say you have debt, and you, being a responsible person, decide to visit with your financial advisor (Masculine Money IQ professional) about this debt. You know what your financial advisor is going to say? Probably something along the lines of, "Best to pay off your debt before you invest; otherwise, you're just splitting your resources. The interest rate on your debt is higher than the percentage of growth you could receive from any of your investments. Why don't you sit down and work with your budget?" Yes, your financial advisor is giving you sound Money IQ advice and this works for some of you. Yet, for the rest, you just got booby-trapped because while the Money IQ side of your financial equation was addressed, your Money EQ side was not. You just received a Money IQ room answer to what seemed like a Money IQ room question, and you were pawned off to a different Money IQ room. But what if your debt was created from another source? A source that exists in your Money EQ room? This means that the Money EQ room containing the potential source of the problem and its potential solution has not been addressed. What if your debt is a symptom of what's living in your Money EQ room? What if your financial advisor's advice gives you a twinge of queasiness in the middle of your stomach?

If anything, you are diligent, so you visit your budgetologist or your debt manager (Masculine Money EQ professionals), showing them how much income you have flowing in and what your expense load looks like, and you ask, "How best to strategize to get this debt paid off?" That is exactly what your budgetologist or your debt manager is going to help you do – provide a Money IQ answer to a Money IQ question. But you're still booby-trapped because your Money EQ sensations are not being addressed. Sure, you're logically aware that this is good money advice and could work, but in the back of your head, you begin to wonder, *Can I really pay off this debt?* It's looking like a squeeze. You don't know. Just about now, the Money EQ room inside of you begins to moan, to sigh, to wheeze loud enough for you to notice and your stomach rolls with more pronounced nausea. Your throat tightens. So, you decide, just to be sure, you're going to visit with your accountant.

You trot off to your accountant (Masculine Money IQ professional) and show them the plan your budgetologist or debt manager has given you, on the advice of your financial advisor. Your accountant reviews your Money IQ plan in the Money IQ room and says, "This looks good, and I can give you a picture of how this is going to affect your tax picture. Would you like that?" You agree and receive this Money IQ information, telling yourself this is important, while at the same time, having an even greater sinking feeling coming from your Money EQ room through your belly that something is miss-ing. Your throat feels scratchy and your mouth goes dry. Still boo-by-trapped! You just received another Money IQ answer in that same Money IQ room from another Money IQ professional, but where is the Money EQ relief?! You know these Money IQ professionals are very good at what they do; they all mean well and paying off your debt with this plan could work because it makes perfect logical sense. But now you know something is wrong because the sound of wailing is coming from your Money EQ room, that other internal place. Your stomach has plummeted to around your knees, you're coughing and you're itching the side of your neck. You are feeling your feels now, even if you don't want to notice them, and the sound from that other room resembles B.B. King singing the powerful blues, unplugged.

Do you dare open the door to that room where the B.B. King of your money blues is wailing with his electric guitar? Do you do what you've always done and tamp it down? Shut it out? Ignore it? Be a good soldier? Suck it up? And do the rational money plan from the Money IQ room just like the professionals say you should?

On the other hand, you know you've been here before with this same Money EQ scenario. You've repeated this debt scene a num-ber of times and you're tired of it. You're wondering if the system is rigged. You ask yourself, "Why can't I just get out of debt? Why can't I just have the money to make it all work out?"

While you're thinking your thoughts and feeling your feels, B.B. King gets a little louder in your Money EQ room. It's beginning to sound more and more like Maurice Sendak's *Where the Wild Things Are*. Do you dare let the weird, wild, strange things you're feeling in your body tumble out of that room? Do you dare look at them? Something cracks in you a little bit, just enough for you to say, "Screw it. I have to open that door! What's in there haunting me and my money relationship?!"

You put your hand on the doorknob. You take a deep breath. You turn the knob and swing open the door to your Money EQ room, and all nature of things tumble out. Your yellow submarine binky from when you were six months old pops out like a cork. The crumpled car fender from the minor accident you had at sixteen that created a fight between you and your dad; it slings up to the ceiling. The silent oath you kept with your mom about family secrets oozes out like slime. The shame you felt about not quite being good enough to win the college scholarship floats out on phantom dust. Bikes with stories, firecrackers with fear and excitement, moldy towels from beach time emerge in swaths. You name it: the random bits and pieces of your story that you thought you'd left behind hover in the foyer of your life, connected to all the unresolved emotion that goes with them. You observe a heap of emotional baggage and clutter that's all connected to your money life, stuffed in your Money EQ room. And B.B.? Oh, he's still sitting there in the midst of the debris, playing away on his guitar with a devilish grin on his face, a glint in his eye and an air about him that says you are finally getting to the good stuff, the root, the heart of your money blues. And Max (or Maxine or a They name) from *Where the Wild Things Are?* He, or your gender and ethnic appropriate power child, is proudly stomping around in her/his/their jammies and golden crown, waving her/his/their staff, leading a few monsters around.

You realize this scenario is not the wheelhouse of your financial advisor, budgetologist, debt manager or accountant. They can't tell you how to financially strategize this one. You're in the wilds now. You're beyond the numbers of your money life, yet you can feel all this stuff pushing up against the budget plan to pay off your debt. ***You're beginning to realize that you're in the emotional and energetic landscape of your body that tells the numbers in your spreadsheets what to do.*** Yet, you're not sure how it all connects and how you can make it work.

About now, B.B. King finishes a song, lumbers to his feet and plants his guitar in its stand. It's time for his set break because he's been playing for a long while. He did his job. He got your attention. As he leaves, he hands the mic over to Dorothy, saying, "You can take it from here." She graciously accepts the mic with a little dip. She's wearing her iconic blue dress and ruby red slippers (or red sneakers), her hair is neatly braided, and Toto is in the basket on her arm. Of course, she's surrounded by the Lion, the Tin Man, and the Scarecrow, with the Wicked Witch of the West lurking in the wings. (If Dorothy doesn't work for you, please insert your favorite epic superheroine (she) or hero (he) or they (they) character and story here. It could be the feminine version of *Captain Marvel* or the Dora Milaje and T'Challa of Wakanda in *Black Panther* or *America Chavez* in Marvel comics or Hermione and Harry in *Harry Potter* or Princess Leia and Luke in *Star Wars*.)

Congratulations! You did the hard part. You opened the door. There's no going back now. It's time for your Heroine's Journey or Hero's Journey, with money in your Money EQ room.

* * *

Hmm. I know, right?! Heroine's/Hero's Journey paired with money? You don't hear about that every day. Yet, that's exactly what each of us uniquely experiences in our money relationships, to greater and lesser degrees. Why is your money relationship, especially when initiated from the space of your Money EQ room, your Heroine's or Hero's Journey? Two reasons. First, anyone who has done this work knows that this path, while totally worth it, is not for the faint of heart. There's a reason it's not necessarily easy to lay your hands on finding and accomplishing your money answers. The wherewithal and illumination to do so is buried in your mind-body-spirit connection of the potentially challenging emotional and energetic places that you probably haven't thought to look. Until you view this landscape, there is a strong likelihood that you're hanging in limbo with the hostage state of your self-made financial picture, as those hidden emotions and energies in your body vibrationally impact the qualitative vibration of the numbers in your bank account.

In the Heroine's/Hero's Journey process of choosing to go to the spaces where you haven't looked and somatically reclaim your money life out of the shadows, you naturally become your own heroine or hero. Remember, you already created this opportunity. You've already set up what you came here to consciously learn about your money life. So, you already have in you all the makings of being your own heroine/hero to heal and reclaim it. You're already wearing your ruby red slippers or your bright red sneakers to click your heels and return home. We just need to show you how.

Second, this path of your financial Heroine's/Hero's Journey naturally unfolds in a way that loosely resembles the patterning of the Hero's Journey as named by Joseph Campbell in the mythology of his anthropological work *The Hero with a Thousand Faces*. This first cross-training concept I'm introducing is that the mythical Heroine's/Hero's Journey of your life crosses into your money relationship. Why wouldn't it? Frankly, money relationship is one of the richest, most alchemical places of cultivating your Heroine's/Hero's Journey — it's tailor-made for it! Initially, Joseph Campbell named Hero's Journey patterning in the male gender, believing that journeying was only for men. I disagree with Campbell and believe journey work is available for all genders. So, I was delighted to discover that Maureen Murdock answered with her book *The Heroine's Journey, Woman's Quest for Wholeness*, showing the feminine gender-specific journey for women. I'll be referring to both journey types throughout the book and we'll outline journey specifics to Somatic Money in Chapter Five.

As I use the feminine and masculine Heroine's/Hero's Journey model in this book, I recognize that the patterning in these models might not fully reflect and resonate for non-binary gender and/or sexual orientation modeling of my LGBTQ readers. I encourage you to define your best journey modeling by internet-navigating "Hero's Journey for LGBTQ." Also, given that Campbell and Murdock are Caucasian authors modeling the Heroine and Hero's Journey models, I encourage all of you to locate the tales of myth from your ethnically rich tribes that best reflect your current journey work for you.

That said, I hope you're beginning to see a greater landscape of how money is not about the money at all. By the time we complete this chapter, I'll outline the basic scope of the Somatic Money map so you may see the tools and aspects you have at hand to adeptly work with your financial Heroine's/Hero's Journey. Before we return to joining up with the gangs of *Wizard of Oz, Black Panther, America Chavez, Star Wars, Harry Potter, Captain Marvel* and the like, I want to ease you in the back door of this landscape. There's going to be plenty of gentle and worthwhile Band-Aid ripping in the near future, so let's begin with a few toes in the pool, shall we?

The "How Much?" Rabbit Habit.

We constantly ask ourselves one question about our money that bypasses our Money EQ room and puts us in the closed-loop circuit of our Money IQ room, quite possibly creating more nagging doubts. This natural question of "How much?" always comes up about our money life, but if we ask it too often, it collects like a bunch of bunnies hopping out of control. Too much of the "How much?" rabbit habit puts us in the closed-loop circuit based on numbers, by numbers, for numbers.

How do we release ourselves from the bright shiny object of money, taking the heat off your Money IQ room to that place where it's not about the money? To create the shift, it's time to ask a new question adjacent to the "How much" question. The new question sounds like: ***"How do I feel in my body with this amount of money? Or this money event? Or this money issue?"*** It's a question that shifts us away from the mentally driven quantitative viewpoints with our money and asks us to slow down, breathe and notice how our body is responding with the qualitative question of how we feel about this financial thing. This opens the door to the qualitative aspects of our money lives. Stepping into the experience of this viewpoint creates breathability and malleability of the thoughts and emotions metabolizing through our money lives, so that we may begin to create better options for ourselves.

With this movement out of financial tunnel vision and into a greater landscape of experiential financial feeling, it's time to explore the continuum of the Somatic Money map for our financial Heroine's/Hero's Journey. Let's unfold a few geographical topo maps.

Where's Waldo? And the Initial Somatic Money Map to Your Heroine's/Hero's Journey.

I love Waldo as a metaphor for finding our money answers. Yet, for the intent of embracing greater gender and diversity identity here, I would like to give Waldo a feminine version of his name and varying skin tones. I can't do that without infringing on the brand of Waldo. However, there is nothing stopping you from giving Waldo your own gender identity-correct name, LGBTQ designation and skin tone version that works for you.

That said, we all want to find our Waldo, the answer to our money dilemmas, but for many of us, Waldo is hiding in a sea of stuff. Sometimes, in everyone else's stuff. Some days, it is not easy to locate that bright red-and-white-striped shirt of her/his in the swamp gas of our money maps. If we even have a money map at all. Which brings me to my first question: Do you have a money map?

More often than not, when I initially talk with people, I find most folks are poking around in the dark trying to figure out their money life. Beyond the systematic, "Have a budget and a financial plan," there is no real game plan to understand your full dynamic relationship with money. Although these two Money IQ elements of our money picture are important, they are not everything. What else is there?

Remember the funny bunny question I pointed out a little earlier? Well, moving beyond the "How much?" question of your budget and financial plan into the, "How am I in relationship with my money?" question opens the door to mapping your more expanded version of your money relationship picture. To explore this expanded continuum of your financial Heroine's/Hero's Journey, you'll need a broader map. Where do we find such a map to help you locate your Waldo? I've been working on it for a while.

Early in this work, I learned that intuitively poking around in the dark with clients was a disservice to all involved parties. I decided that we need landscapes; we need maps. Thus, began my first data collection to see where my clients were, what they had, what they needed, where they wanted to go and what we were intuitively guided and told. These tactile basics served me well, giving me a rudder, especially when my powerful empathic channeling and intuitive gifts kicked in. I knew then that the *Where's Waldo* map was nearby. Documenting this new terrain and learning how to locate ourselves in this terrain became paramount.

After deeply visiting with hundreds of people in thousands of conversations about their money relationships, from both practical and intuitive perspectives, the common ground that we all share in financial somatic patterning eventually rose to the surface as a map. This step-by-step process, collecting data piece after data piece, with individual after individual, is how I turned what looked like an ocean into a methodical map of creeks and rivers with stepping stones and bridges to navigate into one doable step after another. This process gifted me with helping to identify my clients' strong suits, blind spots, weak spots and courses of action for development and solution. Whereas once I used to weave all over this unknown map, I now know where we are in the map because I've covered the landscape thousands of times. In this process, you could say I've finally found the patterning of the Heroine's/Hero's Journey in our money map. I've finally found our Waldo.

Now it's your turn to step inside your initial Somatic Money mapping process. Come with me as I walk you through the initial conversation of our Somatic Money Visit. This conversation is the general schematic of Somatic Money from one polarized end of the continuum to the other, with a connective backbone running between them. We will find out what you already have, what you're good at and what you need for improvement. It's time to find your Waldo.

What's Your Compelling Money Issue? Your Journey Quest.

Pssst. Hey you! Yes, you. Over here! I want to let you in on a little secret. That money issue or money question that is rattling around inside of you? You know that one that's been driving you crazy? Yeah. That one. Guess what? It's not about the money. Nope. That issue, that question you've been asking yourself, has more to do with your financial Heroine's/Hero's Journey than calculating a numbers answer. That's why it's driving you crazy because the place where you're looking for the Money IQ answer, it's not there. Nope. Waldo is in a completely different spot.

You know, we need to talk about this, but you don't like visiting about your money life with anyone else very often, or at all. So, I get how courageous it is for you to even consider having this type of conversation with me, a total stranger. I mean, money conversations are vulnerable because they're about the intimate financial experiences we have inside our partnerships, agreements and exchanges. It doesn't get any more private and personal than that! For you to have this conversation with me takes big courage, so thank you for being here.

When it comes to my first conversation with potential clients in a Somatic Money Visit, I always begin with a warmup in how we know one another, where you live, what you do. Then, I guide the conversation into deeper money relationship space. I want to find out where you are in your Somatic Money map and how I may help. That leads us to the big question. "Now that we're here and visiting, *what is your compelling money issue that you'd like to visit about?*" Although this is a specific question, there are no right or wrong answers. No judgment. As I listen to the answers that you and others might give me, I not only compassionately observe the elements that are happening in your lives, I closely monitor how you frame your answers. The latter tells me as much and more about your money life and how you are financially creating.

I encourage you here, as you continue to read this passage, to move from being a passive bystander to one who is involved in this conversation. I'd like you to join in the process. This is a good spot in the book *for you to identify your own compelling money issue that you'd like to work with.* Imagine me asking you to tell me about what you're financially working on. Here are a few examples to kick start your process. It could be about:

- How you're trying to collect your courage to ask your boss for a raise but continue to hedge around the issue.

- How you're confused about what to do with several recurring debts that never seem to go away.

- How you're trying to clean up your money space and can't ever quite get to it.

- How you're not able to get a handle on your finances no matter how many money books you read.

- How you need to have better financial boundaries with your kids, but you don't know how to start.

- How you wish you could close a big business deal, but it's always just out of reach or around the corner.

- How you never seem to be able to get customer service people, financial people, fellow business colleagues to listen to you, no matter how much you're in their face.

These examples are direct money issues that might help you see your own, or even open more complex issues. Whatever it is, focus on your compelling money issue and imagine your conversation that describes it. What does it sound and feel like? Perhaps record it, write it down or take mental note of what you'd say to me. If it would help, maybe give your descriptive answer to a trusted professional or friend. What you are doing is beginning to lay the tracks of collecting your data for excavation inside your money relationship. This is how you use your compelling money question or issue to become the catalyst for your financial Heroine's/Hero's Journey.

As I listen to you share about your inner money life through the viewfinder of your compelling money issue, I begin to track your Somatic Money markers. I want to know which way you are leaning in your Somatic Money landscape. As you go through the following list of initial Somatic Money markers with your compelling money issue, please begin to track how you are leaning. As you describe your compelling financial issue, are you:

- Leaning toward **Masculine Money IQ** elements in the description? Is your answer filled with how you keep trying to manage your money with budgets and tabulation, but you can't get your money picture under control? How something seems off, but you can't quite put your finger on it? How you'd like more support, but you're not sure how to get it? How, perhaps, you don't feel fully financially protected?

- Leaning toward **Feminine Money EQ** elements in the description? Is your answer filled with how you feel about the money events and situations in your life? Perhaps how you keep trying to have better money consciousness, but the financial flow is just not where you need it to be in your life? How you're always working with different money mantras or Law of Attraction devices or manifestations with vision boards, but you can't quite get the financial traction you'd like to see? How you keep scrambling with money, but you don't fully have the emotional resilience to catch up and truly take care of yourself?

- Leaning into certain repeating **Money Language**? In your description to me, do you find yourself unconsciously using the same set of words or phrases over and over again? These are words that slip right past your awareness, yet you embed them everywhere. By reviewing your writing, recording or having someone listen to your description will help you bring these tell-tale words to the surface.

- Leaning toward the fear side of **Money Empowerment** elements in the description? Is your answer filled with mentions of how nervous, worried, fearful or anxious you are about your money life? How your stomach is nauseous, it cramps or regularly feels out of sorts? How you might feel overpowered by other money players in your life right now? That you have no control? Or that you feel you have to overpower or manipulate others just to make things work? How you believe you're trying to do the right physical and mental things to take responsibility for your financial life, but internally, you don't know how to claim emotional responsibility for the financial things that are happening to you?

- Leaning toward **Money Value** elements in the description? Is your answer filled with mentions about how you are trying to raise your sense of self-worth? That you know you're worth it, but you just don't know how to get from where you are to that place of having a better money life? You frequently think about "fear and scarcity," punctuating it at the end of your answer to me. Perhaps, who you thought you were professionally in the past with the plan of how you were going to get to your financial destination is not true for you today? That now, you're a different person and your sense of self has changed, but not in the way you make your money? The two don't fit any longer and you're not sure how to bridge your identity and financial gap. (If this professional disconnect is true for you, I encourage you to seek a life purpose or soul purpose professional who can help you out.

My work regularly attracts people moving through identity and career change. Make sure you receive the accurate support you need.)

- Leaning toward **Money Story?** Do you share with me how you've been doing your Money Story excavation work and how the current money issue that you're dealing with relates to the home of origin Money Stories that you grew up with? How your boss is the spitting character image of your mom or dad, and you feel like you've surrounded yourself with co-workers who might resemble one of your sibling's habits? Or perhaps, you tell me how you've repeated one intimate partnership after another with similar money patterns in each of those relationships?

- Leaning toward **Money Drama or Money Trauma with aspects of Shadow Money?** Do you spend a lot of time in your description blaming yourself or others? Or describing how you feel resentment for your feeling of being in a financial imprisonment or hostage situation? Or describing how much you are taking care of others financially, emotionally or physically, and how you feel so drained? Or describing how you don't have the power to speak up for yourself in financial situations? Or describing how hard you work, but that you never seem to be able to get ahead? Or describing how you are frequently guilted and shamed into financial situations that you'd prefer not to be in? Or describing how you seem to get close to a financial success and then blow it up with self-sabotage?

The way you uniquely lean with the description of your compelling money issue shows the tell-tale signs of what you're experiencing inside your financial Heroine's/Hero's Journey – how you're relating with the Feminine Money EQ aspect of your money life that directly affects your wallet. Your description shows us how it's not really about the money at all.

As you review this information, what is the diversity or uniqueness of how you lean with your money relationship? You do not have to pigeonhole yourself into any one of these compartments. I encourage you to mix and match, seeing the hues, colors and textures that are creating who you are with your current money journey.

How Your Compelling Money Issue, The Quest, Is Your Financial Viewfinder.

As you begin to look at your compelling money issue through the viewfinders that I'm giving you, assigning more emotional and energy weight to some elements and less to others, I hope you're beginning to notice a slight shift. That shift is about you beginning to see how much emphasis you've placed on your compelling money issue – and perhaps that emphasis and the issue are not what it's really about. Let me put it in light of a partnership argument example. Let's say you and your partner have a tiff about the garbage not getting set out in time for the disposal service to pick it up this week, and you're arguing about who was supposed to do it. The argument descends into something that has nothing to do with the garbage in the first place. It turns out that the garbage on the curb is a placeholder, a symbol, for a deeper emotional dynamic that you're working out in your partnership. When it comes to money, *your compelling money issue is a placeholder for viewing and interacting with the deeper layers of your life that ultimately drive your money engine.* Similarly, the trash can discussion reveals the bigger issues of responsibilities, expectations, fault-finding, forgiveness, and love.

Most of us are so wrapped up in the logistics of solving our money issues and feeling our compelling survival trigger in our bodies as we do, that we forget to let go and allow the patterning of our compelling money issues to be a viewfinder into the very solutions we seek. I'll give you an example. I was working with a local newspaper publisher who was locked on to the perception of:

"I have to find my perfect salesperson so we can create the cash flow we need to keep the publication alive." She was churning in this mantra, triggered by the two-set solution she'd given herself of finding a perfect salesperson and keeping the publication open, or not finding the perfect salesperson and shutting the publication down. For weeks, she'd been teetering back and forth between her two options, unable to make a decision.

When she and I spoke, I gradually coaxed her out of the compelling money issue she'd set up for herself, and I asked her, "What is this really about?" I encouraged her to loosen her grip on what she thought she had to do, and we used her compelling money issue as the viewfinder to go deeper and map out what she was really struggling with: her value, her voice, her confidence in her ability to raise advertising funds. Her deeper compelling question was, "Is the paper of value? Am I of value? And do I have the confidence to be present here and take action to raise funds?" Those were tough and vulnerable questions for her to get clear, calm and present in her body with, because the newspaper was her baby, her life. That's why she was masking her deeper emotional issues with the surface-level compelling money issue of getting a perfect salesperson or shutting down the paper entirely. Once she saw that this was not a question of: "Do I get a perfect salesperson or do I shut it all down?" but rather a question of her confidence with her own value and her value with the newspaper – everything shifted. She began kicking ass, stepping up to the plate with her own ad sales, along with the Universe responding by synchronistically and spontaneously dropping ad renewals and new advertisers on her doorstep, along with people in the community randomly mentioning how much the paper meant to them. In the end, she not only infused new life into her newspaper, the publication bumped up to an entire new level. It wasn't about the money; it was about how her compelling money issue placed her in the viewfinder of her Heroine's Journey, her quest. By being present with the vulnerability of her Heroine's Journey, her quest, she located her answers, her Waldo.

In your money life, the key is to loosen the hold you have on your compelling money issue and allow the issue to become the prismatic viewfinder, showing you the way through. This shift is your courageous step across the threshold into the vulnerability of your financial Heroine's/Hero's Journey. It's where you'll illuminate the players of your story, discovering your villains, victims and rescuers in how you assign emotional weight to each element of your compelling money issue (Karpman Drama Triangle). In the story I just shared, the newspaper publisher's rescuer was her imagined perfect salesperson. Her villain was having to shut the paper down. And she had assigned herself the role of victim. She became the heroine of her journey when she became present and vulnerably embraced her value and her paper's value with confidence, dissolving the rescuer-villain-victim triangle. She had the courage to face the unknown in her shadow by pulling the curtain back from the Great Oz like Dorothy, lifting her lightsaber in front of Storm Troopers like Princess Leia, wielding spears like the Dora Milaje pros, unfurling her cape like Harry Potter in the face of he-who-must-not-be-named. She reclaimed her value in the face of her shadow, infusing the power of a whole new life into her publication.

If you're willing to let go of your compelling money issue enough so that it can show you the fantastical tableau that you're already creating, then the rich land of your money map and the many Waldos you'll find there are all yours. All you have to do is be willing to step across your threshold into your financial Heroine's/Hero's Journey.

* * *

Have I sprinkled enough carrots to entice your rabbits out of your "How much?" Money IQ room into your Money EQ room of "How am I in relationship with my money?" I hope so, because the mythical land living through your checkbook, your bank accounts and your monthly spreadsheets is extraordinary and holds keys to your money puzzle that you might not have imagined. I am tickled pink to get to share all the cross-training Somatic Money connections in this territory that will infuse your money relationship with a whole new life!

Now that we've established a connection between the description of your compelling money issue, and its greater movement of energy and emotion in the Heroine's/Hero's Journey of your numbers, let's get back to a little more business. During my first Somatic Money visit with you, once you've shared the description of your compelling money issue, we don't stop there. Since your description tells me the directions you're leaning, the patterning you're building, I continue by asking you a series of specific questions geared toward the basic building blocks of Somatic Money. I usually ask these questions in the nature of confirming the money relationship strengths that you're already exhibiting, and then gently lean into the more vulnerable areas where you might be missing a few links. The elements in the conversation follow this pathway through the mind-body-spirit connections of money relationship:

Primary Somatic Money Building Blocks

1. Do you have a presence practice? (Integrated body-money relationship)

2. How is your Monthly Money Game Plan working? (Masculine Money IQ budget)

3. Are you tracking and processing your emotional experiences with money? (Feminine Money EQ processing with body)

4. Energy Medicine for Your Money: What conscious, faith-based, energy or spiritual money tools do you work with in relationship with money? (Integrating Feminine Money EQ tools with Masculine Money IQ tasks)

5. Are you practicing being present in your body when and where you transact money? (Cross-training body-based money relationship, Masculine Money IQ and Feminine Money EQ)

6. Are you excavating your Money Story? Are you actively identifying with your gender, racial diversity and sexual identity in relationship with your money? (Identifying financial home of origin with workplace identity and money relationship)

7. What are the money words and intent you are using in your money relationship? (Further excavation stemming from home of origin)

8. Do you regularly call in your Money Allies? (Financial allyship)

Now that you've reviewed these eight highlights of the primary Somatic Money building blocks, the following are brief descriptions of each to help you initially map your overall landscape. We'll be covering each step in-depth through the rest of this book.

1. Do You Have a Presence Practice? (Integrated body-money relationship) Whenever I ask this body-based question during a money conversation, it usually causes pause. I feel my conversant pull back on the unspoken thought bubble hanging in the air: "Wait a minute. We're in a money conversation. What the hell are we doing talking about a presence practice?" That is exactly the point. Welcome to the first primary cross-training practice between your money practice and your body practice creating a presence practice in money relationship.

Why is a presence practice so important for your money relationship? Triggers. It's all about the triggers. Most people I work with are not running their money life. Their somatic triggers (body-based triggers) are running their money life in obvious and subtle ways. Our biological response systems are powerful, and when they are engaged in protecting us against survival money issues, our entire system tends to run out of control like a team of horses gone wild. When this happens, our energy field tends to fly out of our bodies and we're not present. At all. And trying to run our money life from a remote location does not work. So? Presence practice it is!

Presence work, as a basis of Somatic Money, means that the more present you are in your body with your money relationship, the more you are there for the important financial events of your life and the more your money relationship improves. It makes sense that a Somatic Money practice begins with a general presence practice. So, do you have a basic presence practice in your life?

What do I mean by presence practice? Overall, I'm looking for a daily practice, or perhaps three to five times per week, when you completely unplug from your digital world, agendas and pressures and take time out for yourself to calmly tune in and listen to your inner-self, your higher-self, opening the way for you to ultimately become connected with your greater being. A presence practice involves these elements:

Daily Basic Presence Practice

Please check the Resources Chapter for resource suggestions.

1. **Slow down** and mentally, emotionally, physically take stock.

2. **Breathe** with conscious in-out, in-out, in-out breathwork.

3. Allow yourself to arrive with your **presence into your core**, your center. This is you releasing from your day and dropping out of your head, rolling your shoulders back to alleviate tension, and gently feel yourself in your heart, arms, stomach, pelvic and leg regions.

4. **Becoming aware** of your inner world and outer surrounding world so that you may carry greater awareness with you.

You may regularly do a daily basic presence practice like I just described, or feel free to engage the elements of this practice during activities like: walks in nature or walking meditations, yoga, meditation, breathwork, stretching routines, qigong, tai chi or exercising in a way that calms you down and tunes you in. The point is to stop your busyness and allow yourself to *be*. Whatever it is that you can do to alleviate or change your pressurized agenda, let go and tune in to your greater awareness, your greater consciousness, while bringing your blood pressure down, your breathwork up and engaging your core.

When I ask this question about a presence practice, the responses run the gamut, and include, "Absolutely!" and then I receive an excited and positive earful about what a presence practice looks like for the person I'm visiting with. I also hear, "What presence practice? I'm supposed to have a presence practice?" and "Not this again!"

Let's just put it this way. If you don't have a presence practice, a strong chance exists that you are going to get left behind in the rapidly escalating consciousness wave that we're all experiencing on the planet. Your presence practice is your technology to stay tuned in without having to always be plugged in. It's your calming device in a chaotic world, your listening device to locate your inner knowing. As for Somatic Money, regularly cultivating your presence practice, no matter how novice or adept you are, is a required foundational tool for Somatic Money.

Here's your carrot. If you already have a presence practice, fantastic! You'll be able to integrate it with this work. If you're a novice to a presence practice, that's okay too! The key is to begin with something that works for you. I have people who begin with several minutes of breathwork in their morning showers; people who listen for their Fitbit when it dings an alarm on the hour, and use that minute to stop and breathe; and people who spend five minutes between meetings during their day to take a time-out. Whatever it looks like for you, begin! Just know that the more you use a presence practice, the more your life will improve. We'll be developing your presence practice in Chapter Three and Chapter Four, and eventually, I'll show you how to take your presence practice right into your spreadsheets.

2. Do You Have a Monthly Money Game Plan? (Masculine Money IQ Game Plan) Once I ask the body-based question about presence practice, I completely switch gears and ask this left-brained Masculine Money IQ question about your monthly money game plan. If you noticed, I am not using the word "budget" because it carries too much constrictive baggage that repels many people from working their monthly money picture. In my work, I've opted to inspirationally rename budgets as Monthly Money Pictures or Monthly Money Game Plans or Monthly Money Visioning to create a softer gateway into the personal accounting practice of your monthly financial in-flow and out-flow.

On a technical note, a portion of doing your Monthly Money Game Plan is your left-brained Masculine Money IQ practice of logically structuring your money thoughts. Keep that in mind as we'll revisit the other portion of this reflection with Feminine Money EQ in the next question.

When I ask this question about a Monthly Money Game Plan, I receive answers ranging from, "Absolutely!" to the sheepish, "I know I should, but I never seem to get to it. It's hard and I'm afraid." So, if you are working your Monthly Money Game Plan, good for you! Please stick with it because we are going to show you wonderful cross-training Somatic Money practices that you probably haven't thought about or tried, especially in Chapter Seven.

For those of you feeling allergic to your Monthly Money Game Plan, it's okay to feel that way, but I'm not letting you off the hook. Your Monthly Money Game Plan is a necessity in money relationship because it honors the structure, the backbone, the vessel-making of your money life (Masculine Money IQ). If we didn't have this, the flow of money wouldn't know where to go, what to do or what purpose it has. Don't you want to be in a position to direct your money traffic instead of it directing you? Don't you want to give your money a purpose?

What might be underlying your hesitancy about your Monthly Money Game Plan is probably connected to a feeling that you're not very good at it. Maybe no one showed you how to do this. Perhaps you feel like you're "bad" with money. All the labels and upset feelings that have piled up over time are now sitting between you and your ability and desire to sketch your Monthly Money Picture. I get it. I used to hyperventilate anytime I sat down with my checkbook, feeling like money structure was one of the worst places of my life. And now, through conscious presence practice with money, here I am writing this money book for you and regularly sketching out my Monthly Money Picture. So, if I can do it, so can you. How?

Your starting point is to read Question #3 on the following pages and begin to lean into your practice of embracing and processing your emotion with money (using your presence practice as support from Question #1) so that you build emotional resiliency, gradually giving yourself a greater ability to connect with your Monthly Money Game Plan. Whittle away at your stuck fear, self-talk yourself with gentle support and focus on the little pieces of the picture that you know you can do. With each step, build it from there. You got this!

As you gain motion and intent, begin to locate models of how you'd like to set up your Monthly Money Picture. Then, either work with your Monthly Money Game Plan in the old-school way with pen and blank sheets of paper, or go digital and set up your Excel spreadsheets or go online using budgeting software. You can do this as simple or complex as you want. I'd suggest that you begin with the basics and each month add aspects to your money picture that make sense to you. If you're a creative, your Monthly Money Game Plan is like painting a monthly picture with numbers.

3. Are You Tracking and Processing Your Emotional Experiences with Money? (Feminine Money EQ processing with body)

I am sure many of you reading this question are wondering, "What the heck is she talking about?!" Right? This is back-side-of-the-moon talk when it comes to money. Absolutely, I'm laughing with you because I couldn't agree more. Yet, this location of our money relationship is a critical juncture that in receiving little to no attention can easily create breakdowns in our finances. With some attention, however, it can be resiliently healed. Let's take a look at four significant factors housed in your Feminine Money EQ that we'll be exploring and strengthening throughout this book:

1. **What are you feeling** or what is your emotion during any given money situation, event, agreement or partnership?

2. The emotion you feel in number one, **where do you feel it in your body?**

3. Are you being **emotionally responsible** with your money during any given financial event, situation, partnership or agreement?

4. What's your level of **embodied emotional resilience** with your money relationship?

Yep. That was a lot in four short line items. Right now, it might be easy for you to tuck tail and run, especially when you see that part about emotional responsibility. Please don't run. We're sketching out what we'll be working with and I'm not here to guilt or shame you. Instead, I want to show you a better doorway and help you reclaim your financial power with information and tools that are rarely found in the financial services industry. To do that, we have to start somewhere, and that's in this foreign land of Feminine Money EQ that has been sequestered to the financial corner of our lives for centuries. It's lumped away somewhere in our bodies where it's wailing like a Harry Potter Howler (a magical audio letter) for attention. So, roll up your sleeves; we have some work to do. It's time to bring out Feminine Money EQ, where financial blind spots and sink holes live, dust her off and give her the respect, power and attention she deserves.

Remember how I pointed out earlier that your left-brained Money IQ process is about the *logical structure* of your money *thoughts*? **In reflection, right-brained Money EQ is where you process how you *feel* about your money, experiencing the *emotion* in your body.** Notice: thoughts and structure in one area, feelings and beliefs in another. As I show you this, can you feel the teeter-totter between your left and right brain, left and right body? Thoughts and structure lean one way; feelings and beliefs lean the other way. Slow it down and check in with this. I've even witnessed individuals visiting with me at trade shows lean and step to one side while they describe their logical money positions, and then lean and step in the other direction as they describe their emotions about their money relationship. We feel these polarized positions in our bodies!

Once you've got this, let me show you the next step in this picture that is key to the success of your money relationship. **Those of you who process your money issues and events logically *and* emotionally between left brain, right brain, and even body, all working *with* one another in greater integration, create a more developed money relationship maturity.** What I have learned through Somatic Money is that the people who work with their money in this integrated way have a greater likelihood of achieving the financial success they are working toward. Those of you who wrestle and fight between your Money IQ thoughts and Money EQ emotions in the compartmentalized, teeter-totter effect, or even shut down your emotions with money, have a greater likelihood of becoming stuck in undesirable and frustrating financial situations. What's the way through? Breaking multiple cultural financial booby-traps (we'll be doing this throughout the book).

Our cultural financial environment regularly practices eliminating one of the legs of our money table: the *emotion* portion of this picture. Why? Emotions are messy! Emotions are vulnerable! They don't belong with rational, logical money! The unspoken belief is that emotions distort money, making them dangerous, so we must keep emotions out of the financial picture. When we do this, we're financially hurting and disempowering ourselves. We throw the baby out with the bathwater and we don't make this single pivotal distinguishing clarity: ***tracked and processed emotion is one of our superpowers that improves and supports good financial decision-making. This process holds the natural result of creating your financial emotional responsibility!*** Knowing how you feel about your money issues and events, tracking and processing them, especially through your body, building your emotional resiliency, gives you illuminated new choices, greater abilities with financial boundaries and a sense of ownership. This new choice of ownership gives you sense of financial emotional responsibility. This is your financial sovereign birthright. This is your Heroine's and Hero's Journey!

What's interesting is that ignoring and shutting down the feeling aspect of money relationship backfires on us! When we ignore and shut down our emotional process with money, we create raw emotion, stuck emotion, stuffed emotion, unacknowledged emotion, unhealed trauma, emotionalism – the type of emotion that gives us fewer choices, lack of self-leadership and warps our money process through our bodies. This leads to poor financial decision-making and actions.

Not that you need it, but I pronounce that you have permission to *feel your feels* in your body with money, notice and then let them go! See your new illuminated choices! This is you embracing, tracking and excavating your Feminine Money EQ. Open the door. Let the mess in. It's time to sort it out so that your money shadow no longer has financial power in the Heroine's/Hero's Journey of your life. Remember, B.B. King did his job to get your attention. Max (or your best power child) is there to stomp around and empower your home of origin roots. And you're already choosing your superheroine or hero self for your Heroine's/Hero's Journey. Now it's your job to identify, process and clean up all those stuffed and unacknowledged financial emotions so that you can create your new financial space.

Since we've clarified the importance of embracing, tracking and excavating how you feel about your money, I can show you the next step. *Your ability to process how you feel about your money, especially through embodiment, improves your ability to be resilient as you logically work with your numbers in your money.* Resiliency is about being able to recover quickly during challenges. When your Money EQ vessel is full (with your presence practice, processing your emotions and arriving into owning your new choices through Heroine's/Hero's Journey), you're far more likely to resiliently process your logistical Money IQ tasks and difficulties (the books, the bills, the income, the decisions). The emotional resilience of your Feminine Money EQ, that you feel in your body, gives you the ability to respond to your money life which is the heart of financial self-responsibility. As this lovely integrated dance between your Feminine Money EQ and Masculine Money IQ strengthens, your financial resiliency improves, your financial responsibility improves, making it possible to take greater and better actions within your money relationship. This is how your Money IQ and your Money EQ begin to work together in positive and constructive cycles. How exciting! (The heart of this work is in Chapter Five.)

4. Energy Medicine for Your Money: What Consciousness-Based, Energy-Based, Intent-Based, Faith-Based or Spiritual-Based Money Tools Do You Use with Your Relationship to Money? (Integrating Feminine Money EQ Practices with Masculine Money IQ tasks) About half of you just read this question and have no idea what I'm talking about. The other half of you are jumping out of your seats, excited that we are finally in your wheelhouse! But some of you might be scratching your head thinking, "I can apply my energy tools directly into my money? My spreadsheets?" Yes, yes you can. But let's start from the top with building blocks.

Let's begin with the traditional money model that the majority of us were taught and conditioned to believe. It says, "The numbers are the numbers are the numbers. They are solid and not transmutable. They are what they are." This financial belief is traditionally housed in accounting, financial advising, budgets, banking, financial logistics. It's the bones of money, Masculine Money IQ.

Then, in the faith-based communities, there is a commonly held belief that money is energy and if we change our consciousness, our energy about money, we can change the numbers themselves. It's all transmutable. Here, consciousness, energetics, intent, faith and/or spiritual tools are used directly in the realm of a person's money life to affect change and create financial benefit. The popular and oft-used tools here are abundance practices, gratitude practices, prayer, Law of Attraction practices, money mantras, vision boarding, manifestation practices, financial journaling, money coding, energy work and more. This is the flow of Feminine Money EQ.

What I have just shared with you is again the dualistic picture of Masculine Money IQ and Feminine Money EQ. Most financial belief systems create these two dynamics as separate entities, sometimes polarized elements, dividing out financial logic and financial energetics like sorting out the peas and carrots on a dinner plate and sending each to their respective corners. They do not touch. Or do they?

I'd like to show you a little magic. So, before my logical people die from terminal eye roll, coughing under your breath, thinking, "Come on! You've got to be kidding me! Energy money tools?!" And before my faith-based money people scurry off to your meditation corner with your energy money tools for safe protection. I want you all to think about meeting in the middle with logic *and* energy.

You see, the logic and structure of Money IQ numbers work so much better when they are fluffed up with things like conscious energy or energy medicine or the power of intent. It's uncanny how well-selected energy medicine tools create transmutational magic in our numbers, helping our finances work out better than we originally expected. And I've had clients tell me about their money and number transmutational magic when they work with their energy money tools, their energy medicine, in their bookkeeping.

The integration also works the other way around. When we are working our consciousness or spiritual money practices, the numbers work so much better when we have a good Masculine Money IQ backbone, a boundary. That's why I'm a huge advocate for basic accounting and budget keeping, no matter what. Structure is invaluable. I've watched my finances spring as I've given them more clarity and purpose in the structures of my spreadsheets. The same is true for the clients who report back to me, salvaging their financial lives, when they were willing to practice a monthly accounting practice with their personal finances.

So, Money IQ and Money EQ are two countries in our lives that need to form a mutual, respectful and compassionate alliance *with* one another. It's no longer good enough to choose one or the other. We get to choose both! This is a large part of our financial salvation to integrate the inner workings of our Masculine Money IQ and our Feminine Money EQ. (We'll powerfully merge Money EQ practices with Money IQ practices in Chapter Seven.)

Now, we're not done yet. Not by a long shot. This is where it gets a little more complicated, but stick with me. We'll be going down two more rabbit holes on the Feminine Money EQ side. Both of these findings are from my data collection with consultees and clients. One is about how we use energy medicine tools with our money. The other is about embracing emotional responsibility, emotional accountability with our numbers (especially when we implement our body-based money relationship tools).

First, let's talk about how we use energy medicine tools with our money. I have found in working with individuals in the consciousness and spiritual community that energy medicine practices with our money are regularly used in a *compartmentalized* fashion *away* from the money areas of our lives. For example, let's take money mantras. Let's say you're using money mantras to augment your abundance practice to improve your financial situation. So, before your daily meditation, you take out the money mantras that you've been journaling and you bring them into your meditation space for intentional visualization work. You do your practice with them in your meditation. You feel good about them, and when you're done, you put them away and go into your day. That's great! But then, during your day, you handle your money transactions, your business, your finances *completely separately, completely away* from your spiritual practice. You never really let the two touch. This energy medicine practice with money is you putting the peas of your conscious money practice over there in the spiritual place and then you putting the carrots of your business, your transactions over here in your money life. Thus, your energy medicine money practices (EQ) and your money-money practices (IQ) are not touching. ***How the heck do you expect to receive leverage with your energy medicine practice for your money if you're not including it directly into the actions and areas of your money life?!*** We'll be reviewing the details of how to create EQ/IQ financial integration in Chapter Seven.

Then, let's move on to your emotional responsibility and accountability with the energy medicine that you're using with your money. For this topic, I tend to find two camps in Feminine Money EQ where people lean in different directions. One camp includes the people who are diligently leaning into their emotional responsibility and accountability with money (as listed in the last question), and either don't know about energy medicine tools for money or do not want to go there. The second camp of people includes those who love working with energy medicine for their money, but have an allergy to financial emotional responsibility and accountability.

Let me show you how these two pictures work out, but first, I'll cut to the chase with a nuanced and powerful secret. When you attend to your emotional responsibility and accountability with money first (especially with a body-based foundation), you get to the root, the heart of the matter. There is no substitute for this. Here, you grow your EQ-based, body-based financial resilience. This is extremely important. Then, when you add in well-selected energy medicine tools with money, your financial space becomes much more leveraged and powerful — BOOM! You're in brand new realms of creating fresh levels of financial results. That's how these aspects of the Feminine Money EQ department work best.

Now that you know the ultimate model, let me show you the two things that usually happen. Back to the first camp of people. The individuals who are working diligently with their emotional responsibility and accountability with money – that's awesome. Please, keep working your foundation, especially with the body-based money relationship tools you'll be learning here. But if you've bookended your conscious money practice here, you're missing the valuable and powerful elements that energy medicine can give you for your financial leverage. For whatever reason you've stopped - lack of awareness of energy medicine tools, no inclination to go there, or a systemic prejudice against magic and what it offers - I want you to know that you're missing out on your greater empowerment with your money relationship. Exploring your best-matched energy medicine tools to apply to your money life is a valuable experience.

Then, for the second camp of people. The individuals who are using energy medicine tools with their money first, skipping over your emotional responsibility and accountability with your finances — I'm good-naturedly busting you — BUSTED! This pretty Band-Aid that you're practicing with your money is known as emotional masking or spiritual masking. In other words, substituting an energy medicine tool with your money where emotional responsibility and accountability work needs to be done first, usually does not give the full financial deliverables you might hope for or expect. Substituting one for the other is the equivalent of walking around with a crutch, a weapon or a mask. If you're not careful how you use your tools, someone is going to get financially crippled, hurt or blinded – and that person might be you.

So, keep in mind that *when individuals pair their emotional responsibility and accountability work with money (especially using body-based tools) alongside well-chosen energy medicine tools, all in the house of the Money IQ landscape, the results can be extraordinary.* This is where I see clients blow the doors off their money picture in a good way. I just gave you critical keys to the castle which comes home to roost in Question #5.

5. Have You Paired Your Presence Practice at Your Money Exchange Space to Track Your Feminine Money EQ Experiences? (Cross-training body-based money relationship, Masculine Money IQ and Feminine Money EQ) Yep, we're talking about chewing gum and walking at the same time. We're talking about simultaneously patting our heads with one hand and rubbing our bellies with the other. This question asks you to cross-train by being present in your body during your money transactions while being aware of what you are experiencing physically and emotionally. Yes, it takes practice, but it's huge. This is the leading edge of inter-personal money relationship development.

If it sounds like a lot, it is at first. But this wash, rinse, repeat practice that will first have you stumbling will eventually become second nature to you, and you'll be running with it before you know it. You'll wonder what you ever did without it! Instead of your old survival money pattern of triggering, flying out of your body and going into fear and scarcity mode about your money phantoms, you'll soon learn to use this practice to chisel away at being back in your body, bring your triggers down to size and diffuse your money shadow. This is your practice in Somatic Money strength training. Like strengthening any muscle and giving it muscle memory, it just comes with practice. We'll be covering this topic at length throughout the rest of the book, but the key here is to *do* the practice. Wake from your deep and passive slumber with money relationship and engage the process.

6. What's Your Money Story Excavation? Also, Are You Naming and Claiming Your Gender, Race and Sexual Orientation Identity with Money Relationship? (Financial home of origin with workplace money identity) These days, working on your Money

Story is becoming so popular that it's moving into the mainstream, and that's good. If you have attended progressive self-help money classes, then you probably already have been introduced to this tool. Yay! If you haven't checked in with your Money Story excavation work yet, here's a thumbnail primer.

Money Story excavation is about returning to the formative years of your childhood home of origin to review your original money environment. It's not only about the amount of money you experienced in your home and the environment this created, it's even more about *how* the money was handled, how your parents exhibited their emotional financial relationship in front of you both verbally and non-verbally, and what you soaked up as a little person sponge. Money Story excavation is about returning to this space and learning how your early money life shaped you financially. This excavation, in and of itself, is powerful, cathartic. But it shouldn't be book-ended here.

The next step of the work is about tracing those financial Money Story threads into your current financial life to see how the pulse of these patterns mentally, physically and emotionally affects your money relationship today. In the spirit of your Heroine's/Hero's Journey, the question becomes: "Have you emotionally processed what happened back then and dissolved the energy so that you may live your more authentic money life today?" Another way of framing it is: "Are you living out the phantoms of someone else's money life in your family, or is your money life authentically yours?" We're talking about identifying and then dissolving emotional baggage, healing trauma and integrating the shadow so that your money relationship can function much more freely and uninhibited from the past. Remember, money is not only physical, but it is also energy, and it exhibits the emotional energy we're lugging around from our history. Money works better in our lives when we're emotionally clear and regularly processing the activity on our emotional bandwidth towards the landscape of healing. This is why Money Story excavation is so critical to engage.

We're also going to initiate the diversity conversation about gender, race and sexual orientation in the workplace and how naming and claiming our identities is an empowered source of personal value within our money relationships.

7. What Money Words and Intent Are You Using in Your Money Relationship? (Further excavation stemming from home of origin) It's like clockwork. I'll be in a conversation with a client or a consultee and, Ding! They drop a certain money word into the conversation. Then, a little while later, it happens again, and then again and again. Finally, I'll gently stop my person, pause the conversation and ask, "Do you hear the word (or phrase) you're repeating about your money relationship in this story?" Usually, they're baffled and don't know. Then I'll tell them about how they are "blowing up" or "getting killed" or "falling through" or "rolling downhill" or any other number of harrowing phrases they are using to describe their money situation, their money life. And I ask them, "Is this what you want to create?" The answer is always, "No." So, this is our wake-up call to get conscious about the words we're using in describing our financial lives and the intent behind those words. The words we use create our money lives. Improve your money words, improve your money life!

Do you truly know the money words you're using to describe your money situations? Your financial life? And do you know what your hidden money intent is that is driving your money engine? Later in this book, once you've secured the basics and excavated your Money Story in your Heroine's/Hero's Journey, we'll unpack the words and intent that have been hiding out in your money life. They've been slipping through your attention, draining your money empowerment. It's time to recharge your leverage.

8. Do You Regularly Call in Your Money Allies or Higher Source to Help You with Your Money? (Financial Allyship) One of the most heart-rending experiences for me in my Somatic Money work is finding out how many people feel so utterly alone with their money relationship. Hundreds of times, I've held space with precious souls in meltdown, who say, "I feel so alone with this financial thing and I don't know what to do!" This very dynamic fuels my engine to stay in the public marketplace if only to deliver this one message: "YOU ARE NOT ALONE." Even though your financial alone-ness might feel very real, being alone with your money is a myth, a pure fabrication that can only keep you in your prison of financial fear.

I am here to tell you that you are not only NOT alone, but that you have an exquisite connection to the Higher Source of your choosing and belief system, even with your finances. You have a complete panel of your own personal Divine Financial Light Team, if you so desire, who loves you very much in your money space and is here with you to support, guide and protect you. Let me repeat that. You are loved, seen, guided, protected and supported in your money space with your very best money allies. If you don't believe me, please review my own bottom-of-the-barrel, alone, meltdown story in the first chapter of this book, where my very own Money Guide showed up for me. Shortly after, my money life began to turn around. I'm not the only one with this gift. Everyone has this gift of money allies for support.

For those of you who are logical and traditional with your money approach, this conversation about allyship might be stepping over the line into more of the wild side of money than you bargained for, but I'm willing to take that risk. I'm willing to ask you to grow a bit more of a backbone, even as you squirm in your chair at the thought of a Money Angel in your life, because money allyship is where we build supportive nets of connection to help those who feel disenfranchised with their finances begin to have more of a support team. Why? Here are the results of this concept brought to life.

The majority of people who learn and experience this message of money allyship initially feel a sense of relief that their money journey is not all on their shoulders and that they have a supportive connection. This relief and connection begins to improve their overall financial outlook and their mental and emotional health. Sometimes, even the numbers begin to improve. I regularly have people tell me, "Dana, when I learned about your story and began asking for my Money

Guide, my Money Team to show up for me, I began to feel better. In feeling better, my outlook is better and I am seeing solutions where I only felt fear and isolation before."

I hope you take this as your cue that God, the Universe, or whatever greater Source that we're all working with wants us to be wealthy, alive, happy and whole... and definitely wants us to find the support, resources and money to help us along the way. Abundance is our financial sovereign birthright.

* * *

There you go! This is your initial Somatic Money map lighting up the trajectory points of your financial landscape, showing where you hold strengths in your Somatic Money picture and what you need to lean into for development. Here is the flow chart:

Developing Your Somatic Money Keys to the Castle

- You are strengthening your **presence and awareness** in your money life with your **Somatic Money Presence Practice** (by slowing down, breathing, coming to center).

- You are bringing your **Somatic Money Presence Practice** into the space of your financial transactions, placing you at the heart of your **interactive experiences** with money relationship.

- These connections will naturally fill your internal vessel with greater **emotional resiliency,** giving you support in cultivating your EQ tracking and processing for better financial choices, boundaries and ownership. This process will help you **reduce your money triggers,** giving you greater ability to develop and respond to your **emotional responsibility and accountability with money**.

- This all means that you're identifying your emotional and spiritual masking so that you may function more clearly in your **Authentic Money Blueprint** and less in your shadow money contracts.

- This will especially make it possible to **strengthen and activate your Monthly Money Game Plan** in your **Sacred Money Vessel and Space.**

- You'll continue to deepen your money relationship as you excavate your **Money Story, Financial Identity, Money Language and Money Intent** — peeling back the layers to function with more empowerment and independence in your money life.

- Don't forget, you have the **allyship of your Money Guides,** your **Money Team** and the extra energy leverage of your **energy medicine money tools.**

Even though this sounds like a tall order, we're going to spend the rest of the book unpacking and exploring what this is all about. Now, it's time to gather your Heroine's/Hero's Journey self, because we're headed into the territory of the core tool that can make a difference in every aspect of your money relationship. Prepare your super suit, magic wand, light saber or best magical ally and read on for the deep dive into getting present in your body with your money!

Spot Check

Yep, we just did a lot. I walked you through an overview of the entire landscape of this book for the basics of Somatic Money. While it might have felt like we were skimming the surface, a few things may have touched deeper spaces inside of you. For that reason, now is a good time to check in with yourself and see what you need for self-support: Is it time to hydrate? Rest? Eat foods in high nutritional value (leafy greens)? Exercise or stretch? Clear with sage or a salt bath? (Selfcare tips are in the Resources Chapter at the back of this book).

As you let the information sink in and you begin to strategize with your game plan, be sure to check in with how you are pacing yourself. The shift into Somatic Money, though wonderful, has the potential to overwhelm your emotional, physical or energy circuits if you move too intensely, too fast. Please pace yourself. It's like my mentor, Linda, used to say, "In time and on time!"

Two Days to Two Weeks. To help gauge your pace, some people are able to process this mapping work within a couple of days while it might take others several weeks. If you're concerned about how good you are at this, don't worry. It comes with practice. Let go of any apples and oranges comparisons you might be carrying around with you. We're all experiencing our unique journeys while being in this together. You are another colorful part of the Somatic Money picture!

Part Two:
Somatic Money Practices

Transform Your Inner Money Life
to Create Your Outer Financial Reality

CHAPTER THREE

Are You Present in Your Body
with Your Money?

*Presence as the Sacred Power
in Your Financial Exchange Space*

It's ironic that the key to Somatic Money, a grounding and earthing tool to use with money relationship, came from an ethereal source. True story.

Even though I was sitting in the middle of the Somatic Money pool in 2014, slapping around in its waters like a happy duck, I still wasn't seeing the obvious. I wasn't seeing the Wyoming Easter Egg sitting on the end of a fence pipe in the middle of the countryside (story from the Introduction). I needed the obvious concept of Somatic Money to be pointed out to me, and the someone who pointed out the obvious was a Divine Soul. The pointing was through a message.

Keep in mind that I'm an empath, energy channel and intuit who sometimes uses my gifts to visit with light beings in multi-dimensional space while helping clients in their financial lives. The discovery of the key Somatic Money tool I'm going to tell you about came from that space. My hope is that even if you're logically inclined, you stay open to the potential in this story.

It was spring 2014, and I was hurtling along in my coaching practice, putting together the pieces of the Money Magic learning curve, which was my first platform. Every session I held was coaching for my clients and data collection with concept development for me to reinvest in the work. Every step I took with clients, I cut and pasted one learning nugget after another into the fabric of the big money picture to re-engage in future sessions. It was in the middle of this intense coaching, research and development when the largest gem dropped in my lap, right in the middle of a session. I am so glad I was paying attention. This is what happened.

I was in a phone session with one of my clients in Taos, New Mexico. She was a Reiki Master for a center in Taos and also had a private practice. We'd been working together for several months, getting into the nitty-gritty of her money relationship, and on this particular day, we were working on a specific money problem set. Then, right in the middle of the session, without warning, I felt the energies of a powerful column of light drop into space to my right side. When I energetically tuned in, I discovered it was an eight-foot-tall Ascended Master, ripe with the energies of a powerful message. (Ascended Masters are connected with the Hall of Akashic Records and the Archangelic Realm. In other words, an Ascended Master arriving into a session creates a high and powerful energetic vibration with profound articulate information.)

I interrupted Denise, my client, to let her know we had a visitor and we needed to tune in for the message. When we quieted and centered, the profound information rolling through was a question. He said, "*Dana, please ask Denise if she was present in her body during her last money transaction.*" I thought it was a zinger of a question, and I translated it to Denise. Her first response was, "That's an amazing question." She took a few moments to tune in and review her last transaction space. She described to me that she'd purchased a few clothing items at a retail outlet and noticed that when she handed the cashier her credit card, she felt her energy fly out of her body. This revelation, that she'd energetically flown out of her body during the transaction and was vacant during the purchase, rattled her.

So, the answer was, "No, she was not in her body during her last money transaction." The Ascended Master, in spite of his mass of power, responded in subtle and gentle tones, indicating that this would be an important space in money relationship to pay attention to. Then, in an anticlimactic way, he dissipated, his energies slipping away.

Denise and I sat like bells that had been rung, vibrating in dumbfounded silence at the great implications of this question and concept: "Being present in your body during your money transaction." Who thinks of that?! I wanted to find out.

The Body-Money Presence Survey.

The session visit from the Ascended Master and his subsequent message shook me up in a good way. I wanted to find out if anyone else in my immediate circle was working with this idea of body-money presence. I decided to run a casual survey with several questions to my audience that week. I framed the survey in the frequency of being present in the now, which is such a popular message and practice in the consciousness community through Eckhart Tolle's work. First, I asked if they had a presence practice with their money. Second, I asked if they were present in their bodies at their transaction spaces. And third, I asked if they weren't present in their bodies at their transaction spaces, where were they?

The overwhelming response was, "I have a presence practice, but I have never thought to apply it to my money relationship or my transaction spaces, and now I'm going to begin to do that. What a great survey!" I found that 70 percent of my responding audience had a regular presence practice, and out of the 70 percent, hardly any had applied their presence practice to their money relationship and definitely not their transaction spaces. Only several had crossed the divide and were working with presence and their money at their transactional spaces.

I recognized that if my audience members, who are regularly aware of their presence practices, weren't doing any money presence work, I wondered about the general population. What did this mean for people who didn't have the foggiest idea about being present, let alone being present with their money relationship? It meant to me that we have an epidemic of people who are vacated from the presence of their money relationship at the space where it is most important – when they are exchanging money for goods and services. The reason why so many people have such challenges with their money relationship became clearer to me. ***How can you have a good relationship with money if you are not present and accounted for (pun intended) in your financial space?***

These key combined events - the session with Denise, a visitation by an Ascended Master with a clear message, and a survey to learn more - was a pivotal turning point in my business research. Here, all the random puzzle pieces I was collecting began to gather around this one element of "Are you present in your body with your money?"

When I slowed this moving picture and took a closer look, three key elements displayed themselves:

1. What is a presence practice?

2. What is transaction space or exchange space?

3. Why is a presence practice important in an exchange space?

It might not look like it, but the three elements I'm presenting here are the ultimate in Somatic Money cross-training. First, we are breaking cultural barriers by bringing a soft-sided and non-logical presence practice to the very technical and logical act of the money transaction space. Second, in that space, by using a presence practice we are helping you keep or return your system to a calm parasympathetic state. Third, we're counterintuitively slowing down the speed-of-light financial transaction space into freeze-frame moments to unpack it. In slowing down your money transactions, you'll be able to better see what happens in those split seconds when you exchange money for goods and services. Slowing down and taking a look at these three pivotal elements combined will show you the space where the quiet power of internal financial healing exists.

It might not seem like the firecracker-money-relationship-break-through stuff you were looking for. It might seem anticlimactic, but these three turnkey areas of Somatic Money are gripping stuff. Let's take a look at these elements in their glory, beginning with "the why."

Why Is a Presence Practice with Money Relationship Important?

When you are working with your money, do you ever notice that as you experience money thoughts in your mind, you also experience responsive and tandem money emotions through your body? If you don't, or if you haven't noticed, I encourage you to regularly pay attention. What I've learned, through layers of Somatic Money work with clients, is that while we might "think" we're running our money and numbers from our brain space, the emotions we experience in our bodies regularly and judiciously tell our financial bottom lines what to do. Then, the more we try to manipulate our logical numbers into place, and the more our emotions speak from the ignored pent-up space of our bodies, the more frustrated we become with our financial pictures. *The pivotal turning point happens when we're willing to vulnerably open ourselves to the energies and emotions we're experiencing in our bodies as we relate with our numbers. This creates connection between the Money IQ and Money EQ processing ability, which is essential to building emotional resilience and financial ability.* This is a picture of your initial leaning into your presence practice with money relationship.

Even though I make it sound so easy, so simple, sometimes it's not, because what I'm sharing with you here is breaking taboo with our multi-generational financial training in our traditionally accepted financial culture. Which means it's even more important to ask the question, "Why is a presence practice with money relationship important?" Even though the idea might seem counterintuitive or out of place, the opposite is true and here's why.

A common understanding in the spiritual and consciousness community embraces this idea through healing work:

**If you want to heal something inside yourself
that is out of balance, of ill-health,
you must first become present with it at the space
where the imbalance exists.
This also pertains to money.**

When you move your attention, or when you move your internal presence, to the space where you are feeling discomfort, disconnect, trauma, confusion or pain, you are practicing one of your most powerful abilities to support and heal yourself. Your illuminated awareness, presence and breathwork at places of internal imbalance or ill-health provides your body with the support and energy to sort things out. It's through this process that you naturally peel back hidden layers, known as unexpected and hidden aspects of your shadow-self, so you may illuminate your unfinished emotional business for embrace, release and resolution — transformation. This process is you embracing self-responsibility for your healing, and this can and does apply to the healing of your money relationship. If your logical management of money is not working for you, there is a strong likelihood the source of your financial ill-health is occurring where you haven't looked — in your body. This is why a presence practice with money relationship is so important. *When you're in process with these intent-driven elements, it can't help but beneficially affect your internal experience with money relationship that concurrently creates your outer financial results.*

During a financial exchange, what we feel in our bodies are the emotional and energy patterns anchored there contributing to creating our financial outcomes, both consciously and unconsciously. So, it makes sense that you would want to be internally present, using your presence practice, to regularly make a positive difference for yourself. This means that to heal an out-of-balance money picture in your life, a financial ill-health, one of your beginning places is to become present with it in your core.

Your daily presence practice with your money relationship is how you heal your money life from the inside out.

As we move forward, it'll be important for you to practice presence when you make retail purchases, when you are in your Monthly Money Game Plan space, when you are receiving payments and when you are in financial conversations. This is how Somatic Money becomes a financial solution through your daily presence practice. When you don't know what to do in any given financial situation, your first job is to slow down and become as fully internally present with it as possible by using your breath and awareness. In allowing the calm to anchor into your body, instead of the triggering calamity of chaos, your body will begin to sort things out on its own. Eventually, through this process, as your resiliency grows and you begin to notice new choices in situations, the answers will appear. It is your job to pay attention, to listen.

This conscious practice of presence, breathwork and awareness within your uncomfortable internal money relationship space is exactly the courageous vulnerability of your Heroine's/Hero's Journey that you'll be developing for transformational shift throughout this book. Now let's take a closer look and unpack the details of the transaction space, your money exchange space.

The Sacred Power of Your Inner and Outer Financial Exchange Space.

For your inner financial exchange space, let's begin with the unlikely pairing of money and sacredness. You never see "money" and "sacred" paired with one another, do you? Nope. They are treated as two different contexts, like they live in two different rooms. If you're in the spiritual, faith-based or consciousness community, you're hardly ever encouraged to directly put money into the middle of the sacred space (except the offering plate). It's sacrilegious. And in the business community, a mention of sacred with money would receive the side-glances of, "That's too woo-woo here." But what if "sacred" and "money" lived in the same room? What if we cross-trained sacredness into your money exchanges? Why would we do that? Because sacred energy naturally lives in the center of your internal money relationship. Sacred and money naturally go together as sacred money. How? Let's take a look.

Mapping Your Inner Financial Exchange Space: Surprisingly, the home of your money relationship lives in your body's second chakra, not in your brain. So, take your hand and place it right beneath your belly button, and that is where the energy home of all of your financial exchanges, agreements and partnerships live. Shocking, right?! We all believe that we run our money relationship out of our mental brain space. And we do. A lot. But the true home of money relationship sits in the second chakra of our bodies. That second chakra is very sacred. Why? Well, track this with me:

For the background definition, "chakra" is a Sanskrit word that translates to "wheel." And chakras represent the life force energy that moves through you as energy centers or wheels — your light field informing your DNA. The life force energy of chakras is an ancient knowledge of our energy anatomy, providing inner vibrational support for our lives. Each chakra represents a different vibrational frequency supporting different aspects of our lives. If you want to learn more about the chakra anatomy, please check out Anodea Judith's *Wheels of Life*. For our purposes here, the home of our money health lives in our second chakra, just below our navel. The second chakra, shown in the diagram, is the second one from the bottom.

At the beginning of my work with money, anytime I ran across chakra information, it perplexed me that the physical object of money was connected with the vibrational center of the second chakra. That never made any sense until I began digging and putting together Somatic Money mapping. When I unpacked the outer-world of money relationship and realized that *physical money is both the commitment glue and the result of partnerships, agreements and exchanges,* it began to make more sense because the second chakra vibrationally resonates in the frequencies of:

- Partnership / Intimacy

- Co-Creation / Pro-Creation / Transformation

- Making Love / Sex

- Masculine / Feminine

- Exchange

- Agreements

- Reflection

The outer-world interactions with money through exchange, partnership and agreement could not be more reflective to our inner world second chakra energies, as listed above. Since this is the case, and since the second chakra is very sacred in housing the energies of pro-creative sex and making love, nothing could be more sacred than that. In essence, when we are in our money relationship, we are in the house of sacred co-creation with the Universe. ***Holding sacred energy in the financial vessel is one of the most important things we can do.***

Unfortunately, our cultural habits in financial transactions are the opposite of the sacred picture I just shared; they are often devoid of sacred space. We exchange our money for goods and services in a predominantly technological sterilized fashion, experiencing the streamlined nature of them for speed and ease, so we don't have to feel or be present. We cultivate our financial transactions in the culture of logic. Yet, all of this is a smoke screen covering the sacredness sitting in the middle of our money.

Let me ask you this: When was the last time you slowed down and felt into your money relationship space or transaction space with a sense of compassion? Perhaps joy? Or maybe loving patience? Most people I visit with are so frustrated, pained, scared or disconnected from their money space that money is "that thing over there that I have to deal with, blech." Well, if some version of this is you, then you are dumping emotional toxicity into your financial well, into your sacred money space. I ask you to stop. It's time for you to redesign that connection because every time you interact in your money space, you have an opportunity to up-level your money game with the presence of the intentional emotional energy you hold with money, which you may now change to sacred energy.

In light of the topic about money and sacredness I'd like to share with you one of my accidental sacred money experiences. It was the winter of 2005-06, as I was in the heart of experiencing my conscious awakening (that means my awareness, intuitive and psychic abilities were fully activating). It was a time when I innocently knew very little about the spiritual realm, while experiencing a huge inner shift. I was exuberant, if not more than a little dangerous riding the wave. That winter, I experienced one of my first energy healing sessions on the Reiki table of a seasoned practitioner. At the time, no one knew how sensitive I was. When I came off the table I was higher than a kite with high vibrational energies (not a drug-induced high, a natural energy high).

After the session, I collected myself, climbed into my car and drove on the snowy streets of Fort Collins, Colorado (not recommended), and slid into a parking spot at a local bagel shop not too far down the road. Between the session and the shop, I experienced my perceptual world tipping ninety-degrees several times and I had to pull over for safety purposes. (Again, I didn't know a thing about grounding or anchoring with my body after energy work).

After parking, I collected my purse, opened my door, got out of my car and stepped into the snow while bundled in my coat, hat and gloves. I felt superb as I scurried happily into the bagel shop for a sandwich. I was famished. And that's when I noticed that I was living in a much different world than everyone else around me. I felt my inner glow, my vibration and how the world, while still gyrating rapidly, had also slowed down. I checked myself with, "Oops, I better 'look normal'" as I queued to give my order. I smoothly moved through the line, reveling in the golden energy glow of my delicious bubble of light.

When I arrived at the cashier's counter to pay, the cashier gave me a funny look, he rung up my bill and I handed him cash. That's when everything freeze-framed as he returned my change and a receipt. Within those moments, as we made the exchange, I felt the energy of sacredness flood through the space. Nearly simultaneously and spontaneously the cashier and I slightly bowed towards one another. We smiled without words. I took my food, turned around and the world returned to its normal pace. That was the first time, in a comical spiritual accident, I recognized that the money exchange holds deep and sacred power.

Remember, you already carry your ancient and inherent sacred power of money relationship within you through your second chakra. While that valuable power is always there, it is not going to reach up and grab your attention. Instead, it is going to wait for you to become more still, quiet and aware. Your sacred power with money is sitting in the middle, waiting for you to arrive into it. The place where it lives is through your inner presence, your presence practice, as you experience outer financial exchanges. This is you integrating your inner and outer world of sacred money as you experience the exchange. The essence of money exchange for goods and services is an ancient, sacred *ceremony*. I often say that exchanging money for goods and services is also sacred *cere-money*. It's time to awaken your sacred ceremonial space of exchange.

In doing so, let's shift from your internal money space and take a look at your external sacred vessel of exchange with money.

Mapping Your External Financial Exchange Space: Prior to my work with Somatic Money, the money exchange space looked shrouded and unclear, but I knew something worth uncovering was there. I found it during the summer of 2016 when I was integrating my research into coherent landscape, yet sensing I was still missing large pieces of the puzzle. I became so frustrated one day, knowing that I was looking at the obvious, but I could not see it. In the heat of frustration, I decided to dissect the financial transaction space, hoping that I could find what I was looking for. I suspected that the place in our money exchanges that we zoom through in the lightning speed of technology was holding a few ripe nuggets. Yes, I went a little nuts for the sake of the project, but it proved fruitful. Here's what I found: a total of eight elements and actions creating the infinity (eight represents infinity) of our ripe exchange space:

Eight Elements of the Money Exchange Space

1. **The money** used in exchange for goods and services (sacred element).

2. **The goods and services** used in exchange for that money (sacred element).

3. **The customer** or client paying to receive goods and services (sacred element).

4. **The business** providing goods and services in exchange for money (sacred element).

5. **The releasing of money** by a customer making payment (Masculine Money action).

6. **The receiving of money** by a vendor in payment (Feminine Money action).

7. **The releasing of goods and services** by a business (Masculine Money).

8. **The receiving of goods and services** by a client (Feminine Money).

As I unpacked this complex technical picture, it became clear to me that our financial exchange spaces hold moments of magical transcendence when the customer releases money and the vendor releases goods and services in the exchange. Here, for a moment in time and space, neither customer nor vendor is fully holding money or the goods. It's in this suspended animation of the in-between place that the Universe holds this space of money, goods and services. This unpack showed me that not only is the exchange space sacred, as we covered before, but it also holds the energy of infinite transcendence. Therefore, in that place of the suspended animation of sacred exchange, we are served best by having faith and trust in allowing for successful transactions.

Also, as I unpacked the picture, I realized that dual actions of receiving (Feminine Money) and releasing (Masculine Money) are directly related to the second chakra. Truly, every financial exchange we co-create with the Universe is our sacred act in financial creational lovemaking!

And last, I hope you're beginning to see that for something as simple as a financial exchange, there is a certain amount of complexity involved every time you transact money for goods and services or receive money for what you provide to clients or customers. What's more, each of the eight elements I mentioned carries its own energy and emotion, which add weight, dynamic, emotional color and texture to the exchange space.

Now, doesn't a courageous presence practice in this space make sense?! Do you see why slowing down, breathing and getting present in your body at your exchange space during financial transactions is so important? When you unconsciously zoom by this experience, you avoid the heart and soul of where your money relationship pulses, where the sacred power of your co-creational money relationship lives. It's time for you to claim your sacred financial empowerment for vital money relationship healing.

Somatic Money Presence Practice, or "When Do We Get to the Good Stuff?!"

When I introduce the Somatic Money Presence Practice to my audience attendees at speaking events, they're enthralled. They love this idea of getting present in their bodies with their money at their exchange spaces. Yes, I clearly assign each of them the practice after showing and doing the practice together during presentations. But then, when I visit with these same people twenty or thirty days later in consultations or visits, and ask, "So, how's your daily presence practice going with your money relationship?" I regularly receive the response, "What? What are you talking about? You mean I was supposed to do something?" Yes. Yes, you were supposed to do something.

The reason I'm telling you this is that no matter how wonderful you think this idea of presence with money is, and no matter how good your intentions are, and no matter how much you might like all the ideas in this book, it won't mean squat if you don't put the practice into motion. **The practice is the point.** The truth is, you're going to have to work to break an invisible barrier because we are *generational-*

ly trained to be emotionally and energetically disconnected from our money relationship. It's true– we all want financial results – but we're trained to stay away from the very place inside of ourselves that can give us that result! So, you must require yourself to not only step up to the presence practice line with your white, bright, shiny new presence practice sneakers, but then you must step across the chalky line onto the green grass and into the field of play. This is not a spectator sport.

Even inside my coaching clientele, the picture of breaking through looks like this: "Dana! When do we get to the good stuff?!" I can almost set a clock to predict when my clients will ask me this during coaching. It's an understandable question that's usually comically premature in the process. It's also a question that infers, "Hey, why do you have me jumping through all these frigging presence practice hoops? I want to get to the wand-waving where we make the money messes and monsters go away so that I can be in my glowing financial moment of TA-DAH!"

As a coach, my inner thought bubble chuckles with, "Mm-hmm. Right on time." Because buried in the seemingly mundane, banal and subtle strength-building practices of Somatic Money Presence Practice is the absolute power of connective leverage, resilience building, that gives us the magical and unexpected tectonic shifts we're looking for. This is the place where we shift away from our conflict avoidance and shift into our inner connective vulnerability, our courageous Heroine's/Hero's Journey, to move us along the path of unexpected results. Perhaps not in the way we want it to happen, but it is there.

So, when my clients ask me the "good stuff" question, I know they're getting ants in their pants for something to happen, because the practices and processes begin to seem a little ridiculous without the "Ooooh" and "Aaaah" of at least one little fire sparkler igniting. And they do have a point.

There's just one thing. That thing is this: all of us have been using our bodies as emotional and energetic dumping grounds for years, maybe decades. We've *especially* been dumping the emotional toxicity of our money lives into our bodies. Every time we sit down to work with our money picture, if we sit down at all, and only work the log-ical mental angle of it, we ignore how the emotions and energies are flaring in our bodies as we dump load after load of emotional gunk into our central nervous systems, throats, hearts, stomachs, lungs, in-testines, colons and pelvises. It's c-c-c-crazy! Yet, this is the emotion-al toxic dump, the emotional load blocking us from our connectivity.

Yet, the painful and amazing secret in the middle of this uncon-scious mess is that the place where we dump our financial emotion into our bodies is the very place where the connecting points of our financial solutions live! *We're dumping where we need to be clear for connecting!*

It's time to reverse the insanity of our unconscious emotional and energetic financial dumping practices. Instead, let's move for-ward with a conscious effort to reconnect inside of ourselves with our money relationship, between the left brain, right brain, hippocampus, vagus nerve, throat, heart and lungs, esophagus, stomach, intestines, colon, pelvis, legs, knees and feet. How do we get there? The practice!

You see... *the practice IS the good stuff.* Every time you engage the Somatic Money Presence Practice, you are quite literally getting out your backend loader... beep beep beep... and layer by layer, you are digging yourself out. Yes, every layer counts, and then you're actively engaging your Somatic Money gym with your strength and stretch-ing practices, training your emotional body into new emotional and energy response patterns. Yes, every turn in the road counts, and then, bit by bit, a few connective wires in your body, your psyche, your emotion and your brain begin to "zzzst, zzzst" with connection. These baby steps, over time, eventually add up to monumental leaps – the good stuff. The fireworks. The wand-waving. The tectonic shifts. The moments of Ta-Dah!

Now, I have to ask: Is digging yourself out boring? No. Is it mun-dane? No. Is it banal? No. It's fabulously courageous. It's the thing of super suits and superpowers and being your own superheroine or hero. *It's your Heroine's/Hero's Journey with your money relationship.* When you engage the ideas in this book into your life, you give yourself the fantastic gift of connectivity, even financial connectivity. And that is something that no one will ever be able to take away from you again.

So, just when you find yourself asking, "Damn. When do I get to the good stuff?" That's your cue that you're close, so close, and you better keep going. So, here's the good stuff:

Where and When Do You Apply Your Somatic Money Presence Practice?

These are my suggestions as to where and when you may best use your presence practice in your money relationship space:

- In your **Compelling Money Issue** space (highly effective, but optional and when you're ready).

- **Retail Transactions** at home on the computer, over-the-phone, or in public.

- **As You Receive Payments** from clients or employers, in person or via your phone or computer.

- As you have **Money Conversations** with others (intimate partnerships and financial professionals).

- During your **Money Meditations**, visioning, mantras and so forth.

- While you work with your **Monthly Money Game Plan**.

- Or **other** designated financial spaces in your life that work for you.

Start small and slow by selecting one or two of these (above). Then, grow and expand your practice to include more. Read on for the Somatic Money Presence Practice.

BASIC STEPS
for the Expanded Somatic Money Presence Practice

1. **HAVE AWARENESS** during any given money event, money exchange, money space, money issue or money conversation that you consciously select to:

2. Let yourself **SLOW DOWN**. S-L-O-W D-O-W-N. Even if you feel rushed or triggered, you don't have to figure everything out right now. You may take your time, your pace, your space with your money. So, feel free to settle things down. Let your thoughts slow down, let your emotions slow down and let your body slow down. Maybe even STOP.

3. As you slow down, or stop, you'll notice that your BREATH begins to return to your body. When you slow down, you begin to **BREATHE** again. So, please give yourself a few minutes to just BREATHE and shift out of your triggered state into your parasympathetic state.

   CHECKING IN with each of your **FIVE SENSES** as you breathe is a great technique to employ as you arrive into your body for #4. This means breathing and tuning in with what you're *hearing*, what your *skin is feeling*, what you're *seeing*, what you're *smelling* and/or what you're *tasting*.

4. As you allow the SLOW DOWN and the BREATHING to integrate into your body, you'll notice that you're beginning to **BE PRESENT IN YOUR BODY WITH YOUR MONEY AT YOUR EXCHANGE SPACE**. Being present in your body with your money is all about, "Can I feel what's happening in my core as I walk through this money experience?" Also, "Am I noticing what's happening with me? Am I aware?" Being present is all about awareness of your thoughts,

emotions, energy and experiences in this space. **You could even check in with:** What do I see? What do I hear? What do I smell? What do I taste? What am I touching? (These are your five senses to anchor you into your body). This is you potentially reversing a lifetime of being shut down and disconnected from money. It's time to gradually tune in.

* Suggestions for supportive breathwork, awareness, presence and/or meditation resources to build your practice are located in the Resources Chapter at the back of this book.

*Also, if you are in trauma recovery, working to manage PTSD and/ or trauma symptoms, it might be a good idea to look into trauma-significant presence practices. There is a growing field of mindful awareness resources being developed by practitioners who recognize that not all presence practices are trauma-aware and could actually re-trigger and damage recovering trauma survivors. If this is you, I suggest you review the trauma-aware presence practice resources I've posted in the Resources Chapter. Also, read the next chapter on Money Triggers and the impact of trauma on money relationship. Please proceed cautiously but confidently as we put the puzzle pieces together, helping you choose what is right for you.

Is that it for the basic Somatic Money Presence Practice? That's it: slowing down, breathing, awareness and becoming present in your body, in your financial exchange space. That's the basic wash, rinse, repeat foundation of Somatic Money. You can keep it that simple and allow your practice to soak into the complexity of your money relationship for shift, healing and constructive change.

As far as initial responses, every person I work with responds to this practice differently. You might be reading this and thinking, "That's it? Why didn't I think of this?! I've got this!" If that's the case, great! Go for it! Have fun! If you're reading this and still wondering what I'm talking about, my suggestion is to begin with the solid two steps of slowing down and breathing during your money events. These two steps will open the door for more connective awareness and presence. And if you're reading this freaked out, that's okay too (see below). Perhaps your first step is to focus only on your presence practice *without* the money. Then, when you're ready, engage your presence practice with the money aspect. Remember, it's all about strength training in baby steps. Overall, begin where you are and take it from there. It takes time to learn how to walk and chew gum at the same time.

Pro Tip. If you're brand new to this practice and concept, finding it daunting or even impossible to do, that's normal. That's okay. Instead of trying to dive into the middle of presence work with your exchanges, you might begin from the edge and work your way in. You can do this by prepping yourself *before* a money exchnage, like gathering yourself in presence practice in the car before grocery shopping or before you open your phone for Christmas shopping or before you open your bank account to check that deposit or before you engage your Monthly Money Game Plan. By engaging your presence practice before your exchanges, you set the stage and make it more possible to engage your presence practice at moments during your exchanges. This preparation might also improve your exchange experience by doing so. Then, you may do the same *after* exchanges. After your money exchange experience, in private or sacred space, come into your presence practice and experientially review the exchange with presence, breath and no judgement. As you strengthen your energy in this space, you'll more naturally be able to engage your presence practice in the money exchange space in real time.

Pro Tip. It helps if you already have some kind of presence practice to soften the edges of your mental mind and bring you into a more relaxed state with your body, your being. This could be time in nature, yoga, meditation or breathwork practices. Anything that can give you a mind-body-spirit foundation is a helpful gateway to the Somatic Money Presence Practice. Again, check the Resources

Chapter for presence practice resource suggestions, as well as mindful awareness resources for those in recovery from trauma-based PTSD symptoms.

As you work with steps one through four and feel yourself adjust into them more frequently and easily, you can move into the more **advanced steps and awareness of the practice, including:**

INTERMEDIATE STEPS
for the Expanded Somatic Money Presence Practice

5. **GROUNDING.** As you feel yourself integrate into your SLOW DOWN, BREATH, PRESENCE and AWARENESS, allow yourself to drop into your center like a plumb bob, becoming aware of your money transaction in more of a slowed-down state. You'll also gradually feel yourself connect with your inner self and anchor in with the Earth in a more grounded way through your legs. This spot right here is your unique vibration becoming present in the motion of a money transaction. *This space is your authentic body-money presence space.*

6. **RELEASE JUDGMENT.** We are our own worst critics, but during this practice, please do not judge yourself. Substitute observation for judgment. Your job is to do your best in the moments, noticing what you can. Remember, this is strength training, resilience building. The more you practice from a place of gentle observation instead of being hard on yourself, the better.

7. **CALL ON YOUR MONEY GUIDE OR MONEY TEAM.** Like my own story in Chapter One, you are not alone with your money. Not only do you deserve ally-ship, you already have financial allies. Since we live on a planet of

free will, your job is to consciously and clearly call in your highest and best Money Guide/s and/or Team to support, guide and protect you with your money relationship, especially during your financial transactions. There is no right or wrong way to ask and no limits to your requests. I like to say the words, "I call in my Divine Financial Light Team to help, guide and protect me and my money with XYZ," and I fill in the blank. This is not a required step in the process, but it certainly helps. We will be visiting in more detail about this topic in Chapter Seven.

8. **IMAGINE YOU AND YOUR MONEY IN A WHITE OR GOLD LIGHT BUBBLE.** I don't know how or when it happened, but at some point, I realized that the white and gold lighting used in regular consciousness-based or spiritual presence practices was paramount for this Somatic Money Presence Practice. You see, programming yourself and your money with white-lighted energies help to tell your numbers, your life, your options, your experiences to line up in the best potential outcomes possible. Gold light is similar to white light in that it provides healing energies. This is not a required step in the process, but it certainly helps. We will be visiting in more detail about this topic in Chapter Seven.

9. **NO OTHER PRACTICES.** It is key here that you do not push or force yourself to insert any other practice. Please, no spiritual masking or spiritual bypassing. Do not insert prosperity, abundance, gratefulness or manifestation practices here yet. *We want to truly find out how your body and psyche respond to becoming present before making any adjustments.* How can we do that if you push another practice in the way? Give yourself breathing room and let this practice work its magic with breath, presence, centering, grounding and noticing your money movement.

ADVANCED STEPS
for the Expanded Somatic Money Presence Practice

10. **GOING DEEPER.** One of my critical check-ins with clients during our work together is, "What does a presence practice mean to you?" During this Spot Check I have my clients walk me through their presence practice and show me *specifically* what they are doing. I want to know how deeply they are engaging their core body space with their Somatic Money Presence Practice. I know this might seem like over kill, but what I've regularly found is that most of us opt for a surface-level presence practice. This means, when I say, "When you became present with the money issue you just described to me, how deep did you go into your body?" Usually, the answer, once my client checks, is that they arrived as deep as their heart chakra (or heart) and they stopped there. My suggestion? GO DEEPER. The home of your money relationship primarily resides in your solar plexus, second chakra and root chakra (stomach, below navel and hips). That's deep in your body. So, as you *gradually* acclimate into your presence practice, please *gently* allow yourself to gravitate through your layers, more deeply into your body, as you're able. That's where you may engage better presence, better awareness and better insight for solutions.

11. **COLLECT YOUR DATA.** As you engage your practice, you'll begin to notice certain experiences, thoughts, emotions and more. Here, your only focus is to collect your data. Do not judge or try to fix your experience. Instead, simply notice and collect it as information. For example, with money transactions: Did you feel yourself trigger in any kind of way? If you did, that's normal. It's okay. Did you feel

anything happen in your stomach or your heart or any other part of your body? Did you feel calm or nervous? Did you have any specific thoughts or memories? Was anything amplified in your environment? Do specific emotions tend to pop up during specific money events? Do you seem to notice a certain memory always hovering around you during money transactions? Are your dreams indicating specific themes? Are you remembering certain things from your home of origin? Collect these notes, no matter how large or small, and if you're in the habit of journaling, write them down. As you take notes and review them, you'll begin to notice patterns.

12. **BUILD A PICTURE OF YOUR MONEY PATTERNS WITH YOUR DATA.** Money relationship is made up of patterns, especially subconscious patterns. Over time, as you work your presence practice and collect your data, you'll begin to notice patterns. These patterns will emerge showing how you think, feel and respond to any given money situation that is driving the engine on your repeating financial patterns. Many times, changing a negative or destructive money pattern that seems to happen to you are at you is a matter of changing your inner response system to the pattern. Tracking your patterns here is the connective work to your Money Story excavation later on in the book.

That completes the core foundation to developing your Somatic Money Presence Practice through basic, intermediate and advanced steps. As always, begin where you are, do what you can with baby steps and build on the process at your own pace.

Over the years, I've found that extra inspiration was instrumental in helping my clients continue with their presence practice until they experienced their first sensations of success, both subtle and obvious, big and small. Here are some of my best juicy, inspirational nuggets. Please use them as carrots to help you continue with your practice.

How Your Breath and Presence Practice Says, "Right Here, Universe!"

One of my greatest challenges as a Somatic Money coach is getting through to people about how their presence practice is sometimes more important than "figuring things out." Several years ago, one of my Washington clients, who was in corporate management, cut through this greatest challenge with a single, booming epiphany.

We were mapping her money relationship, and even though this was helping, time and again, I reminded her, "It's your presence practice, your presence practice. That mental and emotional drama you're trying to figure out in your head? That won't work. Please stop and breathe and drop down into your core."

Finally, after several push-pull sessions, she got it. She let go. She stopped describing her money drama mid-tirade and said, "Oh, I get it. I get it! Dana, what you're trying to tell me is that if I drop the drama, and drop figuring it out in my head, and get very present in my core, then the Universe can see the bright shining bull's-eye of where to deliver my financial solutions!" She continued by saying, "It's the equivalent of standing out in the open with my arms wide open, all lit up with my presence, saying, 'Right here, Universe! Right here!'" Bingo.

It wasn't much later and she fully shed the drama and embraced her presence practice that I began hearing about her results: Her boss began listening to her, she applied for a title upgrade with a raise and got it, and extra monies showed up as interim solutions for several debt vehicles. Her financial stranglehold began alleviating.

It's like my client said in afterthought, "If I'm not authentically present in my body, how does the Universe know where to deliver anything to me?" That is the point, spot on, with the Somatic Money Presence Practice.

Your Presence Improvements Are Visceral and Visible.

Throughout my career, first as an intuitive coach and now as a Somatic Money coach, I've energetically looked into the energy picture of thousands of individuals. What do I mean by this? It means that one of my intuitive gifts is an ability to energetically scan the light field or energy field of a person's body. When I remotely look at these energy scans, I see the energy flows and energy dynamics happening through a person's body that are not only creating that individual's money situation, but also the person's life dynamics.

I can feel a lot of you reading this with question marks over your heads. Here are some answers. No, I don't read minds. The information I receive is on a "need to know" basis. No, I don't do this work randomly in public because that would be a disaster for me as well as others. No, I don't do this work unless I have full intent and permission from the individuals with whom I'm working.

With that clarity, once I energetically scan or read a person's energy field in session, I have a pretty good answer to one primary question: Is this person present in his or her body, or not? I can literally see the evidence in front of me about a person's energy-body presence. Individuals who are more embodied with their presence exhibit light flows moving through and around their physical and energetic light fields. These people usually have better financial pictures than those whose energies are vaporized, dark or floating outside of their bodies. Literally, as individuals do their body-money presence practices over time, and I see their light and energy beautifully integrate with their bodies, the money picture begins to improve. This is the wonder of the work — how light, energy, presence and intent are so closely related to our money lives. It's a gorgeously beautiful picture that I live in awe of every day. I love seeing my clients illuminate the dark holes of their bodies with glistening light, filled with the amber threads of a gossamer rainbow of colors. We truly are beautiful beings, especially when we engage our presence and become incandescent torches.

Once individuals begin to embody their presence practice of awareness, slowing down, breathing and becoming more present, their overall money relationship picture begins to shift. This is how it starts to look.

The Money Picture with a Presence Practice

- Triggers begin to dissolve. Fear and fight, flight and freeze begin to transform into a sense of calm and groundedness. Money decisions and situations become more responsive instead of reactive.

- Your sense of enough-ness, value and worth begin to improve.

- You dial up your ability to be in the present time and space, in the here and now, to make better financial decisions (rather than being scattered and pitching into past and future places).

- Your literal presence begins to help light up the cracks and doorways of better and higher potential with money. You give yourself options you didn't see before.

- As you feel better, your money voice ignites, and you begin to speak up for yourself in money situations.

- Your internal sensations of empowerment increase.

- You create greater value with yourself, and your money follows the constructive cues you are giving it.

- You have greater sensations of support that help you increase your positive energy with money.

Twenty-one days of a new practice makes a habit. I've witnessed clients move the needle with their money relationship in twenty-one days and begin to make big shifts. *Give yourself an initial twenty-one days with your presence practice.* And watch what changes, because every bit counts.

Claim Your Somatic Money Genie!

When we talk about this anomalous thing of being present, we're talking about the proverbial genie in the bottle. The funny thing about the genie in the bottle is that you can't really see the genie. You can't truly quantify the genie, but the genie is still there because you see the qualitative results of what the genie does. What is the genie? The genie is the unquantifiable yet qualitatively authentic force that is ***you***. The magnificent energy of who you are is your genie, and the bottle is your smart body. Putting your authentic genie in your smart body is the daily celebration of embodying your unique imprint. It's your process of being present with your endless sets of three wishes.

Can you see how your invisible, colorless, odorless (or sometimes odorless) presence of who you are, connectively vibrating in the wonderfully unique unit of your smart body, is the precious dynamic that makes everything in your life possible? You're the genie and you've got your smart body!

However, there is just one caveat I need to whisper to you. Do you know what the genie's kryptonite is? The genie's kryptonite is ghosting – that pop culture name we have for describing the phantom-like vaporization of disappearing. Yes, ghosting, and especially *self-ghosting*, is the very thing that will take the wind out of the genie in your bottle. ***For your genie to create magic, you have to be present with yourself in your body.***

Let's show you a "for instance" situation about ghosting. Please imagine only your body being in a room without your presence in it. It's as if you're there as a figment of your body, but where are you? Creepy, right? That is the equivalent of ghosting your body. Yet, we actually ghost more than we realize. Have you ever been at a meeting or event where someone you know is physically present, but they don't seem "there"? Their body is there, but the rest of them seems elsewhere, checked out. Maybe you later learned they had experienced a serious life event, and so their thoughts, energy and emotion were in another place. Maybe you've even done this yourself, and someone said to you, "Are you all right? It seems like you're not really here." It shows how being physically present is one thing, but being emotionally and energetically embodied is another.

Now, imagine yourself practicing ghosting on a regular basis. This self-talk might look like, "I really don't want to be here," or "I'm not here," or "Does it matter if I'm here?" If you are ghosting yourself on a regular basis, chances are your genie is not in the bottle, or only part of your genie is in the bottle. Can you see how this could eventually build into a destructive practice? If this is you or some aspect of you, please stop ghosting yourself. We need you. We need you here. We need your amazing genie illuminating the intelligence of your smart body!

Now, how does this apply to your money life? Simple. Instead of only ghosting yourself, imagine ghosting your money. Imagine your ghosted finances. Imagine vacating the scene of your money spaces. This creates fragmented, confused, hurt and cracked money that disappears. Now, turn it around 180 degrees. Imagine your authentic genie igniting your smart body in all of your money spaces, in all of your finances. You are there, showing up! That is money healing, coalescing, appearing, configuring and being there for you because you are there for yourself.

Ghosted money or genie-in-the-smart-bottle money: You tell me where the magic happens.

Client Money Story - How a Colorado Waitress Increased Restaurant Business and Her Tips

One of my favorite getting-present-in-your-body-with-your-Money Stories is about a waitress on the Colorado Front Range.

This young woman's mother attended one of my Somatic Money presentations and loved the work so much that she purchased a Somatic Money program membership as a birthday gift for her daughter. Her daughter loved the work, too, and dramatically took to it like a fish to water, working with her Somatic Money Presence Practice diligently.

When I spoke with her on the phone about thirty days after she began her Somatic Money Presence Practice, she was ecstatic to tell me her story. She described how the practice made so much sense to her that she began her practice the next day after reading the initial work about getting present. At first, she saw little external change, while she tracked her powerful internal change of feeling more grounded and positive during her overwhelming life of juggling several jobs and school.

Then, between Day One and Day Twenty-one of the practice, she noticed an uptick at the restaurant where she waitressed in the mornings. She said, "It wasn't the best shift, and so we usually didn't have decent customer flow. That meant my tips weren't as many or as large as they should have been. But around two weeks into the practice, I noticed that we began to have a stronger flow of customers than normal, and there was no logical reason for the change. More people just began showing up. I'd say we saw a 30 percent bump in consistent business for my shift. And, on top of it, my tips increased in size. So, I began receiving more tips and larger tips."

She could not logically explain this change in business and her cash flow, but she was thrilled. She also noted that the practice helped her be more grounded, focused and calm so that she could manage her daily life and finances in a much better way.

Client Money Story - Somatic Money Improvements for a Colorado Western Slope Entrepreneur

In the autumn of 2017, I spoke with a holistic practitioner group on Colorado's Western Slope. As with all my attendees, each one has their own unique hidden Money Story. When I visit with them individually, I learn how their Somatic Money practice is transformative.

On this particular night, one of the young women in the audience, Addie, was recovering from an accident. The accident profoundly changed her life from being an avid outdoorswoman to having to work indoors and have more internal focus with time for self-healing work. Even though this event was challenging for her, it wasn't slowing her down from living her life. She had more irons in the fire than most people.

When I spoke with her on the phone in consultation several weeks after the presentation, I found she had avidly taken to the Somatic Money practice of getting present with her money. She wasn't just working the practice once a day, she was working the practice as often as she could, at every financial corner of her life. The results were astounding. When we connected over the phone, she wasted no time in ticking off a list of changes in her life that she accounted for with the practice. Before the practice, she was stuck.

With the practice, she created multiple breakthroughs. Some of them included a spontaneous raise at work; access to medical financial assistance that had been blocked; landing a grant she'd applied for and more. All of these results, including feeling more confident, focused, grounded and positive, were a much-needed wave of change for Addie. The basic presence practice of Somatic Money was a key piece to help this budding entrepreneur unstick her life so she could receive the support she needed!

Spot Check

This is a great start with the basics! Now is a good time to take stock and establish your daily Somatic Money Presence Practice and partner your process with your self-care habits. This is just the beginning and securing good habits now will provide you with the support you need as we take deeper dives into Chapters Four and Five. (Self-care tips are listed in the Resources Chapter at the back of this book).

One Month: To gauge your progress, the information outlined in Chapter Three takes about twenty-one days to a month to integrate into your life. I like to assign the practice to clients and say, "Gently and consistently apply your presence practice in your financial exchange spaces and areas of significance in your money relationship for twenty-one days. This is the time you need to create a new habit. Then, let's check your progress." So, give yourself a month to work your program, exploring the nuances of the practice, integrating it into your life. Watch for subtle and potential powerful shifts.

As you feel yourself engage with the practice, it's time to step into your money triggers.

CHAPTER FOUR

About Gentling Wild Mustangs and Your Biology of Money

Unpack Your Somatic Money Triggers
to Reveal Your Authentic Money Relationship

Living in Colorado's backcountry a considerable distance from any metropolitan financial center has afforded me a unique perspective about money relationships. Sometimes that perspective arrives through random and unexpected vehicles. During the summer that I was in the depths of writing this book, one of my community members on Colorado's Grand Mesa, George, caught my attention with his work in gentling wild mustangs. His commitment to his equine practice gathered my interest through his social media video blog. I learned how he works with nonprofit organizations to rescue mustangs from the kill pens of our Western United States. Then, at his ranch, George works with each mustang in his gentling practice to mitigate their triggers and heal their trauma. George is one of the few who is working to solve this brutal and unintelligent policy of getting rid of "problem" or "unwanted" horses. He sees the potential in revolutionizing a garish system, not with brute force, but with a gentle hand.

It was the richly colored bay mare he worked with named Luci who initially caught my attention. Luci was short for Lucifer because of her dangerous and aggressive behavior towards people. According to George, with his twenty-five plus years of equine experience, this was not natural but learned behavior that was a result of her poor experiences with the people in her past. She'd been conditioned to react fearfully and defensively to keep herself safe, but this landed her in a kill pen. That's when George partnered with Evanescent Mustang Rescue and trailered her to her new home at his ranch.

On his video blog, George began referring to Luci as *I Love Lucy* because she was a tiny horse, the smallest one in the herd, who revealed her huge heart. He released one video after another on social media, showing his gentling process with *I Love Lucy*, who stole all of our hearts. These videos showed how she wanted nothing to do with George when she first arrived at his ranch. She stood surly on the other side of her pen, as far away as she could get from George, and the other horses in adjacent pens and fields. What was his solution to this behavior? He simply let her be and let her get used to her space without forcing any agendas with her. Gradually, over days, not weeks, the distance between *I Love Lucy* and George naturally closed until she was breathing her huffy warm horse breath in and out of his hand, learning who he was. From there, George was able to enter her pen and with simple body language and gentle, permission-based touch, communicate the language of trust with her. This allowed her to calm down her heart and central nervous system that had been filled with triggers and trauma. I'm sure I wasn't the only one who was brought to tears watching this amazing equine story unfold.

Eventually, George let Luci join with the herd in their field when she was ready. She immediately connected with several other mustangs as best buddies. Luci, once labeled as a "bad" and "problem" horse who couldn't be tamed, who was slated for the kill pen, transformed into a horse who peacefully connected with others. It turned out Luci wanted what we all want: be treated well, have friends, be loved and feel safe.

What does this story about gentling wild mustangs and Luci have to do with our money relationships? Everything, when it comes to our systems' sensitivity with financial triggers and trauma. The process that George implemented to calmly and peacefully connect with Luci in breath and body language and to soothe her somatic and central nervous system is a very similar process to the one I use with clients in triggered money relationships. Each of us can use this process to calm our inner wild mustangs and peacefully breathe connections with ourselves and others, even in financial relationships, to the biological root of our souls.

The journey begins with the tell-tale signs of the cultural labels we apply to horses and humans. These are labels like "problem horse" or "bad horse" or "problem money person" or "bad with money person." The obvious question we need to ask here is: What's the difference between a "problem" horse and a gentle, well-balanced horse? Or a "problem" financial person or a well-balanced financial person? It turns out that it's not the horse; it's the handler and environment. We're a lot like Luci when it comes to our money and money environment. When we get forced into agendas, threatened with consequences or financially beaten in subtle and overt ways with our money, which our regularly punitive financial system tends to do without explanation or question, our sensitive systems trigger into survival mode and sometimes fill with trauma. Our bodies trigger into red alert with our money, and some of us systemically live on red alert, even unconsciously. When we do, we tend to treat our money from unbalanced and destabilized places while getting labeled and labeling ourselves with words like, "I'm terrible with money" or "I hate money" or "I'm a bad person with money." I'm sure some of us sometimes feel like we're at the edge of our own financial kill pen. But we need to keep in mind that we're not taking into account how we've been taught with money, treated with money, especially from authority perspectives, and how we've treated ourselves with money. Remember, it's not the horse; it's the handler. It's not the money; it's how we handle ourselves with money, and how we allow others to treat us with money. Since we are our own best keepers, it's time for us to become our own best gentle handlers of ourselves with our money.

I was inspired by George's work, as I felt it closely reflected the body-based money work I do with people in money relationship. I contacted him and asked for his best book suggestion on the horse-gentling topic. George recommended Mark Rashid's book *Horses Never Lie* that describes a soft-sided and inside-out approach to horse training. Remarkably, Rashid's insights about horsemanship seem to have reflective value into money relationship! Plus, horses could not have chosen a better equine envoy than Mark Rashid to speak their truth.

Let's take a look through Mark's horse-training viewfinder, which is actually about human training through the perspective of a horse. As Mark unraveled his horse stories, wrapped in the richness and warmth of horses' musky smells, velvety noses, powerful bodies and beautiful manes and tails, I fell in love with the idea of reading a horse's body language so well that it can speak its own private messages to you. Your only job is to become internally still and silent while you listen with your entire being. You may notice the illuminations of ears turning, manes shaking and tails twitching, speaking volumes in horse language, telling you how best to respond respectfully. I read account after equine account of Mark leaving behind the old parochial dominant horse-training leadership style that has a lot to do with telling the horse what to do, with no two-way communication. Instead, he displayed a gentler style of authentic or passive leadership horse training, where, with a firm but gentle hand, he listened to and witnessed the horse first, taking into account what their behavior and actions were saying to him before he asked anything of the horse. In doing so, he brought horses out of kicking fights, down off riding rails and out of the center of riding rings with ease, grace and without any force. And I thought, "This is what we all need to learn how to do with ourselves and others to handle our sensitive systems in gentler ways with our money relationships." While horses are sensitive and responsive, so are we. Yet, in the human arena, we're used to emotionally and physically bludgeoning ourselves and our sensitive systems in the old-school way, forcing ourselves into financial submission while trying to make ourselves do what we believe we have to do to get the job done at work and in our budgets. How's that going for us? Let's take a look.

Imagine a horse trainer who uses the traditional dominant horse-training method, where they snap whips over a horse's head with excessive authority and demand horses learn certain things in certain ways without a say-so. Imagine a horse's highly sensitive system in this parochial and punitive method being crushed under the weight of demands of performance with no breathing room and no conversation between horse and rider/trainer. Mark says that when he observes a horse who has been thoroughly trained in this dominant style of horsemanship, he tends to find that while the horse might be able to perform, there is an emptiness in the horse's soul. Their spirit is gone. Sound familiar?

Now imagine yourself, with your own sensitive body-mind-spirit system, with a demanding whip being cracked over your head (self-imposed or job-imposed) to make a certain amount of money in a certain amount of time with a certain variety of job performance requirements and very little say-so in what you think and how you feel about it. This situation could be happening in either your workspace, your money space or both. While I'm providing you with a more extreme version of this example, use latitude here and feel free to locate where you are in your money relationship and workspace continuum. Use this as a thumbnail:

- **Greater Environmental Latitude:** Authentic, valued, expressed, interactive, empowered, rewarded, creative, self-growth workspace and money relationship.

- **Limited Environmental Latitude:** Rigid, unexpressed, unvalued, punitive, unresponsive, disempowered, non-creative, limited workspace and money relationship.

What happens to you in a workplace and money environment with the more limited version of what I described above? Because you want to do a good job and reach your highest performance levels, you try your best. But in the process, you get over-stressed, you might feel unheard, the spirit or light goes out of you and you feel your body taking the brunt of it into your central nervous system and your adrenals. Your brain shuts down and your sense of survival goes on high alert. If you continually condition yourself in this kind of environment, your sense of survival and high levels of triggering become the norm, not the exception. This is where you might even cultivate living in the red line zone with your adrenals and your finances. Eventually, you lose track of your authentic self, your own spirit, and you don't know who you truly are. The spirit goes out of you. Again, I'm providing you with an extreme example and I suggest that you monitor where you live in this work-survival continuum.

From here, the situation rapidly grinds to the epicenter of survival patterning for both humans and horses. Our fight, flight or freeze triggering mechanisms of survival and self-defense to keep ourselves safe turns on high alert. As confirmed by February 2020 Healthline Article, *Fight, Flight, Freeze: What This Response Means,* written by Kirsten Nunez and reviewed by Timothy Legg, PhD, "The fight-flight-freeze response is your body's natural reaction to danger. It's a type of stress response that helps you react to perceived threats..." This can even include financial perceived threats.

In the case of horses, the survival response system appears as rebellious running away during haltering time, kicking at danger in defensiveness to feel safe, laying ears back and baring teeth as a warning, not listening to commands during training or horse shows and doing something else entirely different in ill-timing.

When it comes to humans and money, when we feel our survival back against the wall, our bodily fight-flight-freeze triggers flare with the tell-tale whirrings of our somatic response system beneath our skin. We wind up with twitchy nerves, elevated heartbeats, sweat, heavy and shallow breathing, triggered thoughts, coursing adrenals.

For humans, the survival breaking point of financial rebelliousness turns into deer-in-the-headlights financial shutdown or freeze, lashing out in financial defensiveness or argument, or blowing off steam and running as far away from financial responsibility as possible.

These money reactions might even continue and develop into habits of poor money management, no money management or over money management. They might turn into the polarity of miserly saving or binge-spending. They might turn into quirky financial self-sabotage patterns that you don't understand. They might turn into shame, blame, resentment, financial hostage situations, co-dependent caretaking and more. This is the place, in the state of the fight-flight-freeze patterning of the trigger, where we run to our shadow world money patterns and exhibit our defensive nature of kicking, refusing halters, biting, laying back ears, running away or acting out. Briefly, shadows are where we internally house our unfinished business and shadow work is when we actively excavate what's hiding in our psyches. (We'll briefly talk about shadow work with money in this chapter, and more definitively in Chapter Five.)

These triggered reactions, in humans and horses, that are often labeled as "bad" are not necessarily so. They are about our deeper selves, at the edge of our survival triggers, screaming out to be heard, noticed and responded to in a decent and empathetic way. Remember what we established at the beginning of this chapter? That it's not about the horse; it's about the handling, the handler, the environment. Remember, it's not about the money; it's about your environment with money, how you perceive your money relationship and how you handle yourself and your sensitive psyche and body with your money life. It's also about how you allow others to treat you financially.

So, for just a moment, in this rattled and triggered space, I'd like you to pause here and remember that the sun is still shining, the breeze is still blowing, there's a blue sky and birds are calling. The internal money horse that you're wrestling to halter is still looking at you in her wisdom from across the paddock, wondering if you'll get it. Wondering if you'll get that the old shadow patterning is only a dead end that no longer serves you. Perhaps it's time to sit down and enjoy the breeze and the bird songs. Allow the horse to feel she can approach you from across the paddock, gently thumping her hooves on the Earth until she's next to you, bending her sweetly curved neck down and breathing her breath along your face.

You do know, don't you, that your money isn't horrible and you're not a bad person with your money. You're just frustrated because you don't know what else to do. You just need more help in determining how you may best handle yourself in a gentler, more nuanced and sensitive-understanding way in money situations so that you may locate your authentic financial self. Yes, we all still need to create a money flow, our money life, but we have choices in *how* we do that. We're talking about a shift from punitive and parochial measures in the limits of logical money to the openings of a gentler hand, a lighter touch and financial empathy with a powerful presence.

It's like this with horses and money relationship. What Mark Rashid talks about repeatedly in *Horses Never Lie* about working with horses is that it's about a light hand, deep internal stillness and profound attention to understand what the horse is saying for two-way communication. He intimates about a slowed pace in training and space to locate an integrated answer between himself and the horse that mingles the best interests of the horse and rider. Though Mark is talking about horses, how easily he could be talking about us and how we treat ourselves, our central nervous systems, our adrenals, our brains, our psyches and our bodies in money situations. We can learn a lot about how we treat ourselves and one another, regardless of whether we own a horse, by looking through Rashid's eyes into the world of non-verbal communication, self-acceptance, a slower pace, breath, and a sense to seek deep understanding inside ourselves for an integrated answer. It's time to set aside the unconscious habits of parochial financial rules, authoritarianism with money and ruthless financial labels. It's time for us to look through a new financial viewfinder with more self-empathy so that the authentic self in our money relationships has an opportunity to breathe, perk up and shine with our own true nature.

To do this, to crack the code into your authentic money relationship, we're going to need to step into your Heroine's/Hero's Journey with money. What I'll be asking you to do through the rest of the chapter is to courageously step towards the belly of the beast, towards your shadow world where unfinished business might be hiding in your Money Story closet. It's time to grab your wand, shake out your super suit, click on your light saber or practice your Super Power Pose (standing, feet at shoulder-width apart, hands on hips, shoulders back, looking slightly up, fill your core with air). Let's go locate and dismantle a few triggers, reducing those detonations down to size so you may get a better handle on your money relationship.

Reduce the Survival Monster by Naming It: Fear and Scarcity.

When you meet a horse for the first time, all their senses are on high alert to learn who you are, what you want, what they can get from you and how you're going to treat them. A horse will sum you up in a matter of moments using all their senses. You can't hide your true nature from horses.

I can say the same about you and your money relationship. Money is one of the most highly reflective healing tools we have to work with in our lives, mirroring our true natures, how we function, our soul growth, our wounds and healings. We're regularly oblivious about this aspect of our money relationship as a healing modality, yet it exists. When we uncover the inner reflective wealth that our money relationship can give to us, we're uncovering one of our greatest assets, our treasures! Our responsive nature of how we work with money, even underneath the surface in our bodies, does not lie. This is a powerful gift. The question is, are you paying attention, using all your senses, to notice what is really happening somatically in your financial life?

Let's cut to the chase and ask the question about your deepest, darkest, financial survival triggers that keep you up at night. Why am

I ripping off the Band-Aid right out of the horse gate? It's just not worth tip-toeing around the monster in the closet of your Heroine's/ Hero's Journey that sets your heart racing. The longer we avoid the monster, the trigger, the larger it gets. Remember, we're here to bring pajama-clad Maxine's/Max's monsters down to size (*Where the Wild Things Are*), so you may tame their unruly wiles in your life. We're not going to do that by control. Instead, we're going to help you manage your triggers and bring your authentic nature to life. It is possible. How do we do this?

The first step in bringing triggering money monsters down to size is to name them, blurt them out, by speaking directly to their juicy survival triggering presence in your life. Sound uncomfortable? Yep. Sound like you might want to crawl behind your couch and hide? Yep. But I promise, you'll live. And afterward? Your money life will begin to improve. In the meantime, let's take the next step where I have something to share with you.

In the thousands of money conversations I've had, where so many share with me one money secret after another in sacred space, most everyone lands on the profound punchline. This punchline, spoken in utter confidence, tumbles out in a way that the speaker feels like they're the only person in the world who is experiencing this. The line goes something like this: "You know, Dana, out of all my money issues, it always comes down to my fear of scarcity with money."

Over and over, from so many of you, this phrase regularly rings in the air as the ultimate private money conversation secret: Fear of scarcity. Fear of scarcity. It's the concern of enough-ness, the anxiety of an empty vessel. And so, I can confidently tell you that even though you might have a very personal experience of your own version of fear and scarcity with money, you most definitely share this private survival money trigger with the collective. Most all of us experience our own shadow-version of fear of scarcity with money. You are not alone.

There. We named it, the juicy money monster survival trigger. We named the illusion of the perceived threat. It's now out in the open.

Are you proudly wearing your pajamas or your super suit? With your golden crown cocked at a jaunty angle? Waving your staff or your light saber or your magical wand? Roaring like Maxine/Max? (Or roaring like your gender and ethnic appropriate power child?) I hope you are. At least a little. Let's break this fear-scarcity money monster trigger down to size.

When Your Biology of Money Is Out of Control: Stop the Fear-Scarcity Cycle.

Chances are that if you and I sat down right now and had a heart-to-heart about your money, we'd distill your money issues down to the brain-triggering, breath-catching, heart-racing, stomach-lurching, throat-tightening, nerves-zinging, butt-clenching, hunched-over, legs-twitching, toes-tapping, "I'm-so-scared-of-my-fear-of-scarcity" money shadow. Although what I just recounted is a bit of an exaggeration, this fear-scarcity trigger description, left unchecked, is your biological system running out of control like a team of wild horses. When the domino effect of your trigger is this big, it's less about the money and more about the experience of your biology triggering throughout your entire body. Can you see how your body is using all of its survival mechanisms to trigger beyond the illusion of what is happening in your mind and feelings with money? This team of wild horses you've let loose to run like crazy through your entire body, triggering everything, is making your money monster situation much larger than it is... and it's time to PLEASE STOP. It's time to claim your Heroine's/Hero's Journey!

Before we get to specific practices that will help you stop, let's bring fear and scarcity down to manageable size with a few anchors of calm. First, I want to share with you what my friend Phuong, a wholistic kinesiologist in Durango, Colorado, shared with me around 2012. She said, "Dana, in the body's intelligence, fear is experienced as unexpressed power." When Phuong shared this nugget of wisdom with me, it rocked my world. I walked around for days reviewing ideas about "When we're feeling fear in our bodies, we're not experiencing or expressing our empowerment. And when we're experiencing our empowerment in our bodies, we're not expressing our fear." It turns out that in emotional energetics, *fear and power are two sides of the same coin*. So, we really need to stop talking about fear of scarcity and begin paying attention to *"Am I in my fear or am I in my empowerment in my body with my money?"*

This informational piece about fear and empowerment was a massive Earth gong in my life. Can you hear it sounding in yours? Ko-o-o-o-o-ng?! I hope you can because whenever you feel the primal sensation of a fear trigger (anxiousness, nervousness, tightening, afraid) in your body with your money, you are full-body registering the disappearance of your empowerment out of your body. This means that if you catch yourself in a tense money situation, and then you *slow down, breathe a little and call yourself back into your body* (hint, your presence practice), you may begin to reverse the trigger and experience and express energies of empowerment, even in the middle of the pool of fear. Even though fear is a natural and normal experience, and this is not about entirely shutting down or bottling up your fear with control, you do not have to live at the whims of your fear. You may cultivate tools to *manage* your fear.

Even though what I'm mentioning to you here is a leap to master-level presence practice - the act of system-interrupting a trigger with presence practice - I believe you need to know the end game now. The place where fear can uncurl from your stomach area, your solar plexus, is the same place where a bit of breathwork, presence practice and your empowerment can uncurl from the center of your soul, as well. This means your awareness about which experience you're cultivating, fear or empowerment, is critical. Keep in mind, right now, we're just planting seeds here. These are ideas and tools creating a new direction for you, because I fiercely believe that you are not a hostage to the financial fear in your life. Not now. Not ever. And just between you and me, I see another Super Power Pose in your near future as you continue to step into your Heroine's/Hero's Journey.

Next, let's talk about scarcity, shall we? Scarcity is fear's dark bride, and oh, do they love to dance with one another, echoing in that empty triggering soul canyon. While fear, by itself, is one thing, throw scarcity down that dark hole and watch yourself rev up into one amplified trigger after another. This patterning is not healthy, so let's pull the plug on scarcity like we did on fear.

When we talk about scarcity, we're talking about one side of the coin of enough-ness. It's obvious that the opposite side of the coin is abundance. Scarcity lives in the constant internal biological switch or question of, "Is it enough?" This is the same question I brought up in Chapter Two about the Rabbit Habit of "How Much?" It's all plugged into the same survival question of "Do I have enough?" Now do you see why I asked you to change that question to "How am I in relationship with my enough-ness?" It system-interrupts a deep survival switch. And there's more.

While fear and empowerment are plugged into a deeper part of the body in the solar plexus or stomach area, the home of enough-ness lives a little higher in the body in the throat area, or throat chakra (See the chakra diagram on the next page). The throat chakra, which is the throat, mouth, nose and ears, is the home of value, the place where we are seen and heard in our personal sense of worth and value. It is also the home to our ability to observe and listen to others in their worth. It's the location where we keenly perceive our enough-ness while we handle the house-of-mirror perceptions and illusions about that enough-ness. Blink, and enough-ness or lack looks like one perception. Blink again, and enough-ness or lack has flipped on its head. We're talking about the paradigm of "Is your glass half empty or half full?" connected to the far deeper second chakra (below the naval) and root chakra (tail of spine or pelvis) relationship of "Am I taken care of?"

Breaking the illusion of your scarcity triggers or your scarcity cycles is similar to breaking patterns of your imagination running out of control in negative ways. How easily we fall into thinking and believing there isn't enough, and abundance seems like a figment of our imagination. By the same token, when we live in the practice of

About the Chakras and Money Relationship

For the background definition, "chakra" is a Sanskrit word that translates to "wheel." And chakras represent the life force energy that moves through you as energy centers or wheels, your light field informing your DNA. The life force energy of chakras is an ancient knowledge of our energy anatomy, providing inner vibrational support for our lives. Each chakra represents a different vibrational frequency supporting different aspects of our lives. If you want to learn more about the chakra anatomy, please check out Anodea Judith's *Wheels of Life*.

For our purposes here, the home of our money health lives in our second chakra, in the color of orange light, just below our navel. The second chakra, shown in the diagram below, is the second one from the bottom.

The Solar Plexus, home to our authentic energy, empowerment, digestion or energy integration, will power, self responsibility and accountability, vibrates in yellow light. The chakra is located in the area of our stomach, above the navel and below the heart. Here, it's the third chakra from the bottom.

The throat chakra, home to being seen and heard in value, as well as observing and seeing others in their worth, vibrates in blue light. The chakra is located in the area of our neck, throat, mouth, nose and ears. It's the third chakra down from the top.

a sense of the calm breathwork of "I am enough, and there is enough in my life, and I am taken care of" our imagination takes that cue and runs with it, and scarcity seems like a figment of our imagination. This is the paradigm of Rorschach on steroids. So, be careful because what you internally believe, you externally see. And even though it might seem like I am naming this easefully, I understand that this type of practice, like catching the fear trigger, is master level work. It comes with time.

Pro Tip: Remember at the beginning of this section I mentioned that you *do not* want to pair the dark bride of scarcity with fear? Well, it works conversely. You *do* want to pair your improved self-empowerment with your improved self-value or worth. Why? This is the pro tip I'd like to leave with you. I've learned, over time, with myself and clients that *it is somatically impossible to improve either your empowerment or your value and not have the other come along for the ride.* Empowerment and value are symbiotic with one another in the human body. Conversely, anytime your value or your empowerment crumbles, the other will also spiral down for the ride into either fear or scarcity. It all depends upon how you want to amplify your money relationship experience.

So, the question I have for you is: Which picture are you most committed to practicing?

<u>Fear</u> Side of the Coin   or   <u>Empowerment</u> Side of the Coin
<u>Scarcity</u> Side of the Coin   or   <u>Value/Enough-ness</u> Side of the Coin

It's up to you which way you're driving your team of horses. Over the cliff of fear and scarcity triggers? Or on a solid trail of empowerment, value and enough-ness? You have the reins. These are your horses. Which way are you going, and how are you leading your team?

The Turning Point of Somatic Financial Safety: Naming Fight, Flight or Freeze.

For many of us, we might "think" we're running our money lives, but sometimes, that's just an illusion. Sometimes, our triggers are running our money lives. How so? When we experience the shadow money sensations of fear and scarcity in our bodies, the moment when the "Stranger Danger!" alarm happens, it creates the singular sensation of: "I am not safe." This I-am-not-safe sensation translates through our bodies as the experience of "No matter what amount of money I have, I don't know if I'm safe." That's when we have tendencies to shift into our fight-flight-freeze triggers. Kirsten Nunez, in her Healthline article *Fight, Flight, Freeze: What This Response Means*, reviewed by Timothy Legg Ph.D. confirms, "The response instantly causes hormonal and physiological changes. These changes allow you to act quickly so you can protect yourself. It's a survival instinct that our ancient ancestors developed many years ago."

Then the inevitable loop begins, even with money. When our bodies, our psyches, do not feel safe, our somatic protection mechanism kicks into gear and does what it can to keep us safe. Here, our money relationship crosses over and impacts our biology. It creates biological triggers, *money triggers*, like a domino effect through our bodies, putting ourselves on high survival alert. This energy wave informs our bodies, and voila, it can be so powerful it pushes us out of our right mind and right body — our sensible money space. Here, our survival triggers are running our money show and shoving the numbers around on our spreadsheets, making decisions for us. When you feel your numbers and money are in uncontrollable movement, what do you do? You usually experience more fear and scarcity triggers piling up in your body, and the cycle perpetuates like that team of wild horses running out of control, creating financial sabotaging situations.

But that's not all. Meanwhile, our cultural habit encourages covering for the triggering wild horses, covering for our flight-fight-freeze and avoiding the tell-tale sensations of those triggers, which create another layer of self-protection. This means most of us are walking around insulating our money triggers in double and triple layers while we wonder, "Why in the heck can't I get my numbers to stick?! Why isn't my money lining up the way I need it to?! Why do I keep creating bad money choices?!" We are walking, talking, self-bamboozling machines. How do I know this?

Regularly, when I visit with people in Somatic Money mapping or exploratory sessions, I notice the nonverbal cues people exhibit about their internal money triggers, similar to the horse-whispering equivalent of tail switches, ear twitches, air blowing, foot stomping, turning your butt to me, pawing at the ground, mane shaking and more. How your body and psyche nonverbally communicate in the language of fear, defensiveness, frozenness, abandonment, speaks volumes, even about your money.

So, whether your money triggers are running wild on the surface, or you have them buried under layers of insulation, it's time for the madness to stop. It's time for you and me to step out in front of your team of wild horses running out of control, slow them down and bring them to a walk, with halters firmly in grasp. Really, horses frothing at the mouth in your financial spreadsheets, pushing your numbers around, is not working for you. Our job is to help you locate your horses gone wild in the root of your bodily fear and scarcity triggers, keeping you from your empowerment and value, that ultimately is affecting your money relationship. You could say it's time we go straight to the horse's mouth to find the solution.

To do that, first we're going to need to have a candid conversation about the role that triggers, potentially connected to trauma and PTSD, play in your money relationship. This is something that is rarely spoken about in money conversations, yet, triggers, trauma and PTSD are at the critical center of potentially derailing us from our financial functionality.

What is the Relationship Between Triggers, Trauma, PTSD and Money?

Over the course of my coaching career, especially with money relationship, I have learned that a majority of moderate to severe financial issues are rooted in cycles of body-based triggers (or PTSD-like symptoms), that are usually connected to deeper trauma and/or systemic trauma. How so? Let's unpack this.

First, what is trauma? Trauma happens when we experience mental, emotional or physical events (small or large) that feel out of our control or are out of control, violating our safety or sense of safety. The body and psyche, in its coping mechanism, usually responds to trauma by self-protecting through internal mental, emotional and physical disconnects, creating a buffer zone of safety, of non-feeling. (This definition is from a combination of reviewing client work and reading varying trauma-definition resources). This definition also translates, in real time session work, with the pictures I energetically witness while scanning clients' light fields. I regularly see picture-stories depicting this trauma pattern: First, an individual experiences traumatic impact. Then, when the experience is too painful for the person to handle at that moment, the person's soul-energy or psyche-energy vacates the body or shifts in the body for protection and pain alleviation.

The result is that these impacts of trauma, with our responding self-protective soul loss, can remain in suspended animation and repeating animation within our cellular code until we're ready to embrace our healing. While we're talking about the at-large trauma events and patterning of our lives, this dynamic also disturbs our Somatic Money relationships. ***Unacknowledged trauma patterning and triggering PTSD is where we lose our emotional and energetic resilience, which we need to give us a stable foundation to work with our integrated Money IQ and Money EQ processes.*** This is what I've come to understand as the living dynamic of *financial trauma.*

What I've found in working with clients as we deeply excavate their money relationship through their bodies, is that there is a profound connection between a person's current money relationship issues and their past traumatic experiences housed in their body. The two are inter-related. Past trauma housed in the cellular code of the body, *especially in the second chakra* (the sex and money chakra), disrupts, blocks and distorts the ability to have healthy and balanced money relationships with partnerships, agreements and exchanges. This means past accidents, sudden emotional trauma, exposure to chronic toxic behavior, unstable or dysfunctional home life, addiction, systemic financial racial injustice, incest, rape, violation, harassment and trauma from institutionalized banking/financial systems — all of these have a strong likelihood of creating internal disconnects that can affect your money relationship today. And especially for women, many of us who have experienced sexual harassment or sexual assault, we are especially prone to this second chakra trauma affecting our second chakra home of money relationship. For reference, the National Sexual Violence Resource Center indicates one in five women in this country report being sexually assaulted. Those are the reported numbers, not the accurate numbers. National Public Radio reports in a 2018 survey that over eighty percent of women in the United States have experienced sexual harassment. This means that women have a much higher likelihood of developing financial issues related to sexual trauma.

In light of financial trauma, there is beginning to be a field of work specific to healing it. Your work with Somatic Money is one of your tools to heal financial trauma. I'm also including several articles here worth referencing, as well as resources in the back of this book. Brianna Weist's article in Forbes, *Financial Trauma Is a Reality for One Third of Millenials,* talks about the recurring PTSD effects of financial stress. She writes, "Galen Buckwalter, the CEO of psyML and an expert on financial trauma, says financial trauma is characterized as a dysfunctional reaction to chronic financial stress. He notes that symptoms often present similarly to those who experience post-traumatic stress disorder (PTSD) from other events. 'It interferes with the person's ability to carry out normal work and home life functions, and manifests in multiple areas of the person's wellbeing...'" Also, Jody Allard chronicles her journey in therapy connecting the dots between trauma she experienced as a child in her dysfunctional home life with the financial difficulties she experienced as an adult. You may read her account in The Guardian article *I spent my life in debt. Now I know childhood trauma was to blame.*

I must also mention, within this discussion about financial trauma, the dynamics of financial abuse. Lindsay Dodgson, in her Business Insider article, introduces Shannon Thomas' work in her book *Exposing Financial Abuse*. Dodgson quotes Thomas defining financial abuse as "... when somebody controls how and when you spend money... sometimes as the breadwinner... sometimes as a financial leech. If someone is able to withhold your finances it is a sign you are completely within their control."

This is critical information that I hope illuminates the appropriate aspects of your money relationship. Many times, when my clients make this connection between past trauma still housed in their bodies and current financial challenges, they have watershed revelations. They say, "No wonder I've had such difficulty with my money relationship! It's as though some unknown thing was standing in my way and I know what it is now!" These revelations make it clear that we don't have to harbor shame or guilt in experiencing or having trauma. We all experience trauma to varying degrees as an aspect of our human life on this planet. Our job is to wield the power of our healing tools to reclaim our lives!

Pro Tip: In Chapter Two, you chose to work with a *Compelling Money Issue*. Chances are, this Compelling Money Issue very likely has aspects of triggers and/or trauma woven within it. There's also a strong likelihood that other Compelling Money Issues you identify are similar in nature. Keep this in mind as you move forward.

There. We did it. Thank you for having the courage to walk with me through the challenging space of financial trauma. Although this is uncomfortable to look at, it's important that we reveal what might be held in your shadow closet that might potentially impede your financial progress and money relationship. Now we may show you the process and possibilities of recovery. If what I have just described powerfully or even remotely resonates with you, then we have some work to do together. It is possible to reclaim ourselves in a recovery process that will even retune, rebalance our money lives.

Now do you see why I asked you to choose your epic Heroine or Hero character to journey with in this great adventure of yours? Now do you see why I'm encouraging you to see yourself, in your especially unique identity, as your own best Heroine or Hero? Complete with magical wonder tools? These are the elements that will help you know that you have what it takes to adventurously journey. And that you're not doing the journeying alone. Let's engage a few more tools and resources.

Presence Practice As a Process to De-Escalate Your Somatic Money Triggers.

While there are many resources, professionals and tools to help you in your process of recovery, small or large, one of the tools I'd like to give you today is trauma's kryptonite: presence, and presence with breath. Here's how it works.

Perhaps, your trauma event and the trigger pattern that resulted, was at a time in your life when you were too small or the situation was too large or you didn't have allies or didn't have tools or you didn't have resources or you didn't have a greater understanding. Now you do. You're learning. You're gathering. You're becoming stronger and larger. You are becoming your own thunder. Now you are showing up as your own best ally, surrounded by more allies, tools, resources and support. Which means that it is much more possible to use your presence practice to slow down, breathe, allow yourself to come to center and breathe through your trigger so that you may reconnect with yourself where you once disconnected and potentially left your body. ***Your Somatic Money Presence Practice is a process that reverses the disconnect and triggering battery drain to reconnect and regularly*** *fill yourself with who you are and your own brilliant resiliency — even in relationship with the dynamics of money.*

This is your process in tracking your (fear and scarcity) triggers within your body to their origin (sight of original patterning), and then being present (using your Somatic Money Presence Practice) with yourself where they are anchored, creating the process of internal reconnection (soul retrieval) where the original traumatic disconnection happened. Sound gnarly? Well, trigger mitigation can be, but it's totally worth it. That's why we call this the Heroine's/Hero's Journey where you ultimately locate the precious internal treasures of yourself after meeting up, perhaps, with a few dragons stuffed away in your Money EQ closet.

Which brings us to my due diligence of professional integrity and accountability. This is my standard user's warning label: If you have not worked with a therapy professional concerning the past traumatic events of your life, there is a strong likelihood that you might have stored trauma or PTSD anchored in your body, waiting and ready to release. *It is very important that if you feel you're at moderate to severe trauma risk with what I have just described above, and you've never done trigger release work prior to now, that you seek professional support and guidance.* The steps I describe in the following pages to excavate your Somatic Money triggers have a strong likelihood to spontaneously release your stored triggers and trauma from your body — and that's good. But, if you're a novice, it is best that you do not navigate this landscape alone. Sometimes, this work can be an energetic and emotional wild horse ride. It would be helpful to have someone to visit with about navigating your trauma, trigger releasing, recovery and healing landscape.

If you need further information to learn more about healing trauma, I list a handful of suggestions in my Resources Chapter at the back of this book. In short, I encourage you to refer to the trauma recovery and healing work of Peter Levine and Gabor Mate´. I've witnessed the EMDR modality as effective and constructive in PTSD and trigger mitigation. Locating your best local somatic-based therapist or psychotherapist is an excellent source for cultivating your private healing work. Also, we now have enough healing therapists in our communities that you could look for professionals who specialize in your type of trauma. I'd especially look for specialists if you're in recovery from childhood abuse, marital abuse, sexual trauma, racial injustice, war-time combat (soldiers) or violence against your sexual orientation identity. Each of these types of trauma carry their own identities, patterns and codes, which handled accurately, can beneficially support you in your healing process.

Also, as mentioned in Chapter Three, if you are in trauma recovery, working to manage PTSD and/or trauma symptoms, it might be a good idea to look into trauma-significant presence practices. There is a growing field of mindful awareness resources being developed by practitioners who recognize that not all presence practices are trauma-aware and could actually re-trigger and damage recovering trauma survivors. If this is you, I suggest you review the trauma-aware presence practice resources I've posted in the Resources Chapter.

Now that we've walked through our trauma descriptions, trauma-healing resources and proceed-with-caution encouragement, it's time to gently begin our work of unpacking your Somatic Money triggers. Remember, you're not alone. You can call on a trusted friend for solidarity or locate your local supportive therapist. If you want, you have your superheroine or hero of choice, along with your Money Guides and/or your protective Angels to assist you in your journey! Let's begin!

We're returning to the center of your body where the two-sided coin of fear and empowerment live. This is the place, in your solar plexus, where your adrenal glands, the organ that secretes hormones to regulate the energy of your entire system, parses out your fight-flight-freeze triggering response system (Sargis MD, R. An Overview of the Adrenal Glands. 2015). We are back in the space where you either systematically "claim ownership of your ability to respond" or allow your energy to be drained with unchecked triggering. *So, when you hold space with your fight-flight-freeze triggers, being in focus with your presence practice and breathing through your triggers, you are deliberately diluting trigger energy while reclaiming your empowerment.* Through this process you'll be able to quite literally reduce the triggering energy drains in your life while reclaiming your empowerment energy, including empowerment with your money relationship! *This process will help you build your emotional resiliency in your body so you have better inner emotional support and energy to focus with your logistical financial issues! This is turning-point stuff!*

This is the process of shifting out of self-protection or self-insulating from your money triggers while bringing them down to size by naming the heart and soul of your somatic vulnerability with money. Ultimately, this will begin to give you a sense of empowerment and increased value that will help you turn your team of wild horses around and engage them to work for you and with you in focused money relationship.

Throughout this process, please keep in mind that triggers are not linear, they are cyclical and layered. Also, the presence practice is not linear, it's cyclical and gradually moves through layers. So, even though I'm writing this to you in a linear fashion, punctuated with step-by-step instructions, all of this moves in repeatable cycles.

What I'll be sharing with you here is a gently firm and methodical way to explore and work with a core part of your Somatic Money triggers. You could even identify your *Compelling Money Issue* here to work with. I use this process with my coaching clients and group coaching. These are effective steps to help you name your money triggers and begin to bring them down to size. If at any time you feel this is not right or not working for you, please stop and seek professional support.

Mitigating Your Fight-Flight-Freeze Money Triggers

Let's begin by setting the stage with an initial basic presence practice. (Again, if you are in PTSD or trauma recovery, please reference the presence-specific resources for PTSD at the back of this book or a similar-related practitioner). Also, I've listed the fuller Somatic Money Presence Practice for reference right after this section. Be sure to work your practice during your review of this money-trigger landscape. *The name of the game is to gently and firmly be present and breathe, as much as you can, as you locate your trigger zones.* Breathe through the rough spots. Feel free to walk away and take breaks if you need to. Get help if you need to. Return when you are ready. Let's begin!

1. Slow Down.

2. Breathe.

3. Allow yourself to come into awareness in your core.

4. Tune in with your energy of empowerment and value.

5. Call in your best Money Guides and/or Angels for support, guidance and protection.

First, What Is the Money Event You Feel Triggered With? I classify a money event rather broadly using the designations of exchange, environment, issue, or person. A money event could be:

a. What's the money **exchange** you're experiencing? (Retail? Paycheck? Bills? Entertainment?)

b. What's the money **environment** you're experiencing in any given financial situation? (Home? Work? Retail? Other?)

c. What's the specific money **challenge** or issue you're experiencing? (This could be your compelling money issue.)

d. What's your experience in working with a specific **person** with financial issues? (Partnerships.)

Second, What's Your Fight-Flight-Freeze Adrenal Response with Your Money Event? Once you locate your money event through exchange, environment, issue, or person, then gently review which adrenal response or combination of responses you have in that space. I strongly suggest that you refrain from judging yourself in this process. Remember, these triggers are your body's way to keep you financially safe, even though the result might be sabotaging, such as:

a. **Fight Response with Money:** A fight response with money relationship is typically displayed by defensiveness and denial in money situations where one does not want to embrace financial responsibility. (Remember, adrenals in the solar plexus are in the home of claiming or not wanting to claim ownership.) Fight response is also displayed in arguments and stubbornness where one does not want to listen and only makes point after point. Blaming and shaming can also powerfully show up here. In severe situations, fight response with money can result in financial retaliation, financial hostage-taking or financial resentment where money is used to hurt others.

b. **Flight Response with Money:** A flight response with money results in financial avoidance, another situation where one does not want to take financial ownership in situations. At a subtle level, a flight response can result in a trauma response of dissociation, where one "checks out" and leaves the financial scene emotionally, energetically or even physically. Energetically, this could mean someone "floats" outside of their body when it comes to money. Emotionally, it could mean a complete lack of response to financial responsibilities. A flight response can also mean a complete physical abandonment or vacating a financial situation.

c. **Freeze Response with Money:** A freeze response with money results in a sensation of financial shutdown, much like a deer-in-the-headlights sensation. Again, this is a situation where one does not want to take financial ownership. Instead, the adrenal response is to become highly immobile or frozen with money, to not do anything even if you know you should do something. Whereas the other two responses have some kind of motion, this response has no motion. It is a state of partial or a complete sense of financial inertness or inability to respond or move. The illusion is, "If I do nothing, it'll take care of itself."

Third, What Types of Triggered Sensations Are You Experiencing? We tend to shut down our sensory experience when it comes to triggers connected to money, treating them almost like they aren't there, even when they are. Getting a handle on your triggers means identifying how you feel in your body relating to money. Here, I'd like you to notice if your trigger sensations make you feel things like constriction, over-expansion, disorientation, uber-stubbornness, grounded-ness, instability, ultra-stability, nauseousness, anxiousness, nervousness, uncertainty, over-certainty, anger, sadness, heat, tingles, cold, shut down, or anything else. There are no right or wrong answers here, only tracking what you feel.

Fourth, Where Do You Feel Your Triggered Response in Your Body? The results of your fight-flight-freeze responses to your money event showing up as certain sensations can impact different locations of your body. It's time to notice where you feel your fight-flight-freeze response patterns in certain locations of your body.

a. Do you feel your trigger through the area of your: Head / eyes / nose / mouth / face / ears?

b. Do you feel your trigger through the area of your: Neck / throat / shoulders?

c. Do you feel your trigger through the area of your: Arms / hands / heart / lungs / chest?

d. Do you feel your trigger through the area of your: Stomach / digestive / intestines / adrenals / kidneys?

e. Do you feel your trigger through the area of your: Pelvis / hips / colon / reproductive?

f. Do you feel your trigger through the area of your: Legs / knees / feet / bones?

g. Do you feel your trigger through the area of your: Nerves / skin?

Somatic Money Practice for Reference During Your Trigger Work

1. Let yourself **SLOW DOWN**. Even here in your heightened state of potential triggers, you don't have to figure anything out right now. You're just exploring, so let it all settle down again. Let your thoughts slow down and let your emotions slow down and let your body slow down. Just stop.

2. As you slow down, I think you'll notice that your BREATH is returning to your body. You're beginning to **BREATHE again**. *If you are in a strong trigger, use your breath to breathe through your trigger.*

3. As you allow the SLOW DOWN and the BREATHING to integrate into your body, I think you'll notice that you're

beginning to **BE PRESENT IN YOUR BODY WITH YOUR MONEY.** *Your practice of directing your attention, breath and presence to be with the spaces in your body where you feel your money triggers, is the turning point. At first it might feel uncomfortable. With time, this practice will help you feel safer and more empowered in your body with your money relationship*

If you are in a really strong trigger: use your breath paired with your presence to breathe through your trigger as best as possible without forcing yourself. If it's intense, this can be somewhat like working with the breathwork and presence used during child birth. Frankly, you're breathing through the triggered trauma and breathing in the presence of yourself (soul retrieval). This practice can and does happen in layers, so please DO NOT expect to "fix" things in one session. Allow the process to unfold.

If you are not feeling safe and need to feel support, please call in your Money Guide/s and/or your Money Angels for support, guidance and protection. Or, having a trusted friend on call to be present as you work your steps is a great form of solidarity. And again, if you feel like this is too much, seek professional support with a body-based therapist or psychotherapist. You got this!

Congratulations! You just made it through the heart of your first steps of system-interrupting your money triggers with Somatic Money so that you may begin to feel more empowerment and value in your body with your financial life. That is no small feat. So, whatever you were able to do, give yourself credit. That's a big first step in the journey!

By regularly working this practice, you'll gradually begin to realize the difference between your aware and unaware reactions to your money relationship. This will help you begin to claim the real you, the authentic you in relationship with money versus the triggered you that reacts to money. As you peel back the layers, you'll naturally reveal and establish your Authentic Money Blueprint to your inner self.

Pro Tip to Put It Together. For many of you who have never done this work, it might be challenging to locate what you're feeling, where you're feeling it and how that connects with your life. Remember, this skill is trained *out* of us early in our lives, so you are courageously reversing that process. It will take time. It is totally normal to feel initially disconnected from this process until you make a few inner connections. In the meantime, I have a Pro Tip that might help make this a little more fun.

Every part of your body is talking to you with meaning, both figuratively and literally. If you'd like to know what the triggered parts of your body are trying to tell you, please check out *The Secret Language of Your Body* by Inna Segal. As a medical intuit, her book references the aspects of our anatomy along with their emotional meaning to us. She also references the meanings of chronic illnesses along with light color practices you might do for healing.

Her work has helped many of my clients unravel the meanings of their triggered emotions in relationship with what their bodies are trying to tell them. This creates illuminating connections between the mind, body, spirit and money relationship. Hint. It's a little like a treasure hunt to make the connections.

Daily Training. For many of you, the landscape of identifying triggers and engaging your first presence practice with your money relationship is more than enough. Please take your time absorbing the highlights of what we just worked with and allow what you are learning to integrate with your daily life, your daily money space. Beginning this practice and working it over time will create results, much like you'd attend to regular training with a horse. Would you train a horse for one day and expect an entire result at the end of that training? No. It's all the regular trainings that add up to the big result. Also, you don't have to "get" this all right now — none of this is a horse race.

* * *

Unravel the Anatomy of Your Financial Triggers to Reclaim Your Money Life.

If anything, I am thorough in my work, which means I have more for you. Oh, so much more. There's only one problem with that: As I give you more, you will need to be careful about how much line or rope you take in. For instance, in horse training, you never want to give a horse too little rope or too much rope, because training can become imbalanced. It's the same here. I'll feed you rope; just make sure you're not overwhelming yourself. When you feel your vessel top off, then it's time to take a break and let the learnings integrate. When you feel hungry again, then it's time to continue.

For those of you who are leaning in and can't get enough of dismantling your money triggers, our next step is to move from the focal point of the adrenal response system of fight, flight or freeze into the full-body view of Somatic Money triggers. What I have for you is a collection of the financial triggers that happen in our anatomy from head to foot. Each of these activate individually and in tandem, in dance with other triggers, sometimes contributing to a domino effect through the body. Your job is to locate your hot spots and how each interacts with one another in any given money event or money trigger. I've described each of the triggers in constructive action wording to give you a stirrup-hold on better positioning. If you need a focal-point as an option to review these elements, you may hold your *Compelling Money Issue* as a working viewfinder for your money relationship. Be sure to occasionally pause and use your *Somatic Money Presence Practice* with each element. Here we go.

Slow Down and Improve Your Money Thoughts. We're going to begin unpacking our Somatic Money anatomy at the top of our heads, in our minds, with our money thoughts.

Over the years, what I've learned with my Somatic Money clients is that when we are in trigger, our money thoughts tend to absolutely race. Then, we compact each of those thoughts against one another like geologic conglomerates, with one money thought right on top of another, until they are in a highly charged and tangled mess. It's what I call "the noodle bowl," where one money noodle is tangled and connected to all the other noodles until it seems there is no way out. But there is always a way through. The first step out of this noodle mess is the counterintuitive move of slowing down. That's right: S L O W D O W N. Got that? It's time to move in the slow motion of slooooooowwwww dooooooowwwwnnn.

When you tumble one money thought right after another and tangle them together, how can you expect to find any positive financial results in your life? Please slow down and breathe air between each thought. Heck. Write. Each. Thought. Down as individual line items. Then, treat each one of those thoughts like a respectable person. As you breathe air between your thoughts, you'll naturally unpack each layer of your Money Story.

Once you've slowed your money thoughts down to a reasonable pace, it's time to lean into the next stabilizing action: consciously decide if a money thought is constructive or destructive. Sure, it's easy to get sucked into shadow thoughts, but remember, our thoughts create our lives, and our money thoughts create our money lives. What money thoughts do you want programming your money life? And what groups of money thoughts do you want to shape your money experience?

Take a beat to locate your clarity, your truth about you and your money. Remember: Your life. Your money. Your thoughts. Your emotion. Breathe. Slow. Consider. Then consciously decide.

Cross-Train by Tracking Thought as Emotion Through Your Body. The thoughts in your mind tend to create a wash of emotional experience flowing through the rest of your body. This is all part of the noodle bowl I described above. Thoughts boomerang into emotions that flow through our bodies and those emotions boomerang into more thoughts.

Well, Candace Pert researched and documented in her book *Molecules of Emotion* this very phenomenon of the connection between lock-and-key receptor sites of molecular flow between thoughts in your brain to the emotions or feelings you experience in your body.

I am over-simplifying the process of how Pert explains these lock-and-key mechanisms, but simply put, at the molecular level in our bodies, a connection exists between how we are feeling through our bodies about any given thought that we have in our minds. Of course, this biological connection and experience also applies to money. Why wouldn't it?! The thoughts you have in your mind about your finances locate as emotion in your body. Your job is to notice how your body emotionally responds when you have certain financial thoughts. Where do you feel your money feelings in your body? This cross-training consciousness will help you track the patterning that you might not have noticed before so that you keep the thoughts and emotions you do want and change what you don't. This is a great place to use your presence practice to get clear about your thought-emotion-body connection.

Breathe During Money Experiences for Your Parasympathetic Nervous System. I have a question for you. Are you breathing when you transact your money? Are you breathing when you're paying bills? Are you breathing when you receive money? Are you breathing when you work your Monthly Money Game Plan? I'd put money on it that you probably aren't breathing. Or you're breathing shallowly. Or breathing intermittently.

When I ask clients this question, they usually say to me, "Oh, wow. I never thought about that before," because who thinks to breathe during their money experiences? And some say, "Oh, you're right, I hold my breath. I just stop." And there it is, the conscious awareness of breath and money.

Do you know what happens when you stop breathing? You throw yourself out of your parasympathetic nervous system, which is the place where you are more relaxed, more conscious, and bust a move over to your sympathetic nervous system, where you tend to be more agitated, nervous and unconscious (trigger-land). When you consciously breathe, especially during your money relationship activities, you are much more likely to keep yourself out of your fight-flight-freeze triggers (sympathetic) and in a better, right-minded, right-hearted space (parasympathetic). (Nall, R. Reviewed by Seung-gu MD, H. 2020. *Your Parasympathetic Nervous System Explained*).

Open Your Throat and Financially Speak for Your Value. We often don't think about how our throat and voice are in relationship with our money, but it is through them that we can be seen and heard in value with our financial lives. If you are wrestling about your sense of "financial deserving," it's here that exercising your voice will help.

When we experience our money triggers, our throats tend to constrict, and it becomes difficult to financially negotiate, speak up or say what we need to say about our money in reasonable ways. What's the best way to break through with your authentic money voice? Practice. Speak your money words out loud, vibrating your throat box, before you share them with anyone else. This practice is your bridge. Speaking your money words cold turkey is never a good idea. And if you want your money words to come from a place of empowerment, make sure you breathe energy into your core, your solar plexus, the supportive place beneath your heart and throat, that can infuse your financial words with greater energy.

Identify and Mitigate Financial Fight, Flight or Freeze. We've already talked about our survival triggers with money and how they are intrinsically linked with our adrenals' fight-flight-freeze mechanism in our solar plexus. Keep in mind that this triggering system powerfully impacts all other body triggers that I'm talking about here. Your triggering adrenal gland, creating your fight-flight-freeze response system, is a powerful full-body web-weaver. That's why it's so important to be clear about its role in your life.

Toning the Vagus Nerve for a Calm Financial Environment. When it comes to money, the vagus nerve is the part of our biology responsible for the domino effect we feel when a survival money trigger runs out of control through our central nervous system. The vagus nerve is the largest and longest nerve in our bodies, running from the base of our neck at the top of our spine, down through the core of our bodies, touching all our major organs until it lands at the base of our pelvis. The vagus nerve is the super information highway of our lives and our patterning. If we have conditioned our vagus nerve to be spiked with reaction, trauma and negative suffering (triggers on overload), then that is what the vagus nerve delivers to our entire body.

I recently read Edith Zimmerman's article *I Now Suspect the Vagus Nerve Is the Key to Well-Being.* She writes about toning (healing, mitigating trigger work) the vagus nerve into calm as one of the primary healing centers of our lives. I couldn't agree with her more. When we practice our healing work, especially in slowing down, breath work, becoming centered in a grounded way and healing our triggers, our trauma, we begin to tone our vagus nerve into calm programming. And yes, this directly affects our financial lives. The more we can respond calmly in our bodies with our money issues, the better financial results we'll have in our lives. It is worth checking into Stephen Porges' work with the polyvagal nerve especially as it relates to trauma mitigation as listed in the Resources Chapter.

Stretching and Flexing the Psoas Muscle for Better Financial Survival. The psoas muscle is an amazing miracle of the body, keeping intact the complex central location of our anatomy. The psoas binds our upper body with our lower body at our spine to our femurs and our hips to our femurs. This intricately connected confluence at our pelvis of hips, muscle tissues, nerves and circulatory system, all in our pelvic region is a marvel of biological engineering.

There are two women who are doing exemplary work with the psoas. Liz Koch, author of *Stalking Wild Psoas,* refers to the psoas as the seat of the soul of our survival. Jo Ann Staugaard-Jones, author of *The Vital Psoas Muscle* refers to the deep connection between the psoas and healing the potential trauma stored there by releasing it. The psoas sits in the home of the red root chakra, also the home of survival and how we manifest in our lives. When the psoas is tight and our butt muscles are also clenched, it regularly sends survival response triggers up the spine, up the vagus nerve, into our brains, telling ourselves that we're in survival mode or survival trouble. When we stretch and flex our psoas muscle in exercise, we tend to incur less sciatica (tight muscles in our pelvis that pinch our pelvis, hip and leg nerves), which is an indicator of financial stress. We also tend to open up the pelvis, sit better, move better and allow our pelvis to send signals up the spine to the brain, letting us know that "We're going to be okay. Everything is alright." (Kundalini yoga is great for the psoas.) You'd never know it, but your pelvis and psoas muscle can directly send signals to the rest of your body that can upgrade your life's financial feeling!

Legs, Knees, Feet and Bones for Financial Stability. When you're thinking about your money relationship, the last thing you're probably thinking about is how connected and grounded your legs, knees and feet feel with the Earth. When was the last time you noticed your physical stability and mobility and how it was in relationship with your finances? That's the funny thing about our legs, knees and feet. They are long-term indicators of how we feel about the way we're moving forward, or not, in our lives and our financial lives. Do we easily trip when we walk? Did we injure ourselves, and it's hard to move? How stable are we on our feet? In our financial life? Take stock of how present and grounded you feel in your feet and legs the next time you transact money!

* * *

Client Money Story - From Curling Up on the Couch with Ben and Jerry's Ice Cream to Kicking Ass.

When I first met Elizabeth Rose, a music teacher in Connecticut, she felt like money was the anomaly in her life, and no matter what she did, she couldn't understand it or get it to work for her in the way she wanted. Regularly, when things didn't financially flow the way she planned or needed, she'd curl up in a ball on the couch and drown her woes in pints of Ben and Jerry's ice cream. This was her money management and coping system.

When we began our Somatic Money discussions together, I interviewed her about her money relationship. She was wrapped up in the drama of her Money Story that regularly included cameo appearances of her mother's presence. As we tracked her Money Stories, we soon learned that the majority of her money dramas, and what she naturally found herself recounting, were the toxic and dysfunctional aspects of her relationship with her mother. This awareness of her mother playing a central role in her money life gave Elizabeth Rose the clarity and leverage she needed to begin to shift her relationship with her mother, shift her money programming and reclaim her power.

I also showed Elizabeth Rose, as she peeled back the layers of drama, how to work with her Somatic Money practices at the heart of her money vulnerability. She literally and courageously, with the heart of a lion, took her presence practice of breathing, grounding and centering directly into the vulnerable center of her money triggers and stopped them in their tracks. She said later, "That was the most terrifying and difficult thing to do - hold presence where I felt my triggers erupting - but it was also the most effective."

Nearly overnight, she stopped eating Ben and Jerry's ice cream on the couch to assuage her money triggers, and her husband was delighted to watch his wife financially kick ass and take names later. She negotiated on auto repairs, set up their emergency fund and began filling it with money, strategized on unexpected expenses and set up their monthly financial game plan.

Even though Elizabeth Rose knows she is not where she ultimately wants to be with her money picture, she knows she's on the road to achieving her vision, and she has the tools to get there.

<u>Spot Check</u>

If you're moving fast through this book out of excitement, the informational uptake might begin to feel a little long in the tooth, especially about now. I understand. It's a lot to take in, especially if you're trying to do it in one fell swoop. This is the place in the work where I've found many people burn out and they begin to feel heavy (their cellular code is jammed with old code leaving and new code trying to come in). Some people say, "Oh, my God, Dana, this is so great, but you have me drinking from the hose!" Is this you? In your exuberance, you might have pushed a little too far, too fast. Since we're not close to the finish line, what should you do?

Yep, once again, it's time to pace yourself. This is where I have people truly take a break so the cellular code in their bodies has time to sort out the deeper inner information that needs to shift. There's no shame in that. Let your body catch up with you! Be sure to take your time, and if you really feel like you need to be doing something, *gently* circle back and review what you've learned and what is happening inside your practice. Let the practice begin to sink into a rhythm in your life.

Also, WARNING, if you push too hard and don't allow yourself to recover, you can make yourself sick (i.e. the old energy and information leaving your body gets jammed up with the new energy and information arriving in). Illness is one way the body has of making us stop so that it can process and catch up. If you are feeling sniffly, sneezy, achy or low energy, take heed! Rest!

For gauging your progress, I'd allow about **two weeks to a month** of combining your deeper Somatic Money Presence Practice into your trigger work (Chapter Three and Four). Truly, this depends upon your existing and previous foundational support and level of experience. You might need longer or shorter.

When you're ready for more, let's dive deep into the next chapter on vulnerability.

CHAPTER FIVE

Make Friends with the Elephant in Your Living Room

Vulnerability as the Heart of Heroine's Journey with Your Money Relationship

Discomfort.

That's the word you're looking for. Here we are in Chapter Five, and we've already ripped off the Band-Aid more than a few times. We've gotten personal, and right in the middle of your money relationship, maybe even your life. My hunch is that by reading this book so far, you've already experienced a few emotional waves. Anxiousness or fear. Maybe anger. A few jolts of happiness. Heavy sadness. A couple of aha! moments. And with m-o-n-e-y, no less!

But what is beginning to settle in is your recognition that yes, the reason this work, this Somatic Money practice, just might be effective is that it's... uncomfortable. Discomfort is sticking out like a sore thumb. You're seriously considering whether or not you want to bite off that big chunk of being present with what makes you truly uncomfortable with your money relationship. It's a big decision, a worthy decision, a Heroine's/Hero's Journey decision that very well may change your life.

I mean, you've probably not heard of anything like this before because most money management books give you logical money equations to get from point A to point B to point C in your practical money picture with a few psychological pointers along the way. But I'm not giving you that. No, I'm moving you to the Feminine Money EQ room of emotional intelligence, adjacent the numbers, where waves of emotion and energy impact your financial picture. And *I'm giving you the open-ended assignment of being present with your emotional discomfort inside your money relationship at the uncertainty of your pain points.* I'm saying look at and be present with how you're *feeling* in your body in connection with that money number, that money thing, that money issue, that money event. And don't just do it once or twice. Regularly use this as a tool, a practice, one or more times a day.

What are we really talking about here? We're talking about the discomfort you're experiencing with the *vulnerability* inside your money relationship – and consciously becoming present with it in your body.

Breaking Financial Taboo with the Myth About Vulnerability.

Our overall cultural relationship with vulnerability is undergoing a powerful and rapid transformation, thanks to the work of vulnerability researcher Brené Brown. Her groundbreaking vulnerability research work is revolutionizing how we view, interact with and experience vulnerability. In her work, she highlights the inaccuracy of the long-held popularized myth in our culture about vulnerability being a weakness. It's not. She assures us that vulnerability is actually a courageous and connective strength.

According to Brown, and I'm paraphrasing here: *Vulnerability is the ability to be courageously unshielded in intimate moments to create a greater connection between yourself and others.* Brown also documents that creating a greater connection is essential to the development of our healthy relationships. So, it's this balance between unshielding or becoming vulnerable, which raises the risk of being wounded, while also garnering the essential greater emotional and physical connection, which cultivates healthy relationships. Although vulnerability might be uncomfortable, scary or even painful, it's an essential root that cultivates the connections of healthy relationships between ourselves and others.

Let's take a deeper look. Being vulnerable is at the heart of connecting in courage with others. Paraphrasing Brown, she says that our connections, especially our authentic ones, are an inherent driving force inside relationships. The desire to connect is hardwired in our systems. But to connect, we must do two things. First, we must have courage. Second, we must be willing to embrace our courage at the vulnerable reveal of our authentic and intimate selves to create that connection. I encourage you to explore Brené Brown's fantastic book series and especially her breakout TED Talk and Super Soul Sunday presentation with Oprah Winfrey called *The Anatomy of Trust*.

In essence, what we're talking about here is that *authentic connection* occurs *in relationship between parties* when we have the *courage (heart)* to risk being *vulnerable (unshielded in intimacy)*. The connections we cultivate through this practice define the quality of relationships we keep. So, we must be willing to practice our courage in vulnerability for greater connection with ourselves and others.

What does this conversation about vulnerability have to do with money and money relationship? Everything, because money relationship, in the home of the second chakra, is all about the intimacy and vulnerability of partnership, exchange, and agreement. ***For us to have healthy financial relationships, it means cultivating our ability to be present with the discomfort, the uncertainty, the vulnerability we feel inside our financial lives.*** We especially must cultivate this at the exchange space during our partnership interactions in light of our existing verbal and nonverbal agreements. When we become present here, at this richly complex and intimate confluence of our lives, where the heart of our financial vulnerability lives, our money relationship naturally heals and improves. Nothing could be more Heroine's/Hero's Journey activated than this!

In my own work with individuals in the Somatic Money arena, financial vulnerability is regularly hidden as the big elephant in the living room of our lives. It's what we've closeted in the shadows of our money relationships. It's the culturally taboo "money weakness" that's actually one of our most powerful financial strengths. Yet, when you become consciously present with your vulnerability, it holds the heartbeat of personal transformation, the healing agent of soul-searching questions and the single thing you've probably not tried in your money relationship that can solve what seems unsolvable. Being present in your body with your financial uncertainty, your financial discomfort, is you practicing the big one – being present with your vulnerability for empowered and voiced money relationship breakthroughs. And is that big? Hell yeah, it's big. It's super suit, Heroine's/Hero's Journey, face-the-dragon big!

Even though your vulnerability with money relationship is a big deal, do you see anyone directly talking about being present with the discomfort, the uncertainty that you might feel in your body inside your money relationship? Nope. That's the anomaly. We're taught to financially strategize in logical ways, in our minds, until we're cross-eyed, but God forbid we recognize how we might vulnerably feel in our bodies about that strategy. The disconnect to avoid the big energy of potential discomfort creates the elephant-in-the-room dynamic. Over time, it creates elephant messes in your living room. So, grab your scoop shovel and put on your rubber boots. We have work to do!

The Truth About the Financial Elephant Mess in Your Living Room.

If you haven't yet embraced presence practices with your financial vulnerability, chances are you've grown a big ass elephant that's swaggering around in the living room of your life. This elephant represents all the vulnerable discomfort you're hiding about your money relationship. Perhaps you don't know about this elephant, but you sense it's there. Perhaps you know about it, and you just don't know how to deal with it or talk about it, so you avoid it. Perhaps you know about this elephant so well that it's about ready to run you out of house and home. Oh, that elephant is tipping over lamps and squashing couches. Noodling up the remote control. Farting on your favorite chair. Eating all the chips you were saving for your special party night. Your uncomfortable vulnerability elephant is making one elephant-sized mess! But don't worry, you're in good company.

What I know to be true about money, after working with hundreds of clients on their money relationship, is that money, for the majority of people, is messy. Money is messy because people's lives are messy. Living is messy. Money always and only reflects our lives. So, if our lives are messy, our money is probably messy too — no matter how little or much money you have.

How does this money mess begin and grow to elephant proportions? It begins by not naming the elephant in the first place. It begins with the nonverbal, subconscious cues from our generational lineage that says: "Thou shalt not name thy financial vulnerability because thou shalt appear *weak*!" That's the first notch in our centuries-old relationship between vulnerability and money. But there's more. The next ramrod of generational cultural programming is: "And we cannot appear weak because then we might not be able to *survive*! So, *thou shalt not reveal thy vulnerability for financial survival's sake!*"

Please, I encourage you to laugh a little here. Please giggle or snort or belly laugh. Something! Because I want you laughing at several centuries of old emotional habits that are ridiculously out of date, untrue and that do not serve you. It's this belief system, generationally woven into the fabric of our DNA, that is harboring your elephant! So, please LAUGH. It's time to break this pattern by breaking a few cultural rules.

Let's get back to our elephant-sized money mess. We usually don't stop there. We tend to exacerbate the making and the having of our money messes by doing what our inter-generational programming tells us to do: "Stay quiet and don't claim how you feel about your money situation. Then, go it alone so that you can *survive*." What actually happens when we do these things – implementing financial silence, avoidance, and isolation? In remaining silent, we self-isolate without practicing the building of incremental trusting support. In avoiding how we feel about our money situations, we abandon ourselves without building emotional resiliency. In going it alone, we become lone wolves and cut ourselves off from our networks. Meanwhile, our money messes just get messier and larger in an unending cycle. Yet, overall, the generational programming says we must be an isolated, abandoned, lone wolf to financially survive... while creating an out-of-control elephant in the living room of our life.

Again. LAUGH! Let's chuckle a little bit, shall we?! I mean, when I lay it out in such a black-and-white picture, it's ridiculous! This is programming from long before the 1700s, the 1800s, and even the early 1900s. But this programming is not for now and does not work today. So, if this programming is you or resembles you, breathe and shake yourself out of it, and giggle. It's time to break it up!

But there's more. We have one more aspect of this old financial survival pattern to break up. Ready? Imagine, again, about *being silent* and *abandoning yourself* and *going it alone* for survival's sake. Got that? Now, time for the extra layer of elephant goop on top of this patterned mess. Right about now is when we tell ourselves, or a close friend or family member tells us, or our culture tells us: "You really need to be responsible with your money." And "Why can't you be accountable with your money?" This is guilt and shame, piled on to seal the deal of silence, abandonment and isolation. This is when the mess really reeks, and there's no denying the presence of an elephant in the room. That, my friends, is the financial hostage chamber echoing in your life with the strains of B.B. King's blues filtering down the hallway with your Feminine Money EQ Room rumbling in the background with years of financial emotional stuffing.

At this point, I'm not laughing or encouraging you to laugh. Why? Because I'm pissed off, and I hope you are too. Sometimes, enough is enough. When it comes to money, what I can tell you about guilt and shame is that they are the biggest morale busters that I have ever seen when it comes to improving self-value and empowerment with money relationship. And I've seen a lot of guilt and shame, since I come from a generational line of Midwesterners who have absolutely mastered soaking and gloating in guilt and shame like pigs in mud. So, from information built on my heritage, to coaching and research with clients, I've learned that one way to not help yourself or someone else with their money is to pile on the guilt and shame. Please stop.

Eventually, you get tired of this entire pattern of creating messes and trying to manage them. Eventually, you get tired of the elephant shoving you around in your living room. Eventually, you get tired of the old programming of being silent, going it alone and abandoning yourself while getting piled on with guilt and shame while being in survival mode. You know there has to be something better, and so, with a liberal dose of self-righteous indignation, you take the unexpected on-ramp.

With a bit laughter laced in dark humor, a flare of anger because you've had enough and a bit of a "screw-it" attitude, you tilt right in the direction you needed to go all along: *your financial Heroine's/Hero's Journey through the gateway of vulnerability.*

Slow Down! To Untangle, Unpack Your Vulnerable Money Mess.

I know! I know! Slow down? How are we supposed to slow down when we all zoom around making lightning-fast money transactions in our uber-technology-driven culture? Slowing down feels foreign and counterintuitive to what we're used to, yet I've found in my coaching work with clients that slowing down is the ultimate gateway into your Somatic Money Presence Practice, and it helps you unravel and unpack your money messes. Look at it this way: It's time to de-clump your money drama! It's like this:

Most people infer from the first step of the Somatic Money Presence Practice that slowing down with their money is the physical act of slowing down. Yes, I definitely do mean this. The habit of slowing down physically with your money in your money relationship space also leads to the natural next step of taking conscious breaths with your money experience. Yet, slowing down with your money goes beyond the physical and encompasses so much more, including slowing your money thoughts so that you might catch them along with the resulting emotions that you're feeling with those thoughts. How so? Take a look.

How about the picture I painted for you in previous pages about the survival money relationship picture, including silence, self-isolation and the non-embrace of your financial discomforts? And about piling guilt and shame on top? And about that darned elephant? Well, imagine being in that practice for years, if not decades. Then, imagine visiting with someone about your money relationship for the first time. What do you suppose happens?

What happens to all the things that have been stuffed away inside that money closet of yours, along with vulnerable emotions in your body, where B.B. King has been playing your blues? Well, it tumbles out all at once with no rhyme or reason in a pile that might include scuba diving flippers from your honeymoon, chopsticks from a meal with your ex, a pamphlet from your nephew's college graduation, dead flowers from your uncle's funeral, a wadded-up Kleenex from crying over what seemed like nothing but was actually a big deal and your favorite heels that busted the night when you tried to run and catch the subway. And the list goes on – all items emotionally connected to your money relationship.

When I visit with my consultees or clients for the first time about their money relationship, what they usually share with me is a deluge of emotionally soaked financial information, clumped together in a drama-mass of geologic financial conglomerate, wrapped around a fuzzy idea of how they are trying to make sense of their money relationship. It usually arrives in a fast monologue, tripping over itself in no apparent order and then drops between us like a hot potato. Most of these Money Stories end with an exclamation of hope, frustration, and the question, "Does that make any sense at all?"

If this is you or remotely you, I want you to know that, "Yes! Yes this makes perfect and total sense." You are in good vulnerable money relationship company with so many others. We've all been here at some point or another. Now, we're going to give the honorable B.B. King a break, and we're going to sit here, plus or minus a Kleenex box, a cup of tea and your favorite treat and unpack your glorious mess. Be of hope. Not all is lost on the hill of your hard-earned noodle-mess. Tell the elephant to scooch over and make room for you.

Now, this is the place, instead of zooming by your mess with a bright-shiny tool, where I take my client's hand, your hand, and say, "Let's take a breath and slow this down, shall we? And let's take it from the top again because I have some compassionate questions for you. No judgment. This is all about dynamics. We're going to unpack this." That's exactly what we do. We slow things w-a-a-a-ay down. I ask you questions about what you meant by this certain person or situation that you mentioned. I ask you questions about what you meant by this phrase or word you repeatedly used. I ask how you feel and what you mean about each of the line items you mentioned in rapid fire sequence. I especially ask you to tune in with your body at different points in the re-telling to identify your physical and emotional sensations. And I ask what are you omitting, leaving room for assumption or interpretation?

We begin to give your Money Story breathing room, space, so that you might see its contours and colors. So that you might see what you're highlighting, holding or hiding. So that you might see what you're good at, strong at and also what you don't feel good about. All of this is so that we may begin to locate what you really, truly mean and how you really, truly feel, and what you really, truly think about all the aspects of what you're describing about your money life. This is de-clumping the drama.

In essence, I am asking you to set up camp *in* your mess *with* your elephant, take the remote control, sit in your chair with your chips and tell me a-a-a-l-l-l-l about it (or tell a trusted friend or therapist or your journal or a voice recording you can listen to). Sure, part of the telling is dumping it all out. Then, the telling turns into an excavation and a claiming, where you lean into it in the most honest, constructive, courageous and open "I-am-claiming-my-mess" kind of way that you possibly can. If you have tears, shed them. If you get angry, rage. If you need to laugh uncontrollably, go for it. If you need to belch, fart, cough, sneeze, laugh, scream, or even have orgasms in private – please do it. And if you think I'm joking about the body releases, I am not. As you emotionally release the things you might have held for years, your body will also naturally want to experience its own releases. Remember, money relationship is second chakra, the sex chakra, so releases might also include bedroom activity. This is a great time to let it all hang out. Release emotionally and even physically all that you've been holding for far too long. Shamelessly uncork the cork!

Once everything has been laid out, talked about and rummaged through, and you feel you've released what you needed to release, then it's time to do one thing: Leave it. Let it rest. Let it breathe, and let your body, your psyche, sort itself out on its own. That means once you've done the great release, then it's okay to let it breathe, walk away and go have dinner somewhere nice. Or go take a walk in the park. Or soak in a luxurious bath. Or take that drive in the pretty countryside with your music playing. Give yourself a little self-care because you deserve it. You just cracked open your financial emotion-based nut and stomped around in your money monster mess wearing your crown and waving your staff like Maxine or Max (or your gender and race appropriate power child). Ultimately, do you know what you really did? You began your Heroine's/Hero's Journey through the gateway of vulnerability. Bravo! This is big stuff. BIG STUFF!

Now that you've done this once and survived it, you know you can do it again with all the different niches, landscapes and hidden places inside your money relationship — when you're ready. Because once you peel back several layers of the onion, there are more layers. Oh, baby, there are more. You're going to be good at this.

It's through this initial excavation that you begin to do something major in the tide-turn of your money relationship. Instead of hiding from the elephant in your living room that drains your battery, your resiliency, and empties your vessel along with your bank account, you are now going to engage your Heroine's/Hero's Journey. This is where you begin to be, holding presence in the living room with your elephant, embracing and filling your vessel with resiliency through your presence practice, charging your battery. You're going to activate your super suit, your Super Power Pose, and with the moxie of conscious boundaries, you're going to butt-bump that elephant over or even out of the living room and begin to tell it what to do. You're going to don your royal crown, take your royal staff and be a little bossy, like Maxine or Max, and put that elephant to work, or at the very least, make it your friend. It's your elephant. You decide!

Do you know what this process is? This is you building emotional accountability with yourself. This is your sense of embracing emotional responsibility to build your resiliency, strength, with your money relationship. More empowerment. More value. More support. More flow. More courage. These are the priceless shifts you'll be making where your courageous vulnerability meets up with your money relationship and your super powers. This is your financial Heroine's/ Hero's Journey that will deliver great rewards.

Now that you have this initial model, I'd like to give you a living example of what this looks like. Let's peek inside a client conversation where I take a version of this slow-down-and-unpack-the-vulnerable-interior with a client in one of her money relationship niches.

I began my Somatic Money mapping work with Sonia, a marketing professional in Denver, Colorado, when she found she would procrastinate with her invoicing until the last minute. She described her Money Story about invoicing in her financially triggered state of frozenness. She said, "I look at the whole picture of invoicing and just go into a state of overwhelm. And then I freeze, and then I shut down. I constantly have a feeling of fear about the unpredictability of what might happen when I send those invoices out." These few sentences that tumbled out of her wholly described on the surface Sonia's money closet and the elephant in her living room. No matter how many different ways I prompted her to describe her situation, her words always returned to "overwhelm, overwhelm, overwhelm" with a few indicators of the word "unpredictable" and then the non-verbal cue of "frozen and shut down."

Once she placed the vulnerable share of her Money Story on the table for us to look at, I honored and acknowledged her for her courageous act of vulnerability to reveal with me the uncertainty and discomfort she felt at her exchange space with money during her invoicing process. The reason I point this out is that acknowledging the act of courage it takes to vulnerably share in this space of uncertainty is how we build trust and resiliency (strength) with ourselves and others. This supported space and practice is what we need to continue to grow.

From here, I asked her permission (because permission-based work is important in vulnerable financial emotional spaces) to continue the conversation by moving into a gentle deeper excavation of the invoicing space. She agreed, and so I returned to the word "overwhelm" and asked her, "Sonia, could you please describe to me what you mean by the word 'overwhelm' in your invoicing space?" Here, she was able to unpack the patterns of thought and emotion she experienced *inside* her invoicing space where the experience of overwhelm lived. Her description tumbled out and we were able to define the different areas inside invoicing that were locking her in place. They included fears of:

- "Is this really happening?"

- The unpredictability of what could happen with each individual client.

- Trusting that people were going to do what they said they would do (pay in certain periods of time).

- The underlying questions from her ex-marriage of "Am I valuable enough? Am I empowered enough to do this?"

- The underlying cultural patterning from her family, questioning whether it was okay for women to not only succeed in business, but thrive in business.

In essence, Sonia was able to voice and name all these emotional layers at the exchange space of invoicing that she had tied up inside of herself and built into one conglomerate picture of "overwhelm" and her somatic trigger of "freeze." This is why airing out the individual elements in your Money Story are so important!

As I reviewed each of these financial emotional elements with Sonia, I took another step in the slow-down practice and had her breathe while checking in with her body during each element, telling me what she felt and where she felt it in her body. As she breathed through these spaces, just being with each one, she felt her freeze trigger begin to relax. She was able to be present with some of the elements during our session. The others she took into her presence practice space to work with. The next time I spoke with her, the procrastination habit with invoicing had dissolved, her freeze trigger had dissolved and she was working with her money, both in invoicing and in new business, in a way she'd never imagined.

This process of slowing down to unpack the emotional layers of your money mess, while consciously embracing your vulnerability and breathing through the space with presence, is the very thing that will naturally help you untangle your financial noodle bowl. Through this process, your exchange space will take on a whole new meaning, feeling and experience. What at first feels like the elephant in your living room can transform into a process of feeling more blessings with your money and you begin to feel better, maybe even good!

Overall, what we just walked you through is the juicy landscape of your financial Heroine's/Hero's Journey. It's time to don your cape and clasp your favorite magician's wand, beam up your warrior's light saber, swirl your spear or slip on your magical traveling shoes because...

Your Financial Heroine's/Hero's Journey Is Masquerading in Your Fiscal Spreadsheets.

Not at first, but eventually, I noticed a rhythm appearing in the cycles of my financial journey and that of my clients. It was like a drum beat or a rhythmic song playing in the background, just out of earshot, but it was there and getting louder. As I helped myself and others connect the symbolic, sometimes mythical, sometimes intuitive, tell-tale signs of personal growth inside money relationships that ultimately lead to breakthroughs, I couldn't help but turn around in certain moments and say, "Hey, Universe. I heard that," as rimshots from the drum's edge ricocheted around me. I couldn't help but sense things were happening just out of the corner of my eye, and I'd say, "Hey, Universe. I see that," as a powerful ephemeral energy flitted just out of view with money work.

What am I talking about? You see, we've all been trained to look at the hard edge of numbers through the viewfinder of our left brain. We've been trained to treat numbers as solid things, and we're told, "Just look at the factual data of the numbers. That's what's true." But I'm not so sure that's the entire story because when I walk people through their healing and personal growth with their numbers inside money relationship, the numbers take on a life of their own, shimmying and shaking, singing and dancing, while they tell a totally different story than just being jammed into squares and columns on a spreadsheet. Sure, you initially need the spreadsheet for the picture. That's Accounting 101. But then, you need to be able to look with soft eyes at the *story* your numbers are telling you within your spreadsheets.

You see, I've found that numbers in spreadsheets are a lot like musical notes on sheet music. Like musical notes, numbers vibrate and sing their story, dance their story and tell their story... if we will only pay attention and listen to the story. If you do, that's about when your Herione's/Hero's Journey screams up on a classic Indian motorcycle on the edge of the Salt Flats in Nevada, hands you a helmet, and says, "Ready to ride?"

I didn't always have this piece, the Heroine's/Hero's Journey piece, to light my way through this rhythm inside the journey of money relationship. Nope, it wasn't until I was into the core of writing this manuscript that two words, like fireflies in a forest, fell onto the page: Hero's Journey. Ding! The thing that's always been just out of reach, the glimmer on the edge of my field of vision, the beating drum rhythms just out of earshot – that. Until the Universe seemed to say, "It's *Hero's Journey*, honey. The utterly glorious journey you and those around you have been on your entire lives." That's when I knew the precious life work of Joseph Campbell that had been sitting underneath my nose this entire time, inside the dusty video jacket of *The Power of Myth*, popped through with the golden model.

When I looked up the *Hero's Journey* model, and Maureen Murdock's answering model of *Heroine's Journey*, I was looking square in the face at the patterning all my clients loosely walk through in healing their own financial journey for breakthroughs. It would make sense that the intimate sacred home where the money relationship lives in the second chakra of our bodies, amongst the vulnerable money relationships of exchange, partnership and agreement, would be ripe ground for Heroine's/Hero's Journey patterning to unfold.

Of note, Murdock's *Heroine's Journey* and Campbell's *Hero's Journey* vary because of gender differences that women and men experience — and I encourage you to review the model/s that are right for you. Also, for my non-binary gender and LGBTQ readers, as noted before, I encourage you to review Hero's Journey LGBTQ models. Interesting, Murdock's work defines how women, to succeed in the marketplace, are required to identify with the masculine viewpoint. Then, upon success, may have varying identity crisis' that require some kind of spiritual resolution to reconnect and heal their inner wounded feminine and masculine. I regularly see this pattern in my financial work with women. I also see resemblances of this pattern in my male clients who lean feminine and have difficulty embodying the traditional patriarchal viewpoints. This all leads, for both men and women, to a retune and rebalance of the inner masculine and inner feminine. This is an entirely large topic to explore, but for now...

If you want to know how to have a breakthrough in your life with your money relationship, grab your magical baton. It's time to dance with dragons, dine with royalty, sleep under stars along the yellow brick road of the Heroine and Hero's Journey pattern. It all begins when you decide to butt-bump aside the elephant in your living room, take the helm of your ship and walk through your threshold of embracing your vulnerability with money relationship. When you do, the micro and the macro patterning of your journey with money relationship begins to loosely resemble this:

Somatic Money Through the Viewfinder of Heroine's/Hero's Journey

Remember to use your Somatic Money Presence Practice as you read through the pattern with slowing down, breathing and becoming aware in your body. Also, if you need a focal point, you might use your current Money Event or your current Compelling Money Issue as a viewfinder.

1. **You begin to notice the call to adventure.** You feel the itch that something needs to change. You notice that "You've had enough of having enough" and the hamster wheel of your current financial pattern is no longer working for you. You are ready to depart the world you know and head for the unknown world. Big, courageous vulnerability.

2. **Initially, you resist or refuse the call to adventure.** At first, you resist the initial call to adventure, listing all your current reasons, excuses and obligations. You tell yourself, "I can't risk changing all this for something I don't know." You put off the inevitable out of fear or responsibility or comfort until the

Universe deliberately sends enough signals that you know you need to pay attention. Mark my words, don't wait for the two-by-four to tell you it's time to journey. Choose when you get the feather gently tapping you, telling you it's time. Inevitably, you realize it's time to make the commitment because it's time for change. Brushing up against vulnerability to take this journey begins to feel more like the norm than the exception.

3. **The mentors, resources, and synchronistic connections materialize during your commitment to journey.** No one journeys alone. Ever. The Universe always gifts you with exactly what you need: the right people, resources or connections at just the right time. That's how it shows up. Make the commitment, and voila, the Universe materializes your wands, boots, backpacks, swords, books, carpet bags, magical pouches or whatever it is that is perfect for you in the time you need it. Remember, courage first. And yeah, it feels vulnerable. Second comes commitment bonded with courage. Third, Universal support, even if you feel like you're in the wrong spot at the wrong time. Sometimes your journey is not what you think it's about, so never stare a gift horse in the mouth.

4. **Journey! You experience challenges, tests and growth.** Your journey might be about learning something new. Or practicing something new. Or putting yourself out there in a new way. Or taking new action you didn't know was possible. Or speaking up in a new way. Essentially, the journey is about being outside your comfort zone, and making those vulnerable connections where you grow, learn and heal. Along the journey, you find that even the challenging experiences, the tests, help you grow resiliency and change you in ways you didn't know were possible. And this all builds until you...

5. **Confront the shadow, your journey's ordeal.** (For description about shadow and shadow work, please reference the next section.) Somewhere in the journey, you come face to face with the one thing that scares you shitless. The one thing you know is there that you don't understand or know how to handle. Maybe it's a dragon. Or a boss. Or a spiteful goddess. Or a co-worker. Or a bear reared up and raging. Or an employee. Or a sinking swamp. Or a troubling intimate financial partnership. Or a ship full of pirates. Or a terrifying feeling at certain places inside your money relationship. Or an overwhelming phantom. Or a financial riddle that's haunted you all your life. Or that one line item in your spreadsheet. You get the picture. Your financial shadow, the thing you couldn't see that you haven't dealt with, flares up in front of you. This is the ordeal in your journey. It's the aspect of intimate partnership, exchange or agreement that is your bane, showing up reflectively on the stage of life. Whatever it is, this is why you sucked in oxygen when you made your vulnerably courageous commitment in the first place. And now that you're here, there's no backing out. It's time to look into the mirror of the confrontation and see what's looking back. *It's time for you to make a new choice about an old thing in the heart of your vulnerability as you face off with the dragon.*

6. **Interacting with or confronting your ordeal.** The moment you're in the middle of the confrontation or the interaction of your ordeal, you are in the middle of your courageous vulnerability. *You're also in the space of your pure creational potential.* This is where time stops and the cavity of the Universe opens up for you to do what you need to do to create in the vulnerable event horizon of your life, possibly in brand-new ways. Possibly in ways that release and complete the old, making space for the new. No matter who you are, you are the heroine/hero of your own journey. You are Dorothy

ripping back the curtain to see the Great Oz. You are T'Challa standing off in battle at the waterfall. You are the female, Captain Marvel, claiming memory and activating into your superpower as you face off with your shadow, realizing the pulsing power of who you truly are. You are Luke standing before your dark father Darth Vader, light saber in hand and the canyon of the Death Star opened beneath. You are Harry Potter activating your wand in the presence of He-Who-Must-Not-Be-Named. Yes! Please choose the story and superheroine or hero character you most relate with because this is your journey. This is your story. This is your time. Make it your own! Whatever your great story is, make sure you are in the middle of your vulnerable courageousness with your slow down, your breath, your presence, your authentic self. You are your own heroine/hero!

7. **The treasure of your vulnerable reveal.** Here, in the middle of your creational ordeal with your shadow, you learn who you truly are, through the vulnerable reveal of your experience with the interactive stand-off. Usually, the thing you feared the most, well... you become one with it by becoming present with it. As you did, you transformed in it and with it while it transformed you. In holding space with what you feared the most, while speaking and doing what you needed to in authentic vulnerability, you created. You became a new version of yourself. Now you are living to tell about it, and in doing so...

8. **It's time for you to seize and embrace your treasure.** On the other side of your ordeal, your inexplicable transformation, your treasure arrives. It could arrive as self-claimed new experiences. Or in the form of financial treasure, resource treasure or breakthrough treasure. It could be new connections for yourself and others with new relationships. Or it

could be an up-level or expansion. Maybe a healing. Maybe closure. You may not know what the treasure is until you arrive there — or even later. The treasure becomes clear when you've found the courage to connect with yourself and others in vulnerability and become present with your greatest resistance, fears, and shadows. And no matter what, when your treasure arrives, embrace it!

9. **Integration: It's time to go home.** Make sure that when you arrive here, after the big storm and the treasure you claimed, that you return home. This is the space where you give yourself rest and time to process. Integrate the precious journey you've experienced. It's time to review and embrace it. So, even though home might be different and you might be different when you get there, that's okay. Just let yourself return and integrate what you've just experienced.

Your money relationship growth, healing and breakthroughs are soaked with the rhythms of your financial Heroine's/Hero's Journey, not just once or twice, but repeatedly in both micro and macrocosmic ways. This shows that money is not just about the numbers; it's about emotionally intelligent risks of courageous vulnerable connections inside your money relationship. It's the journey of building your emotional resiliency (strength) into greater self-trust and greater self-faith, giving you a greater sense of financial emotional responsibility and ability to hold financial boundaries as needed. This is your experiential transformation, especially in the middle of uncertainty, where you claim your authentic money blueprint – not the money life pre-defined for you by others, but the real one living inside of you.

How Shadows and Shadow Work Impact Your Money Relationship.

I've mentioned shadows and shadow work multiple times throughout this book and there's a reason for that. Now is the best space to connect the dynamics of shadows and shadow work for trigger and trauma mitigation while empowering your embodiment and Heroine's/Hero's Journey to constructively impact your money relationship. It's time to define what shadows and shadow work are, and how they relate with our money relationships.

Our personal shadows are a bit of an enigma. While you might think your shadow is your negative side, your dark side, that's not entirely true. Your shadow, housed in the twilight-ey, dimmed-down region of your soul, is an aspect of yourself that provides the service of holding what you can't see about yourself or what you don't want to know about yourself until you're ready. Another way to look at shadows and shadow work is that they are our blind spots, holding that space for us, until we're ready for the great reveal. Our shadow self, worked with constructively, is a healthy and important aspect of our psyche. But that's not how it usually goes.

Shadow work regularly gets a bad rap because we tend to believe that shadows are only negative and nasty and the big, bad, boogey-men hiding in the shadows will jump out of the bushes and snatch us if we go looking into the dark nether realms of ourselves. We're a culture that would rather ignore our shadow self and wrap ourselves in the blanketed idea that if we only hold a positive attitude, looking only at the good stuff and staying only in the light then everything will be okay. (Snort! I am holding back ruthless laughter!) But that's not true. This dynamic of "only stay in the light and be positive" is exactly how we end up with elephants in our living rooms running the show and professional blues players riffing for us as emotional shit tumbles out of our emotional closets. Ignoring your unfinished business, including the emotional drama in you Feminine Money EQ closet, is a great way to bog down your life. Besides, staying in the light only lasts as long as the sun is in the sky. When the sun goes down there is the potential for balance and integration. After sunset, eventually, you're going to have to navigate and deal with your shadow by walking around in a darkened landscape with only the moon and stars to light the way. And there you go. Even in the dark there is still a little light, you never have to go it alone, and you always have support just a conscious "ask" away. And eventually, the sun rises in the morning.

For the constructive aspect of working with your shadow self, you need to know that shadows and shadow work tend to be closely linked with the unhealed, unreleased, triggering trauma held in the envelope of suspended animation in our bodies (small to large), much like we talked about in Chapter Four. Healing trauma, which is ultimate shadow work, is truly an in-time and on-time process with no forcing or pushing. We tend to embrace our self-integration, our self-healing and reconnect or integrate the disconnects inside our trauma when we're ready. So, what does our psyche do in the meantime? The envelope of suspended animation holding the disconnect of our trauma has to go somewhere. So, the body decides, "Hey! Let's put it out of the way in the closet, in the blind spot. It'll still be there, but we'll act like it's not until our person is ready. Begin the cover music! And, to keep them occupied, let's go ahead and release the elephant into the living room as a stand-in distraction." (Frankly, it doesn't have to be an elephant distraction. It could be an alligator, a snake, a spider, wild lions – whatever it is that best matches your slightly dangerous and highly annoying distraction).

From this angle you can see that the systematic process of shadow work is a necessary constructive action along the Heroine's/Hero's Journey of redemption, healing, integration and reclaiming your true self. So, when someone mentions the shadow or shadow work, they're merely saying, "I'm talking about what hasn't been revealed, recovered or looked at yet from your blind spot that might be in need of help or healing." If you need further reference on shadow work, check into *The Dark Side of the Light Chasers* by Debbie Ford. This is also the area of work best supported by a somatic therapist or somatic psychotherapist.

I hope you're beginning to see that just by taking a look at shadow work it plays large in powerfully shifting your Feminine Money EQ department. Imagine it like this: all those suspended animation contexts that you keep hidden away in your emotional closet while the elephant dances in your living room? This is your opportunity to unleash your can of Heroine's/Hero's Journey whoop-ass on:

- The unpaid bills you can't look at. (Potentially linked to your version of Judeo-Christian guilt and obligation that you've let leak into your finances.)

- The salary raise you keep avoiding, keep meaning to ask or negotiate for at work. (Potentially linked to your frozen voice from never being able to speak up to your father or mother.)
- Feeling like you can't have a financial boundary with your kids and spouse. (Potentially linked to early patterns of always trying to please someone else to receive your greater sense of self-worth.)

- Running and working so hard, but never feeling like you can catch up with work or money. (Potentially linked to early memories of wondering if you can survive.)

- With these examples, feel free to review your own personal version of these types of patterns, both small and large and the deeper emotional and relationship issues they're linked to.

These are just a few examples of the connective emotional blind spots affecting your financial picture that you might have stuffed away in your shadow, your closet, for safe keeping. You're keeping them there until you feel strong enough, valuable enough, confident enough to pull them out and redeem them, Heroine's/Hero's Journey style, for the raise, the debt dissolvement, the financial boundary, the peace of mind.

Remember, Somatic Money Presence Practice is your foundation to fill your vessel of resilience so you can do the work of breaking the patterns. Remember, pace yourself. Like my mentor, Linda, used to say, "In time and on time. We're ready when we're ready." Are you ready?

Defining Your Vulnerable Money Pivot Points Through Inventory.

Now that I've shared with you the concepts, stories, and data about the vulnerability in money relationship, what does it mean for you and how do you work with it in a practical way?

Let's define the primary places where you might experience potential vulnerability with your money relationship. As you comb through this inventory, you might come up with a couple new inventory items of your own. I've broken the money vulnerability inventory into the three activated locations of money: exchanges, partnerships and agreements. **Please locate your hot mess money zones and your secure, confident, value-based money zones. Then cross reference your information to build a landscape of your particular brand of money vulnerability and strength.** It's important to know what you're good at even when you are tripping over your challenges. As always, please use your Somatic Money Presence Practice of slowing down, breathing, getting present and noticing how you feel in your body through this inventory. Initially, I encourage you to use this checkl list below for your entire money relationship. Then, as you become familiar with your landscape, you may use this tool to trouble-shoot the Compelling Money Issues that arise in your life. That said, let's go ahead and begin:

Identify Your Hot Mess Money Zones AND
Your Confident I-Have-My-Act-Together Money Zones

- **While <u>receiving</u> money in EXCHANGES** - Identify the items below that pertain to you, and please describe your strength and vulnerability relationships with:

  ○ Invoicing or negotiating for rate of pay.

  ○ The amount you charge for goods/services when you receive money.

o   The technical and emotional process you experience when getting paid.

o   Communicating about invoicing.

o   How you handle situations that might arise in accounts receivable.

o   Enough-ness in receiving payments.

o   Allowing yourself to have money in receiving.

o   Systems or protocols to receive money.

o   Other.

Are you slowing down? Breathing? Being present?
Are you checking in with your body
about how you feel concerning each line item?
I hope you're being kind with yourself.

•   **While <u>releasing</u> money in EXCHANGES** - Identify the items below that pertain to you, and please describe your strength and vulnerability relationships with:

o   Paying bills.

o   Spending money for fun: entertainment, travel, clothing, self-care.

o   The experience you have reviewing the pricing and value of services or items that you spend money on.

o   Your ability to make payments.

    ◦   Financial planning and the building and keeping of your Monthly Money Game Plan.

    ◦   Enough-ness in making payments.

    ◦   Allowing yourself to have money to make payments.

    ◦   How the money works for you in spending.

    ◦   Other.

Yeah, I know. I'm a pain in the ass,
but are you slowing down? Breathing? Being present?
Are you checking in with your body
about how you feel concerning each line item?
I hope you are being gentle with yourself.

- **About the quality of your <u>money environment</u> or EX-CHANGE SPACE** - Identify the items below that pertain to you, and please describe your strength and vulnerability relationships with:

    ◦   Retail spaces? Do you feel safe, confident, secure or vulnerable?

    ◦   Your home budget / bill-paying space? Do you feel safe, confident, secure or vulnerable?

    ◦   Your digital financial connections? Do you feel safe, confident, secure or vulnerable?

    ◦   Your place of business or employment? Do you feel safe, confident, secure or vulnerable?

○   Or do any of these money environments have vulnerable niches or pockets in them, as well as safe, confident and secure places? Get clear and define for yourself.

○   Other.

It's me again with your friendly blunt reminder:
Are you slowing down? Breathing? Being present?
Are you checking in with your body
about how you feel with specifics?
I hope you are being supportive with yourself.

• **About the quality of your intimate to professional money PARTNERSHIPS.** Identify the items below that pertain to you, and please describe your strength and vulnerability relationships with:

○   What is the nature of your intimate partnership/s with money? How would you define them in relationship with the vulnerability topic? This might include identity roles and conversations about earning, income, financial priorities, emotional dynamics with money, and communications.

○   What is the nature of your family/friends with money? How would you define them in relationship with the vulnerability topic? This might include identity roles, conversations about who pays for what and who receives/gives what. It might also include financial status, emotional dynamics with money and communications.

○   What is the nature of your employer, employees, colleagues, or co-workers with money? How would you define your working partnerships in relationship with the vulnerability topic with money? This might include salary negotiations, financial work environments and pay scales. Pay attention to the undercurrent about emotion, money and vulnerability in the workspace.

o   Other.

Alright, I know this seems like it's over the top,
but do I give up? No, and neither should you.

You're in the thick of it, but please be sure to:
Slow down and breathe. For a few moments, just be present,
while checking in with your body about how you feel.
And, of course, have patience with yourself.
But who am I kidding?
This is where I'd break out the chocolate or the ice cream!
Sheesh! (Seriously. Keep going.)

- **About the quality of your intimate to professional money AGREEMENTS.** Identify the items below that pertain to you, and please describe your strength and vulnerability relationships with:

   o   Within your relationship with YOU and money, what are the money agreements that you keep with yourself? Where do you feel the most vulnerable or confident? Are you strict, reasonable, lenient, methodical, rational or irrational with yourself about money? Do you pay things early or on time or wait until the last minute? Do you receive money in guilt and shame or in confidence and value? Do you have arbitrary money rules with yourself or irrational ones or rational ones? What's your money method of agreement with yourself? This is an extension of money environment in that how you agree or disagree with yourself about money sets up how you engage with money and how you engage with others with money. In your agreements with yourself, do you feel vulnerable, uncomfortable, clear, unclear or something else?

o   Within your intimate partnership/s, what are the money agreements that you've officially committed to, either in writing or verbally? Or what money agreements have you committed to out of pattern or habit? This is akin to a financial division of labor. Who is responsible for what? Are things open for discussion or reasonable negotiation? When changes or surprises happen, can you communicate? Do you feel vulnerable or confident about these working partnership agreements?

o   Within your circle of friends and family, how is the agreement of money handled verbally or nonverbally? What financial roles or financial agreements do you verbally or nonverbally keep with your friends or family members. Are you always the one who pays for meals out? Or do you always allow others to cover the tab? Or do you rationally split the bill or fight over the bill? Is money an issue or nonissue? Do you financially receive help from others or provide help to others? Is money a status thing or a nonissue? In essence, what money agreement environments have you set up with your warm circle? Where do you feel confident or vulnerable with these agreements?

o   What are your money agreements at work or in your place of business? Is money matter-of-fact? Is it a power issue or not? Is it clear or unclear? Are you fairly compensated for the work you provide an employer or the services you provide for your clientele?

What is the money environment? Is it confident or undermining? Toxic or clearly supportive? How would you describe the types of verbal and nonverbal money agreements in your workspace? What's your level of vulnerability or confidence?

o   Other.

You did it!
You gradually worked through all the primary areas
where your money vulnerability is potentially exposed
and you also located your strengths.
Good job!
Be sure to breathe, take a time out and
reflect on all you excavated. That was a lot!

With this inventory, I hope you can begin to see the themes and patterns inside your vulnerable money relationship - both your hotspots that are creating your money messes AND your money relationship confidence, strength and empowerment - that are keeping you financially afloat.

Now that you've mapped this landscape, what next? My first suggestion is to take a breather. Like I mentioned before, you did a great job excavating and that in and of itself shifted your energy, emotions, psychology and body with your money relationship. It's time to let go and let your inner self and body catch up with one another. Let the feathers settle. Once you allow yourself a bit of breathing room (a day to a couple of days), then it's time to return and refocus your practice into your big pivot!

Putting It All Together for Your Money Relationship Pivot.

No doubt, you're probably already experiencing shifts in your money relationship with the applied pieces of the puzzle that I've given to you so far. Yet, these pieces are still sitting in loose association with one another. Now, I want to show you what they look like engaged together. We've arrived at your powerful pivot point with money relationship! I'm super excited for you because you've had the courage to walk through daunting space, you're still here and we're ready to put it together! Here is what the connective pieces look like working together:

Combining Your Somatic Money Tools for An Empowered Pivot

1. *Gently lean* with your **Somatic Money Presence Practice** of slowing down, breathing, becoming present/aware and center/grounding in your body into ...

2. *Into* your identified **Hot Mess Money Zones** where you feel vulnerable. You may either do this one item at a time OR into specific patterned locations.

3. As you're *aware* and holding space with your Hot Mess Money Zones, notice if your body's potential response shifts into **Fight-Flight-Freeze Triggers.**

4. This might *indicate* past dis-connective or **Unhealed Trauma** that is being held ...

5. Being *held* in your **Shadow World or Blind Spot.**

6. This is your *indicator* of where to **Fill Your Inner Vessel With Resilience Energy** from your Somatic Money Presence Practice, preparing you ...

7. *Preparing* you for your **Heroine's/Hero's Journey** to transform your money relationship.

In seeing this bigger picture, it will help you know where/how to refocus your Somatic Money Presence Practice to your specific Hot Mess Money Zones with your money relationship. As uncomfortable and messy as this might be, what you're doing is bringing your can of presence practice whoop-ass to beef up your empowerment and value, support and flow where you need it the most. And this creates pivot energy into financial transformation and new money choices.

Without trying to solve anything in your head, this begins to fill up your reservoir of resilience where you've felt challenged. It begins to give you a little more room in your psyche, a little more empowerment in your soul. Your sense of self lifts with a little more value. You feel your legs return to support your entire self. Flow begins to arrive with hints of potential illuminated solutions. Before you know it, you're beginning to feel the pulse of your Heroine's/Hero's Journey and a willingness to take back the reins of your life.

What I'm asking you to do is to be gently present at your financial pain points, a counter-intuitive act of faith, so that you may allow an authentic unfolding inside your money relationship. Without a shadow of a doubt, this is super courageous of you to be willingly present with the vulnerability, the discomfort of your money relationship. It's time to be present right in the middle of the hot mess of your money life and make friends with the elephant in your living room. This is how you begin to tip the scales, quite literally. It's your time to fill your glass beyond the halfway point!

* * *

Reminder Warning: As I mentioned during the Money Trigger work, please keep in mind that consciously working in the areas of your money vulnerability might create triggers into existing or past trauma. So, if you are recovering from mild to severe trauma, including accident trauma, physical abuse, racial injustice, war-zone combat, mental and emotional abuse or sexual trauma, I recommend that you seek a supportive body-based trauma/healing therapist. The steps I outline here might directly take you into trauma release, and if you don't know how to constructively manage your symptoms in a healthy way, these steps might be more difficult or overwhelming for you. Please take extra care of yourself during any vulnerable money relationship processes. If you find yourself in the severe zone, please do not go it alone. Seek professional support.

* * *

Review Your Money Vulnerability with Your Four Sacred Money Elements. As you begin to collect your data, your patterning from your Somatic Money Presence Practice, your fight-flight-freeze triggers and the hot spots that you inventoried in the previous section about your financial vulnerabilities, you'll begin to notice patterning. This patterning, within your exchanges, partnerships and agreements, will more than likely begin to take shape in the four following areas. These four categories gradually revealed and illuminated themselves to me over the course of thousands of client sessions, appearing as The Four Sacred Money Elements.

The Four Sacred Money Elements Defined

- **Masculine Money:** financial logistics, analytics, logical thoughts (IQ), structure, protection and support. The structural legs of money.

- **Feminine Money:** financial intuition, flow, emotional intelligence (EQ) and self-care or nurturance. The flow of money.

- **Money Value:** financial worth, esteem and value along with identity, voice and being seen. The vibrational value of money.

- **Money Empowerment:** financial empowerment, financial "I am," ability to respond and claiming ownership. The power center of money.

These four elements and their respective subparts are a reflective financial balancing system, showing where we are in and out of balance with our money relationship. The quality of our money lives is determined by how we work with each of them at our exchange spaces with partnership and agreements. Although I'll be spending a great deal of time covering this topic in Book Two of *Somatic Money Mapping*, I want you to know about these now to give you compass settings with your money relationship. Take a look at how these break down with the vulnerabilities you located from the excavation you did earlier. Do any of these resonate with your hot spots?

Illuminated Vulnerabilities
within the Four Sacred Money Elements

- **Masculine Money Vulnerability:** Am I *supported and protected* with my money and money relationship? Am I able to *logistically*, mentally, work with my money?

- **Feminine Money Vulnerability:** Is my money *flowing* into my life and out of my life in a healthy way? Is there enough flow? Am I *valuable enough to be cared for* no matter the amount of money I have?

- **Money Value Vulnerability:** Am I *worth* it to myself? To others? Are others of worth to me? Do I have substantial *esteem*? Do I have *value* in my own eyes? Do I matter to others? Are others valuable to me? *Am I seen and heard? Do I listen? Do I observe?* Am I seen and heard in business? Am I seen and heard in value with my money?

- **Money Empowerment Vulnerability:** Am I able to *claim ownership* of my financial life? Am I able to financially *respond?* Am I financially *accountable?* Do I feel *empowered* enough to manage and work with my money? Do I feel empowered with my money relationship?

Then, if we take the next step and create the natural pairings, you'll find what you might have found yourself asking about *trust* and *belief* in yourself with your vulnerable money relationship.

- **Financial Trust:** This is the confluence of Masculine Money and Feminine Money where the yin and yang dance in co-creation with the Universe. This is where the vulnerabilities of support and flow combine to create a greater and better whole, but in doing so, require the practice of trust. This is the "No matter what happens, I know I'm always taken care of" place.

- **Financial Belief:** This is the confluence of Money Value and Money Empowerment in the dynamic of claiming ownership (empowerment) of who you are (value). This combination gives you the penultimate financial practice of belief that says, "I claim ownership of who I am."

When I arrive at this place with clients in the mapping process, showing the elements as stand-alone features, but then combined into our financial trust and financial belief, there is a resounding feeling of, "This might be the balanced space of the Financial Holy Grail." Financial trust and financial belief are what we're all searching for inside our money relationships through the gateway of vulnerability into the land of the Heroine's/Hero's Journey. We just want to know that we can trust and believe in our lives, our partnerships, our exchanges, our agreements and how our money is going to work out along our yellow brick roads. So, our job is to be relentless in the practice of embracing ourselves in our value, our empowerment, our support and flow — even if that might not always be clear or apparent to you or modeled to you. In ripping back the curtain to reveal the Great Oz, after the grand journey, we find that we're our own best answers. Here is where you'll find your Authentic Money Blueprint of who you truly are, waiting for you without fail.

Client Money Story - How Claire's Slow Down With Money Positively Changed Her Money Life

One of the most powerful and profound somatic connections is the one between money relationship and slowing down during money transactions. Most of my clients don't recognize how fast they're actually moving with their money until we unpack the transaction point. In Claire's case, this proved very profound. Let me set the stage.

When we met and began working together in our first session, I began by interviewing Claire about her recent money transactions. As we slowed down and peeled a few layers of her spin cycles with money at her exchange spaces, we began to find out that she simply could not remember her money transactions. At all. At first, it was a stretch for her to recount her most recent exchanges – like receiving checks from clients. And then, it was really a stretch for her to recount the details of depositing those checks at the bank. Claire was blanking out and disassociating in the middle of her money transactions. Her hamster was running full tilt on the money wheel and she wasn't there.

We spent one entire session helping her re-create and re-associate herself back into her most recent money transactions step-by-step to show her where she needed to slow down and be present. In unpacking these situations, she experienced profound moments of revelation, understanding why she was having deep moments of disorientation with her money and why money seemed so challenging for her. The exercise helped her understand how much she was missing in action with her money relationship, which was both exciting and terrifying for her. She was excited because she was able to see how she could reclaim in her money life, and she was terrified that it had been so bad for so long. She wondered how she had managed to stay functional with money.

Claire took her practice of slowing down with her money transactions to heart and initially, she found she wasn't able to remember doing the practice until after the money event. Her disassociative instincts were tightly clenched, but daily, as she practiced intent and focus, gradually, she was able to circle in closer and closer to the exchanges with her money.

Then, the breakthrough arrived! She experienced the first intermittent waves and then steady moments of slowing down in transactions with her money. These moments profoundly affected her and she gradually made more and more progress. Then something magical began to happen. *She felt her internal vessel begin to fill up.*

After several units of coaching she was able to report this to me, "Oh, my God, Dana. I've stopped racing around with my money. I can even stand on my porch and take in the sun, the air, the birds, the leaves and grass. I'm remembering my money transactions and I've stopped being frantic. I've even stopped thinking I have to be on the hamster wheel to make the money I thought I had to make. Instead, I'm in my body, more grounded, at a more reasonable pace, *and the money is still flowing to me.* I'm working so much less and feeling a lot more calm."

These profound connections between Claire's money exchanges and her overall presence in connecting with her five senses to enjoy life all wonderfully came alive and profoundly changed her life.

Spot Check

Congratulations! You just read and worked through the juggernaut of Somatic Money! Your Somatic Money Presence Practice engaged at your Money Triggers while embracing the vulnerability of walking in the shadow world of your Heroine's/Hero's Journey — that's the juice. Even though we'll continue to add elements, fine tuning for greater leverage as we go, that was the true confluence where the meatiness of the work connects. It may take time to review and allow the rhythms to sink in, but the core is right there and you did it!

This is the place in my coaching practice with clients, in the heat and thick of the work (at least three to four months in), where individuals begin to get a real taste of the magnitude of what they've truly been doing inside their money relationship without even realizing it. This is the place where empowered, leveraged, illuminated shifts begin to happen.

So, if you've made it this far, you're doing awesome! And for incentive, things begin to be a little more fun with the magical money tools in Chapter Seven. Please keep going. You got this!

For gauging your progress, as you peel back the layers in your "slow down" with financial vulnerability and embracing your Heroine's/Hero's Journey, this can take about **a month, maybe more**. Be sure to take your time in a way that works for you. This is the chapter where you'll regularly circle back to excavate the layers. One layer might bring up three more layers. Allow the process to work itself so the greater clearing and revealing may happen.

Also, keep up that self-care. Please hydrate! Your cells need water to lubricate your deep changes. Rest! Your body needs a chance to catch up. Eat those leafy greens to support the change in cellular code. Move around in nature. Stretch. Breathe. Limber up.

Now, let's go fine tune your Somatic Money Presence Practice and bring your Authentic Money Blueprint to the surface.

CHAPTER SIX

Clearing Your Way Out of the Weeds, Into the Flower Patch

Strategies for Cultivating
Your Authentic Money Blueprint

Do you feel we're about to get lost in the weeds? Because I feel we're about to get lost in the weeds. We've covered a tremendous amount of landscape and it's time to highlight the basics of the wash-rinse-repeat process of Somatic Money. Once we re-secure the process, then I'll point out a few spots where it's easy to end up in the weeds, and you don't want to do that. Afterward, we'll spend the rest of the chapter methodically outlining the next steps of leveraged cross-training in the Somatic Money process to help you move out of and stay out of your financial weeds. It's time for you to cultivate your Authentic Money Blueprint, which is you living your authentic money life instead of your money living you. This is about unearthing your financial sovereign birthright through these Somatic Money processes. Remember, every time you cycle around the Somatic Money medicine wheel (process), you learn a little more, deepen your practice and gradually gain the footing of your structure, flow, value and empowerment with money. Ready? Let's go!

Wash. Rinse. Repeat.

No matter how many new concepts I give you throughout the rest of this book, the foundation of Somatic Money always returns like a homing pigeon to these washable, rinseable, repeatable steps. It's like my mentor said to me on a number of occasions. She said, "Dana, if all else fails, go back to the basics." Here are the basics:

1. **Physically slow down** within your money exchanges (receiving income, retail spending, budget strategy, bill-paying, financial issues) so that your money relationship may catch up with you! Don't fly financially faster than the Universe can keep up. Also, emotionally and mentally slow down with your money relationship **to unpack** your authentic money thoughts and vulnerable money emotions in your financial Heroine's/Hero's Journey, revealing what might be hiding in your blind spots, your shadows.

2. **Please breathe** during your money experiences so that you may shift out of your fight, flight, freeze adrenal responses of triggered biology and instead, shift into your parasympathetic state for **greater calm**. This puts you in a better financial physiological space that supports better decision-making and helps you naturally become present in your core.

3. **Awareness. Intent. Presence.** The presence you hold in your core, closer to the home space of money relationship in your body (second chakra), helps you increase your sense of self, presence, value, support, flow and empowerment during your money transactions. This is you improving your emotional resiliency with partnership and agreement within the sacred vessel of exchange so that your money works better.

4. The first three steps of the Somatic Money process naturally support you in **presence and energy at your vulnerable**

money hot spots in your body, shifting the elephant out of your living room while allowing you to **claim your Heroine's/ Hero's Journey** with money relationship. All of this helps to dismantle what's been hiding in your shadows, holding you back. You begin to grow with greater resiliency in light of your money relationship. Here, with time and practice, your Authentic Money Blueprint gradually reveals itself to you.

Like I said, use this Somatic Money process to wash, rinse, repeat with your unique money experiences, partnerships, agreements and situations. Wash, rinse, repeat using these steps with any new tools that I or others might give you. Wash, rinse, wash, repeat as you work with solving your money issues and experience triumphs with your money. Wash, rinse, repeat into deeper understanding, insights and layers of your money relationship as you improve with the process. See how this practice is never really over? It becomes a part of you, always unfolding new aspects that you hadn't seen before, unless you unknowingly detour right into the weed patch. Let's take a look at these blind spots to help you clear out of the weeds.

The Weed Patch of Spiritual and Emotional Masking.
Our first detour into the weed patch is through emotional masking or spiritual masking, also known as emotional or spiritual bypassing. This ever-so-popular habit happens when we insert a cover-up emotion or a cover-up spiritual practice or tool of what we *think* we *should* be doing during a practice or a life experience. We do this without first checking in with our authentic selves, our intuition, our deeper knowing. The telltale sign we might be in the weed patch is feeling guilted, obligated, shamed or pressured into feeling a certain feeling or doing a certain practice that might not be entirely right for us, or right-timed or right-intended. Yes, that might also include Somatic Money! That said, emotional and spiritual masking inserted into the Somatic Money Presence Practice usually triggers in the area of Step Four as I outlined in the previous section. It looks something like this:

You're consciously slowing down and experiencing your money relationship exchange space (Step One) and you're consciously leaning into your breath (Step Two). As your breath helps you shift into your core, you're becoming present there (Step Three), and if you're deep enough and focused enough, you might even be feeling some of your vulnerability (Step Four), some of your emotional and physical sensations.

Right here, this is the detour where we trip into the weed patch. For some, it's an echo in the air of emotion that says, "I *should not* be feeling this way. I *should* be feeling another way." For others, it's a subtle inner "click" where something tells you, "Well, I'm here, I *should* be doing something." So, you begin to insert "This is where I *should* bring in my abundance practice." Or "This is where I *should* be doing my manifesting energy work." Or "This is where I *should* be doing my list of gratitudes..."

Please, no.

No no no no no.

Please STOP.

Why?

This is emotional and spiritual masking that covers up what is authentically happening inside of you. This segue assumes, in your brain, that you already know what your psyche, your soul, your body needs. But do you? It's also paired with the subtle guilt trip of "I'm not allowed to feel this way," or "If I'm a correct spiritual and conscious person, I have to be doing something good here." Well maybe, but let's drop the martyrdom cloak on the floor for a moment.

This emotional and spiritual masking is a detour into the land of the shoulds, woulds, coulds of guilting and possibly shaming yourself into a preconceived notion of the emotional and spiritual practice you need here. ***Emotional and spiritual masking or bypassing eliminates your authentic opening to discover what is real and true for you in your physical and emotional core space.*** No matter how much you want to cut and paste another emotion or another spiritual practice into that spot, please don't. Give yourself a fighting chance to locate the potentially critical vulnerable connection that might have been previously dropped – no matter how small or large. This is your opportunity to reconnect, to begin to reclaim your inner authenticity with emotional accountability (take a stand for yourself, your emotional truth, have a boundary) and grow your emotional resiliency. So, please don't fill in the precious space of your psyche with someone else's idea of what you should feel or what you should do. Instead, please claim your authentic inner space for yourself. Which means you're going to have to step up to the plate and be there for yourself, claiming your vulnerability to find out what is truly unfolding for you. And I promise, there's a special and empowered spot for you to select your emotion or spiritual practice, but *not yet*.

So. To repeat, when you arrive into your Somatic Money Presence Practice space, where you feel yourself tipping into the land of your vulnerability (Step Four) deeper in your body with your emotional intelligence, this is the location where it's most important to:

Break Down Step Four of Vulnerability in the Somatic Money Presence Practice

1. **Just be.** Allow yourself to be there and notice your emotions, your psychology, your physical sensations and any triggers. Please resist the urge to buy into any should, would, could trigger of guilt, shame or blame.

2. From here, if you want, you might ask, **"How do I feel?"** and notice how you feel without doing any fixing, strategizing or Band-Aid mending. Just embrace yourself and acknowledge your emotion.

3. Or you might ask, **"What is this about?"** and notice what comes up without assigning any judgment. Embrace yourself, acknowledging what comes up.

4. Your job is to **observe, embrace and allow** your body to sort things out as you hold presence with all that is happening physically, mentally and emotionally. Breathe.

5. Let there be a pause. There is no rush. **Let things settle**.

In this space, let me ask you this: When was the last time something happened in your financial life where you didn't rush to fix it? To throw money at it? To lean into taking care of it for yourself or someone else? To go into more debt and put it on a credit card? To run away or shut down or fight to defend yourself? To avoid looking at the financial impact? The first layer of our triggered financial instincts most likely to happen in Step Four usually screams to us, "DO SOMETHING! ANYTHING! PUT OUT THE FIRE SO WE DON'T HAVE TO FEEL THIS VULNERABLE THING WITH MONEY!" Well, that's our survival talking. Our shadow talking. Our original wound talking. Our emotional and spiritual masking of guilt, obligation and shame talking. They are telling us about our fear, lack of safety, lack of power, lack of know-how, burning pain and lack of value. This is where we'd rather let the money go haywire than look at what is truly happening, be present with it and experience our vulnerability. Simply put, the overwhelm is too much. This is where we insert the elephant, cover with another emotion and put on the mask, detouring off the path of our Heroine's/Hero's Journey right into our weed patch. But we don't want to do that, do we?! No. (A gentle sidenote. In the spirit of in-time-and-on-time, building your emotional resiliency to do this might take time, some false starts, as you acclimate into this process. Careful the pitfall, or self-masking trap door of self-sabotage where you might beat up on yourself if you can't do it at first. Gentle here. Be kind as you acclimate.)

So, as I continue to freeze-frame this spot in the presence practice, illuminating the interior of your small to large money patterns, let me ask you, "What if?" What if, for once, you don't do anything?

What if, for once, you remain in your authentic and vulnerable space, allowing yourself *to be?* Just *be and embrace yourself. Breathe.* Even if it's for a short while. Even if it's for the baby step that you can do. What I'm asking you to do here is to potentially **be with the trigger, the vulnerability of the event, without doing anything except breathing and experiencing.** I know, that's like asking you to stand in front of the symbolic locomotive and experience the impact. That's like asking you to stand in the symbolic house as it burns down. That's asking you to stand and hold presence in the shadow-world work of the de-construction as it naturally unfolds, without you controlling it. What I'm asking you to do here is trust in the nature of the Universe to catch you, hold you. And I agree, that is not easy. Sometimes, it's messy, it sucks and it's the scary and uncomfortable part of shadow work, because you don't know what is going to happen. Yet, this is where the mask begins to fall away. This is where the elephant pauses mid-step in your living room and says, "Oh, shit, she/he/they is taking the reins. I don't have long here. My stay will be ending soon." This is where we clear out of the weed patch into the Heroine's/ Hero's Journey, into embracing our emotional accountability, our resiliency. What a turn around!

On a personal note, so you don't feel like you're standing alone at the edge of this cliff, know that I have a boatload of heart-rending financial empathy for you. I've regularly walked through the vulnerably challenging financial steps of this space and so have many of my clients. I began reclaiming my financial journey with these presence tools in the basics of my checking account space. Here, I'd previously embodied waves of panic attack energy, making it nearly impossible to balance my checking account during bill-paying time. I ran from my shadow monster, feeling like it was a life and death situation when I worked with my money. I understand now that I had built cycles of triggers, harboring them in my body in connection with my money, especially as I balanced my checking account. To break the cycle, I used the presence practice steps so that I could just be, breathe and sit through the energy wave with my checking account, allowing myself to come present with it, vulnerability intact, until I could regularly balance my monthly statements into a greater state of calm. Now this space is second nature and I have multiple accounts, multiple financial strategies at play, and remarkably, they vibrationally sing their messages and my money path to me! (Instead of me cratering into the collapse of fear and scarcity triggers.)

But that wasn't the only financially difficult space in my life. I also carried loads of putrid fear concerning my personal taxes that blocked me from filling out my 1040 tax forms. I avoided those forms for years. Here, I also used the presence practice steps, especially at the vulnerability points, to tame the 1040 tax beast, just by being and breathing through the rough space until I was present enough to log onto irs.com, download and print the forms. Then, I again used the presence practice, especially at the points of vulnerability, to help me fill out the forms, filing each year sequentially until I was caught up and paid in full.

You name it, I've done some pretty stupid financial shit because my money monster was too big, too shadowy, the emotional collapse was all-too consuming, and the easiest coping mechanism was to use whatever emotional and spiritual financial masking I could find to pull the veil down, cover the mess, and live to fight another day. So, I know what it's like to be in a fragile financial position, a fragile emotional state, while considering staring the dragon of your Heroine's/Hero's Journey in the face. It's not easy, but I also know the positive things that can happen when you do: Things like getting a grasp on your monthly numbers, breaking destructive financial patterning, finding the hutzpah to voice your financial boundaries and give yourself a raise that works, gathering the internal support and courage to make a big money move. All of this while cultivating a sense of knowing that you're financially nurtured and valued by the same Universe that created you.

I believe it's worth mentioning that these vulnerable, turning-point presence practice tools are not only helpful for digging out financially, they are also useful for breakthroughs to the topside.

Once I righted my financial ship, I began using these steps to gradually build my business, speak in front of audiences, raise my rates, attract and land new clientele — and even have the courage to write this book. It's important to keep the dream in front of you, even as you dance with dragons.

So, I would not ask you to do what I haven't already done a number of times and also walked my clients through a number of times. You're not alone in this process and many have come before you. When we embrace ourselves in our most vulnerable interior spaces of our finances, even in trigger, and we stop reaching for the emotional and spiritual masks that will shut it down, we are internally claiming the confrontation and integration space of the shadow in the Heroine's/Hero's Journey.

Remember back in Chapter Five and Step Five of the Heroine's/Hero's Journey where it's time to hold space with the shadowy presence of the monster? This is the spot. This is it! This is where we win, even if it momentarily feels like we're losing, because the win is the embrace of our authentic vulnerable selves, even in the face of our scariest dragon. This is where we hold presence for redemption, healing and integration with ourselves in our here and now of the trigger connected to the original wounding event. It's here, that sometimes our dueling dragons become our greatest allies, our friends. They are the catalyst to help us step up to our greatest level of being in our lives, our greatest heroine or hero self!

What I'm asking you to do is simple, yet utterly heroic. What I'm asking you to do is brilliant, yet it can be one of the hardest things to do. All because most of us train ourselves to avoid this scary, vulnerable, painful, messy space by spiritual and emotional masking to self-protect. Ultimately, what I'm asking you to do is choose your precious sacred self at the vulnerable confluence of the exchange space in your money relationship. Even if it feels like you're facing a monster, a shadow, a dragon, a death, an unknown – because you are. But you know what? You'll live. You'll do more than live. You will come through it to the other side and have more of yourself. You'll be holding the sacred love of your soul inside of you, beating more strongly and clearly than ever before. Every single baby step you take on this journey counts. You count.

Do You Know What You Need? Clearing Unwanted Weeds to Claim Flowers.

Many of us get financially lost in the weeds, losing sight of why we're doing what we're doing with our work and our money. It's easy, through the routine of life, to lose our way and get stuck in the financial weed patch. Eventually, we begin to realize we're not necessarily creating money for ourselves or for the purposes that we originally intended — if we even knew what that intent was in the first place. Sometimes, we find ourselves creating money for everyone else and everything else except ourselves. This is why we all occasionally need to know what we really, truly need in our lives. In the Somatic Money Presence Practice, there is such place to ask about and entertain these ideas, and the question regularly tends to pop up in the middle of unpacking Step Four that I reviewed with you in the previous section, as you're clearing a few dragons, a few monsters or a few toxic weeds in your life.

Asking yourself, "What do I truly need?" is a fantastic question to ask after you've settled into the *being* part in the practice, after you've asked yourself what you *truly feel* and after you've asked what this is *really about*. You might even be in the middle of letting the trigger feathers settle when you ask what you *truly need*. As you arrive into your vessel in this more grounded and sound space where you unpack your vulnerability, usually the authentic soul rises and becomes very clear that it is in need of something that it has not been receiving. Thus, it reveals the imbalance in your life that caused the chaos, for attention, of a financial event, financial issue or financial person. Remember, we create from the inside out of our deep spaces, even financially. Money challenges usually arise from the deep space of a specific deep need – energetic, emotional, physical or mental -- that was not met in the first place (from home of origin or past lifetime or trauma event). As we familiarize ourselves with our internal self, through our presence practice, it's important to locate what we are craving in our depths and give ourselves the emotional attention we deserve.

As you are in your process of slowing down, breathing, getting present and deepening your vulnerable connection, your internal bubbling pot is answering as to how you truly feel about any given financial event, person or agreement — the unpacking. Listen to what your body, psyche, soul have to tell you, and believe it. And then, when you ask, "What is this about?" your soul answers into your internal bubbling pot with information about whether this is connected to current wounds or events, previous wounds or events, other drama or that it doesn't belong to you at all. Again, listen to what your body, your psyche, your soul have to say and believe them.

If arriving into these spaces with these layers peeled back does not create a greater calm or peace for you, then it's time to ask: "Soul, self, what do I really, truly need here? What support, protection, energy, resource or guidance is most helpful for me?" The answers could be anything from "I need more respect!" to "I need more money on this project!" to "I just want to feel peace." Or "Wow, it's time to buy that new car." Or "It's time to lean in on my abundance practice." Or "I need some time alone." Or "I don't know why, but I need to pay attention when I water my plants." Or "It's time to totally focus on my vision boarding and manifestation practice." Or "I need to finish my taxes early this year." Or "I need a deep feeling of nurturance right now." Or "It's time to purchase that professional outfit for a job I haven't landed yet." Whatever answers come to you, whether physical needs, emotional needs or energy needs, your job is not to judge, not to dismiss, but to acknowledge and pay attention to what your authentic self is revealing to you. Then, move in the direction of giving yourself what your soul is asking for. Your deeper needs could be:

1. Answering to a physical need that is random, rational or irrational.

2. Answering to an experiential need, including a spiritual practice.

3. Answering to a mental need.

4. Answering to an emotional or psychological need, including an emotion-based energy or practice.

5. Answering to a deeper unconscious soul-level need.

6. Answering to a completely random or irrational need.

As the answers come to you, my first suggestion is that you acknowledge what your inner self is asking for, no matter how plain, obvious, irrational or random. Then, allow yourself to be present with what shows up to see how it feels, how it fits. Believe me, your deeper, authentic self is more plugged in than you know, and it can lead you to your better life with powerful answers than what might first seem possible. The key here is that we usually never stop long enough to tune in and listen to our deeper soul needs. When we do, we might be surprised how specific our soul requests are and how much leverage we receive in life by answering to those needs. This is powerful co-creation with the Universe.

When it comes to answering to deeper emotion-based or energy needs, I'd like to share a practice with you that an experienced practitioner, Karen, in Durango, Colorado, revealed to me years ago. Karen showed me that when you ask yourself the "What do I need?" question, especially in relationship to emotion and energy-based needs, then it's helpful to practice giving yourself that emotion or energy answering right then and there. As you're in your presence space, slowed down, breathing, coming into center with your deeper self, it's in this space that you can imagine, breathe and allow the energy of the emotional need that your soul is asking for.

For example, let's say your psyche, your soul is asking for more financial peace. As you're in your presence practice, breathe and allow your body and energy to feel the experience of peace flowing through you and filling you up. Then, be sure to practice the energy of peace in and around your money. Let's say you ask yourself, "Self, what am I in need of here, especially with my money?" And your soul answers, "I really need more patience in the money space." Then, that is your cue to, right then and there, breathe in and out and allow yourself to feel into patience inside yourself and then feel patience in your money space. This will help begin to build the foundation to be more patient with yourself in your finances and attract more patience-filled dynamics for you, in and around your money. If you need more ideas of helpful, uplifting emotional energies that are supportive for your vulnerable interior and money relationship development, here they are:

Peace. Patience. Sacredness. Honesty. Acceptance. Love. Embracing. Confidence. Wisdom. Purposefulness. Connectedness. Grace. Restoration. Focused. Attention. Revitalization or Renewed Energy. Clarity. Surrender. Resiliency. Belonging. Adaptability. Initiation. Security. Supportiveness. Responsible. Relaxed. Stable. Calm. Harmony (Har-money). Balanced. Respect. Worthy. Forgiven or Forgiveness. Courage. Boundaries. Cheerful or Happiness or Joy. Grateful. Abundant. Whole. Uplifted. Comforted. Nurtured. Hope. Gentle. Tolerant. Committed.

All of these, and energies like them, which are aspects of love, are the supportive, protective, flowing, nurturing and improved value and empowerment elements that come with improved money relationships. These are the types of up-leveled energies you want in and around your money life, so it's a good idea to practice the unique energy-blend or emotion-blend that you need, that is right for you.

The idea behind the "What do I need?" practice is about cultivating more of what is aligned for you to create, while you clear what you don't need. *The key is that as you release low vibrational money agreements, partnerships and enviroments, you begin to attract better ones. This creates uplift, a spiral up, as you release from low vibrational*

money energy to higher vibrational money energy. This says to your body, your soul, that you're paying attention and you want to help yourself. This process of literally letting go of low vibrational elements in your life (or letting go of garbage) while claiming better choices, opportunities and partnerships, is akin to clearing weeds you don't want, while making room for the flowers that you do. Fewer weeds, more flowers. Less work, more pay. Less drama, more results. Less clutter, more clarity. You get the idea.

Speaking of more flowers, I need to make mention of a short, but very critical and powerful aspect of answering to your needs: celebrate when things work!

Positive Imprints: "Happy-Thank-You-More-Please-of-This-Universe!"

Most of this book focusses towards supporting you in identifying, managing and growing through the challenging aspects of what is emotionally and energetically creating your financial life. We're working on helping you cycle out of what you don't want to create and cycle into more of what you do want to create. That's some heavy lifting at critical pivot points. So, it's natural that we're primarily looking at the tough stuff and healing or shifting what's not working. Even though this is our focus, don't assume that this practice is always about picking at unhealed wounds and shadow world.

It's important to regularly pause and celebrate your wins, your breakthroughs, small and large, as one of your vital allies for imprinting your new patterning into your life and your money relationship. Why? Your celebrations help to constructively and biochemically imprint into your body and soul the somatic foundation for the continued direction you'd like to create in your life. I like to call this type of breakthrough celebration the "HAPPY-THANK-YOU-MORE-PLEASE-OF-THIS-UNIVERSE!" celebration. I took it from the 2010 movie *happythankyoumoreplease* that embraces this concept of pausing to celebrate the good stuff.

For instance, when I'm on the phone with my clients at the front end of a session and they are recapping their between-session practices and life events, many times successes, breakthroughs and the big wins get buried. I call this "burying the lead" which is a term from my journalism background that means, "hiding what needs to be first!"

Regularly, I encourage you to bring your breakthrough leads to the front of your life and celebrate them with an attitude of "Happy-Thank-You-More-Please-of-This-Universe!" Your breakthroughs might be an easier time of becoming more present in your body. Or noticing that you're speaking up where you weren't before. Or receiving an extra bonus out of nowhere. Or noticing more support easefully showing up in your life where you had to go it alone before. Or noticing that a utility bill wasn't nearly what you thought it would be. Or noticing that little signals from the Universe are appearing more readily for you. Or noticing that one of your debts was easily paid off. Or noticing that someone went out of their way to do something kind for you. Or... fill in the blank. There is much more bountiful magic happening in the world around us than we know. We may easily align with it if we're paying attention. More magic. More colors. More flowers. More celebrations of things working out better than we ever imagined for ourselves and those around us.

These steps of answering to your needs and celebrating your wins will help you more easefully clear out of the weeds of your Shadow Money Contracts and walk you into the flower garden of your Destiny Money, your Authentic Money Blueprint. To add to that good mojo, there isn't anyone I'd like to introduce you to more than your Money Guides or your Money Team or your Divine Financial Light Team or your Money Angels.

Your Divine Financial Light Team: Keep Them with You.

Okay. I know for some of you, this segment is a stretch because you live primarily in your logical aspect with money, but like I said in Chapter Two, I need you to be curious and humor the process. This one concept has utterly changed and healed people's financial lives for the better, and I am not going to hold back a decent tool out of fear that I might rankle a few egos. So, buckle up, buttercup, because this is good butter to put on your financial toast. For those of you leaning in, curious, you're in the right spot.

For starters, I would not be here today writing this book to you if it weren't for the tremendous team of Light Beings on the other side of the veil in higher dimensions who support, guide, protect and message me in this sacred work of Somatic Money. My belief is that if they are here for me, oh baby, they are certainly here for you. As a matter of fact, you don't have just one Money Guide working with you. If you want, you may develop and have an entire team. Before I lose us in the weeds with too much excitement, let's keep it simple.

First, given that money tends to be taboo in the consciousness and spiritual community, the thought of having Money Guides usually doesn't cross people's minds. Yet, I can assure you, our financial sovereignty is our birthright, so why wouldn't we have an Angel, a Guide, an Ascended Master or two helping us with our money? (Reference Chapter One.) Your first step with direct financial Divine Guidance is to entertain the idea as not only possible, but most likely probable.

Next, let's switch financial cultural polarities. If you work in the business and money sector, the idea of a Money Angel, a Money Guide? It's not only outrageous, it's completely dismissible. The business community's strong prejudice against anything intuitive or faith-based knocks out some of the greatest help we can cultivate in our money relationship. Sure, we could go it alone, but why should we when we can have great help?

Now that we've established how the Money EQ community and the Money IQ community regularly ignore and block help from the Divine Council when it comes to money, do you want to see how amazing it is when we let Divine Guidance in the door of our finances? Great! Let's break a few cultural rules!

I'd like to establish a few definitions so you know who you're working with. A Money Guide is a light being who spent time on Earth incarnated as a human and understands the trials, tribulations and stresses that we humans live with on the surface of the Earth.

When I first met my Money Guide, his presence alone lifted a weight off of my shoulders so that I was no longer a lone wolf with my money stresses. Next, he made it very clear that I was and am loved in my money picture, and I was forgiven for every money mistake I'd ever made. That gave me the freedom and confidence that I could succeed with money instead of feeling guilty over how terrible I felt about money. Then, he was present with me as I took baby steps in putting my money life back together again. I naturally felt his loving presence and guidance looking over me as I leaned into methodical and practical steps with money, including my presence practice, that seemed to bring my finances back to life. That's what a Money Guide in action can do. Imagine having a being with you who understands your personal finances, is holding you in patience, kindness and love (no animosity or judgement), and is willingly supporting you as you develop your money relationship. That emotional and energy environment could create a huge difference for you in how you work with your personal finances! (Feel free to imagine, see and experience your Money Guide as the appropriate gender, ethnicity and sexual orientation that works for you. How we identify, even in our money matters!)

Let's talk about Money Angels, especially the Archangels, who work with us financially by bringing in specific energies. For instance, Archangel Uriel is a profound presence with a commandingly protective and supportive energy with money, while glowing in gold light that helps to warm and open the cold spaces where money might be locked or frozen. He opens financial avenues that might not have been available before. He's like the sun who warms rocks from the inside out with great love. A Money Angel might be assigned to you for a great length of time, or she/he might arrive and work with you on specific projects. I've found that Archangel Raguel likes to come and go with people working on sticky estate issues. We know how estates can get tangled with families and our government system. Archangel Raguel tends to locate the fair aspects in the estate project, answer to everyone's needs, create flexibility, assuage egos in the process and untangle the toughest knots. Then, there is Archangel

Raphael who is good at encouraging you to letting go of working so financially hard so that you can trust an easeful shift into an up-level of your work and finances. He brings a feeling of less work and more pay while sustaining vitality and healing. Angel energy working with us in money tends to come from the higher realms, so be ready to step up to the plate with your greater financial courage, accountability and responsibility. No more financial slouching when the Archangelic realm shows up!

Again, identity matters as you imagine your Money Angel/s. I find most pictures of angels are depicted with white skin tones. It's time we changed this and additionally see our angels in varying skin tones of chocolate and olive that suit our best identity needs. Also, most angels in our pop culture are shown as heterosexual masculine and feminine. For non-binary gender and LGBTQ readers, I can guarantee that when the diversity of Spirit World shows up for me, they are just as gender-diverse and sexually diverse as we are. You have your identity match in Spirit World so don't be afraid to imagine or ask!

Then, the Ascended Masters arrive, helping us navigate through our Shadow Money Contracts, moving us into our Destiny Money Contracts or Authentic Money Blueprint. Ascended Masters hail to us from the Akashic Hall of Records, where all of the experiential coding of our lifetimes is held. Ascended Masters help to support, guide and protect us as we choose to move out of old money patterns or old money coding that no longer serves us (shadow coding), and help us move into higher consciousness and better money coding that serves us (Destiny Money Light Codes). For reference, imagining or seeing your Ascended Master/s as your appropriate gender, ethnic and sexual orientation identity is also important here.

For those of you who are interested and wondering, "How do I get some of that magic?!" Simple. You ask. That's it. We live on a planet of free will, which means spirit beings cannot interfere with your life, so you have to ask for the specific help that you want. It looks like this: When you are in your presence practice, right around when you've begun to center into your body after you've slowed down and you're breathing, that's where you say, *"I call in my highest and best Money Guide (or Money Angel or Financial Ascended Master) to help me, guide me and protect me in my financial life for the best possible financial outcomes with highest intent."* Notice I use the words "highest" and "best" several times, because we deserve to have the highest and best help. (Please do not use "greatest good" because it is middle-of-the-road energy.) We also need that help to arrive in the forms of support, guidance and protection, resulting in the best possible financial outcomes in the highest intent. The very cool thing about this wording is that you don't have to know the details of the outcome, but you do need to create your best programming. So be very careful about the wording you use with your Money Team. Weave this practice regularly into your greater Somatic Money Presence Practice and begin to watch for signals and signs from the Universe as confirmations and encouragement towards specific actions you might take along your financial path.

Once you've begun your daily practice of calling in your Divine Guidance with your life and money picture during your presence practice, then it's up to you to pay attention to how your new team member/s is interacting with you. The Divine Realm works through subtle hints, messages, synchronicities, symbols, sign boards and random resources. They even anthropomorphize money to make it fun and engaging. As an example, I once worked with a client who had a client that was a professional baseball player, and all the messages showed up in terms of baseball puns. Even though the work was important and serious, we laughed a lot with baseball jokes, and that helped my client lighten up and do better work for her client. The same went for working with my horse trainers. During our sessions, we tended to have more horse references with the money topic than we knew what to do with.

Also, don't be afraid to ask and invite your Money Team Member/s directly into traditional financial spaces. I regularly encourage my clients to take their Angels, Guides and Ascended Masters right into the courtroom, into business deals, into financial advisors' offices, into accounting offices and into the salary negotiation room to help out. The fun secret is that you don't have to tell anyone. They don't need to know that an eight-foot Ascended Master is giving commentary only to you, while standing over the legalese that an attorney has written. They don't need to know that an even larger Archangel is standing and watching the stock market reports on TV as you review your accounts with your financial advisor, giving indicators on best account decisions. The wonderful and crazy thing is that it helps. It works. Good Lord, we need all the help we can get!

Most of all, if you find that you're experiencing big life money lessons from the Universe, that you know you need to learn, heal and grow from, your Money Team members are some of your best peeps to help you clear through the weeds.

As you attune to working with your individual financial guides, when you're ready, feel free to open up your space and work more broadly with your larger Money Team. My team gradually showed up over time as I became more adept with my practice and needed more help with the different areas of my money and business.

Most of all, have fun! It's a fun kick-in-the-ass to financially co-create with your Money Team!

Client Money Story - How a Colorado Western Slope Attorney Transformed Her Money Relationship

Money relationship transformations take time and this short story might give you an idea of what that looks like. I worked with an attorney here on the Colorado Western Slope for about six months when she began to experience shifts with her money relationship. When we first began our work together, her money relationship was filled with anxiety and guilt and she felt like her money and numbers were disconnected, cold and distant from her. This was her experiential relationship with money and how she expressed with her money. Then, after moving through a bulk of her money relationship work, during a time that she claimed her power, shed insulated layers, left behind a primary toxic relationship, sold her home for a substantial profit, spontaneously dissolved a chunk of debt and received a pay increase at her firm, she described her transformational expressive money relationship to me. She said, "Dana, my money now feels like it has a connective vibration. The guilt and anxiety are gone and my money relationship feels lighter and filled with glowing warm energy. This is so different and good!" This is an example of a dramatic transformational shift in money relationship and experiencing a new and empowered form of financial expression.

Spot Check

The big pressure of "the work" begins to alleviate as we turn the corner, leave this chapter, and turn towards a bit of fun. That's the whole point. Once you establish your foundation and know how to use your elbow grease at critical junctures to better your money relationship, then it's a great time to add in the lift. The wonder. The ease. The magical bang. It's a balance that keeps everything in perspective.

About Progress. Integrating information from Chapter Six into your practice by weeding out your emotional and spiritual masking, dialing in your needs, along with inviting in your Money Guides takes **about several weeks.** For some, the process might be faster, some longer. Add these elements as they fit and as they feel appropriate.

Also, depending upon your foundation, you might find yourself circling back to do layers of heavy lifting from the earlier chapters. It can take a little while to work out those layers. I have some clients who do the work in as early as four to six months, others might take several years. Even after the bulk of "the work" is done, we all regularly do maintenance. So, whatever time it takes to work the process, it's okay. You do what works for you. We've all been there, so allowing yourself to patiently and methodically move through the layers at your own pace (with systematic breaks) is one of the healthiest things you can do.

Key: Just when you think the heavy lifting will never end, that is usually right before big breakthroughs.

By all means, be sure to celebrate your small wins and your major breakthroughs! See how far you've already traveled?! Way to go! And now? Let's go rearrange some furniture...

CHAPTER SEVEN

Rearrange Your Somatic Money Furniture

Break Through Financial Compartmentalization and Toxic Money Environments

Moving furniture is never graceful. It's a clunky, onerous and sometimes an overwhelming task that can lead to cussing, pinched appendages, strained relationships and sore backs. Yet, the results can be quite splendid with old furniture leaving and new furniture snuggled into its new space. Or it can be a move to an entirely new location for a fresh start. Or it can simply be about rearranging a room for a fresh perspective. Whatever it is, moving furniture does provide benefits.

Moving furniture is similar to what it feels like when I coach clients out of their old, sometimes toxic, money environments of compartmentalized money space into new cross-trained Somatic Money space. At first, it's awkward, disorienting and maybe even overwhelming. It's like picking up one end of a couch without knowing where you're headed, letting a few cuss words fly, until you realize it's time to swing the couch around and set it down in a new spot. It's like unplugging the lamp and re-plugging it into a new location to shed light in a new way. It's realizing the carpet really does need cleaning and when you give it that lift, everything changes.

During this chapter, I'm going to ask you to walk with me through the clunky and awkward changes of learning how to cross-train your money relationship out of the compartments you've never questioned and rearrange it in a brand new way with many of the Somatic Money elements that I've already given you. We'll be adding a few new pieces to flesh things out, but the primary focus in this chapter is to show you how to break from stale and unconscious money convention and reassemble your money relationship puzzle pieces in new ways. For direction, here is the quick list of our furniture rearranging process:

1. Identify your official **Money Space** for a *better financial environment.*

2. Consciously create your **Sacred Money Space** for *better financial experiences.*

3. Consciously build your **Money Vessel,** your Monthly Money Game Plan, to *cultivate emotional resilience for greater financial support.*

Don't worry. If these elements don't make sense to you, we'll be covering them in detail. I would, however, like you to notice that we'll be working to build your money space from the outside, or bigger picture, into your internally focused money relationship. That means, as we take steps and get closer to your physical and emotional center with money, if you feel yourself getting wiggly or jiggly or nervous, that's okay. That's normal. Please come with me as far as you can in your own pace, carving out your best money space. If you get stuck, be sure to use your Somatic Money Presence Practice to provide yourself with gentle support to build your resilience. For some, these steps we take together might create breakthroughs and celebrations

– Woot! For others, we might be peeling back a few vulnerable layers and you'll begin to realize more about why things are the way they are with your money! Your best bet is to be as aware as possible in the landscape we're navigating and notice what is coming up for you. Allow your psyche and body, with the Somatic Money process, to naturally resolve issues that used to block you as you arrive into claiming your Somatic Money Sacred Space.

Old Furniture:
The Default Zone of Toxic Money Environments

Let's begin our furniture moving adventure from the perspective of the *money environment* you have currently established for yourself. In Chapter Two of this book I walked you through the initial standard money relationship conversation I have with most of my consultees and clients, giving a sense of mapping out the initial money relationship. It's a good place to begin. What I did not share is the conversation I have after that, still fairly early in the coaching relationship, that gives me a better idea of the environment and psychological state my client is consciously or unconsciously cultivating for themselves in their money space. Let's cut to the chase and talk about the specifics of what I normally find when I ask my client the question, *"Could you tell me about the space where you work with your money?"*

Old Furniture Response #1: What money space? I have no money space. I do all my financial activity on the fly with my phone.

Old Furniture Response #2: Yes, I have a money space, but it's (one of the following)... at the kitchen table in the middle of family traffic, in the living room on the coffee table in front of the television, on the bed in the bedroom, on the floor, or moves around depending upon circumstances.

Old Furniture Response #3: Yes, I have a designated money space where I always do all my money work and it's (one of the following)... mixed in with my business stuff, antiseptic, stuffed with clutter or doubles as a multi-activity space.

Are you able to locate yourself in any of these descriptions? If you are, we have a *money environment* make-over to help you with. We'll be moving furniture for you to create a money space that is specific, has clarity and is perked up with energy you love. If you already have a designated money space that feels good and that you love? Congratulations! You're a rare bird and you're doing awesome!

New Furniture:
Breakthrough to Your Authentic Money Environment

Let the furniture moving begin! And yes, I mean that figuratively and potentially literally.

For starters, the quality of your *money environment,* or lack thereof, affects your energy with money. Vibrational energy is embodied through money, and so money mirrors the emotional patterns and energy we keep, as well as the environment that money is housed in.

From an emotional housing perspective, it follows that if you have a crappy money environment, chances are you have a crappy relationship with money. If you are uptight with no frills in your money environment, chances are you and your money can't breathe. If you aren't paying attention to your money environment, how do you expect money to pay attention to you? If your money environment is adversarial, chances are your money relationship is adversarial. If your money space is a mess, your financial books are probably a mess. If you have clutter everywhere in your money space, chances are you're missing or losing money in the clutter of your books. From these examples, please take a look at your environment along with your money relationship and finances and see if you can see the reflective mirror between the two.

Do you truly want to do better with your money? Then clean up your money environment both emotionally and physically! If you clear the clutter and mess, chances are you'll find money and open space for new money to arrive! If you consciously upgrade your emotional state in your money environment, those new attitudes and emotions will likely bring in new financial options. If you eliminate drama from your money environment, you'll probably eliminate the need for crisis financial management. If you bring in breathing room to your money space with color or flowers or music, chances are a fresh flow of financial energy will come in too. It truly is remarkable how powerfully our money responds to its environment!

Next, let's talk about your *designated money space*, the place where you work with your money. Point blank, if you do not have a designated money space, that is like you saying to the anthropomorphized version of your money, "Sorry dudette/dude, I don't have the time or the space to make you a valuable part of my life." How does that make your money feel? Money shrinks and then slinks off into whatever corner of your life it can find to make do with whatever little you give it. You have just disempowered and devalued your financial relationship, making your money homeless. In essence, you're saying to yourself, "I'm not enough. I'm not important enough to take up space and time." If this is you, I hope you call bullshit on yourself and define that you are enough and you have enough: ***This is your financial sovereign birthright to take up empowered and valuable time and space, even with your sacred money relationship.*** This is reflected in making the commitment to the importance of you and your money relationship in the form of your *quality* money space in your home or business.

Take a moment, even as you're reading this, and determine where your best money space is. ***Imagine how you want to create your new conscious money environment.*** If you already have a money space, great! Perhaps consider if this money space is working for you. Do you want to make a change? As you consider your options for new money spaces or changes, I'm going to remove a handful: DO NOT place your money space on the floor or on the bed. Your floor is the foundational place where you walk, not where you work with money. Elevate your money off the ground. Your bed is the foundational place where you sleep, dream, rest, recover and make love, not where you work out your emotional and mental issues with money. Give your money the clarity of its own space. Do you work with your money on the fly with your phone on the train, in meetings, on the subway, in the airport or on the freeway? Please stop. Locate your *stationary position* with money, in the most beneficial space that works for you so your money may find you, come home to you and snuggle in. It's time the two of you have a mutually beneficial relationship.

Perhaps your designated money space is a sacred corner of your office or home. Perhaps it's a new table by a window, specifically for your money work, where you include sacred money altar items. If you truly are mobile, maybe it's a new and colorful file folder set that is only for your money paperwork, financials and printed/written goals that you keep in your business satchel. Along with it, perhaps you keep your mini-Altoids tin, transformed into a travel money altar (you can make one or find one on Etsy) to set up whenever you do your money work to improve the sacred energy of your mobile-designated money space. Whatever choice you make for your designated money space, make sure it's special, sacred and an up-level from your previous money space. Keep in mind that setting up your designated money space is the structural aspect, the Masculine Money aspect, of consciously creating your money environment. Once you do, your space is ready for you to fill it with the Feminine Money aspect that is defined by color, tone, emotional frequency or vibrational frequency of your money environment. And that begins with... your presence.

Old Furniture:
The Default Zone of Stale, Compartmentalized Money Habits

Now that we've helped you either designate your money space or consciously reassemble your money space for improved money environment, it's time to take a look at what you do when you're *in* your money space. ***How are you consciously interacting with your money space?*** What do I mean by this? Let me show you with an old furniture money picture.

I am going to take a wild guess, based on thousands of Somatic Money sessions with clients, what your current conscious (or not so conscious) interactions look like with your money space. You finally stop to work with your Monthly Money Game Plan, resignedly plunking yourself down after procrastinating with household chores or other activities you'd rather do or hanging out with other people you'd rather be with. You brace yourself with the feeling of "just get it over with." Or maybe you work your money management on the fly with your phone, avoiding any sense of getting a clearer, bigger picture with your money. Since you can only stand to be around your money for a short period of time, you only do the bare minimum. Or maybe you're overly responsible with your money in tight, restrictive and controlling ways. You've set up your money picture with double, triple or multiple financial checks, weekly or even daily. You just don't want to get anything wrong, fearing financial mistakes.

As we focus into your money space, we continue with the question of "what is really happening here?" When you work with your money picture, do you direct your attention to your mental process of calculating the income you've received and processing out your bills, getting it done as fast as you can? In the meantime, has the rest of your body ceased to exist to you? Does your breathing stop? Do you stop noticing your emotional and physical sensations from the neck down? If you feel your heart rate jump or your stomach churn, do you ignore it, putting your head down and curving your shoulders against the financial space, hunched over to get through it?

Remember how I've spoken previously about how deeply we've trained our brains and our bodies to disconnect from one another when we sit down to work with our money? Here it is displayed, the non-verbalized disconnects creating the toxic compartments. These compartments cycle between mental money calculations while the body roils with anxiety, insulated emotions, fear of scarcity and somatic shut downs as the tension rises.

This picture I'm painting, with variations, is a fairly standard American picture of how many of us work with our money — unquestioned. Few of us ask "Is this healthy?" and "Do we really need to do this?" Honestly, the answers are no, this is not healthy and no, we do not need to continue this fruitless cycle. We have choices. Before I paint a picture of our new choices, I'd like to ramble down memory lane a little further. We need to take a deeper look here so that you may unravel a few more pieces of the toxic family furniture.

These unconscious interactions in our money spaces, where did they come from and how did many of us unconsciously land in this space? For most of us, we witnessed our parents' financial patterns and behavior. Without even thinking about it, many of us were little sponges soaking up what we saw. Later, when we began working with our money, we drew from our most immediate data banks in our bodies and modeled our parents' behavioral experiences, mimicking the actions and emotions of what we witnessed and felt. Even though we'll be taking a deep dive into your Money Story in the next chapter, we begin now because the central location of building your Sacred Money Space is deeply affected by your childhood, your Money Story. Please take a few moments and review the experiential financial environment of your childhood home. What did you financially witness and feel then, especially nonverbally, that might be impacting how you interact with money today? Especially when you work with your Monthly Money Game Plan.

To help you ignite those memories, here's an example from my own life that I'd like to share. Like many middle-income American households, my parents did the best they could with what they had to work with both financially and emotionally. My folks are Baby Boomers, raised by staunch Depression Era and World War II stock from the Midwest. With this lineage, when it came to money, there was no messing around. Over the course of a month, my parents stuffed their bills into a file labeled "UNPAID BILLS." The print was bold and the file was big, inspiring serious awe. Now, when I think about the unconscious intent of languging the bill-paying file as "unpaid," it seems oddly comical because wouldn't you want those bills to be "paid?!"

As the month progressed, the file grew thick with billing notices sitting in the kitchen desk nook across from the kitchen table where we ate our meals. I looked at this file folder regularly as it was in my line of sight from my seat at the table. By the end of the month, to me, the file was so conspicuous that I felt like it also had a seat at the table. Then, once a month, both my parents sat down with the collection of bills, a calculator and the check book and whittled through the pile. Sometimes, paying the bills worked out peacefully with a stack of neatly stamped and labeled envelopes ready for the next day's outward-bound mail. Sometimes, arguments broke out. All I knew is that the "Unpaid Bills" file was regularly connected to tension and anxiety in the household that semi-regularly erupted into verbal fights between my parents.

Gradually, I came to understand that the arguments had something to do with "enough-ness" and "fear" and what was "important" or not. That's when I non-verbally began developing a sense of wondering if there was enough money to pay all the bills. Once I became a young adult and had my own "Unpaid Bills" to pay, assuming the context I'd grown up with, I began with the anxiety and tension I'd already lived through. It set the stage. I did not question it because I'd already soaked up the program through my body in my formative years. It wasn't until I began interviewing people through Somatic Money about their formative financial years, listening to descriptions of their parents paying the bills, that I connected the dots between our early childhood stories and our present-day adult relationships with money management. Making this connection helped me and my clients shatter some of the financial myths that we'd been holding in our bodies about money since childhood. I hope similar reviews do the same for you.

The story I just shared with you is surrounded by so many other stories I've heard from people who, as children, watched their parents go behind closed doors, shrouded in secrecy and weight, to "do the money." Stories about parents who sat at desks with single-bulb lamps, lighting the family's financial landscape as they wrestled with money in front of their children for hours. Stories about bribery and guilt and shame with money. Stories about parents who began paying bills at the kitchen table, appearing emotionally fine, only to cry part way through the bill-paying. They finished the money work in an emotional heap of helplessness — unknowingly terrifying their kids. Even as I write this, I tear up, because there could not be more pain, fear, love, heartfelt trying and vulnerability in one place in a household. This is where we all share a critical emotional and financial crossroads that regularly unfolds for all of us in our homes — such a valuable and vulnerable human experience of money relationship.

That's why one of the most important things we can do in the sacred space of our money relationship is to navigate this part of our lives with as much emotional intelligence, unconditional love, self-forgiveness and compassion as possible, especially around our kids. It's our turn to exhibit tools and ways of being to our offspring that our parents might not have had. Our financial lives might not be perfect, and that's okay, but we now have emotional wherewithal to better handle what is financially happening in our households so that we can gift future generations with new ideas about money.

Quite frankly, generationally, most of our families, somewhere in the lineage, have lived through financial hell at one time or another. These energies continue to live within us, within our bodies, until someone in the family makes a change. The stories vary, but they are regularly there, somatically hidden, waiting to be unearthed, honored, cried about, yelled about, hugged over and walked through. It's time to release the relentless financial grief of the generational past and bring ourselves into present space with a financial freshness our families have possibly not had for generations. It's up to us to stop the cycle.

If you're uncertain about this unearthing and excavation, please

know that this is not about blaming our families. It's about revealing the raw, vulnerable childhood moments when we knew our
parents loved us and were doing their best, but unfortunate things
still happened that imprinted into us deeply — even about money.
The inner children living within us, carrying unfulfilled needs, deserve our loving adult attention and honor now. It's time to release
as much of this toxic generational family energy as possible, even
in light of money relationship, so that we may reclaim our whole
selves, even financially.

Now, when you consider the interactions you experience in your
own money space, within your own home, can you see how it might
be emotionally colored and textured from your family's generational financial emotional influences? The non-verbalized money habits,
emotions, energies and stories held within our generations have gone
unquestioned and unspoken about for too long. It is our job, now that
we have these Somatic Money tools, to identify the emotional and
behavioral money environment we inherited from our parents and
rearrange the furniture to create something new.

It's time to break these cycles so that we may live in greater peace
and harmony (pun intended) with our money relationships. It's time
we shift the old patterns, toss out the old furniture and teach ourselves new ways. We all deserve to have better financial experiences,
not only for ourselves, but also to pave a new way for our children.
They too deserve to have empowered behavioral financial tools so
that they may move beyond this legacy of fear, secrecy, victimhood,
weight and scarcity. We'll be talking at length about transforming
your Money Story in the next chapter, but it begins here, in the center of creating and experiencing your Sacred Money Space.

New Furniture: Breakthrough Financial
Compartmentalization with Your Sacred Money Space

When it comes to money, what few seem to notice is how so
many of us wall ourselves off at home in our toxic, rigid compart-

ments with our money relationships. I mean, if you were to imagine the millions of homes across America, how many of us, do you suppose, are shut down in our tiny, compartmentalized holes wrestling with our money relationships?! I don't have numbers, but my hunch is that there's more of us wrestling than not. Which means, we all need to be coming up for air with our better emotional and energy space to improve our financial experiences! To do that, I've identified two of the buga-boos standing in the way. It's time for us to move through them with more compassion than force.

About that quality-of-money-environment discussion: Most of the time, when we make incomplete, poor or stressed decisions with our money, or no decisions at all, it happens because we don't feel good about ourselves or feel safe to process our inner vulnerable money thoughts and emotions. When we feel unsafe about how or where we are going to process our emotions and thoughts regarding our money, that's when we get stuck. If we don't have safe, secure space to process our vulnerable thoughts and emotions about money, how can we come to sound financial experiences and decisions? Although it might seem like I'm going to great lengths and being methodically meticulous about the basics of setting up your quality money environment, there's a reason. *I want you to have the most safe, secure and sacred space so that you may feel supported to mentally and emotionally process the vulnerable aspects of your money relationship. This is about building your resiliency.* When you cultivate a quality money relationship environment, you're able to grow your financial strength and resiliency, grow your value and empowerment and heal what you haven't felt like you could heal.

Then, about that quality-of-emotion-or-energy discussion: On that note, let's walk you through the process from transforming "icky" money experiences into more constructive ones. I'd like to begin with how you feel. Do you know why most of us don't like to sit down and work with our money? Why we cultivate a distaste, or even "hate" for it? Most of us don't like working with our money because we've developed an experience of "working with my money doesn't feel good.

Sometimes, it feels terrible." Perhaps we're experiencing emotional residues from childhood or we've built up layers of PTSD-type triggers inside our money experiences. Even though we do our best to blot them out, there they are! So, why would we want to do something that feels bad? Good question. There's another reason we abhor working with our money: in our core we don't feel emotionally safe. For many of us, the moment we open up our numbers we feel as if the boogey-man might come and get us. Vulnerability wails. More potential sensations from childhood trigger, along with unresolved emotional layers. So, why would we want to voluntarily do something that doesn't feel safe? Another good question. What stands between us and getting our financials done for the month? Distaste, vulnerability and lack of safety.

If you are feeling like you want to check out, dial for food and go get pizza right now, I'm with you! Buuuuuut. Not so fast. What if. Just what... if... you could gradually cultivate a little bit better and a little bit better and a little bit better money experience until you begin to feel *good* about it? What if you begin to have little tingles that working with your money is a good thing? And those good-feeling tingles begin to lead to actual positive financial experiences? Well, it is possible. And that possibility begins with your willingness to consciously cultivate your experiential sacred space with money, breaking up the old financial compartmentalization that had you feeling so crappy, so unsafe in the first place.

This means no more plunking yourself down to "just get your money done." This means checking your anxiety at the gate with conscious breathwork (all the great tools I've already given you) before you even begin your Monthly Money Game Plan. This means being willing to work a little bit of magical elbow grease. Humor me, because it's time to move more furniture around, cross-train and begin to consciously create your Sacred Money Space. Let's do this in story form.

The Story of Creating Sacred Money Space

Let's say it's time to work your numbers for the month. The moment you begin to think about, "I'm working my Monthly Money Picture or my Monthly Money Game Plan," what do you feel through your body? How are you emotionally responding? This is the exact space where you begin consciously co-creating your Sacred Money Space. If you feel yourself trigger and you allow yourself to go down the rabbit hole of bad feelings before you even begin working with your money, you've already set the stage. This old theatrical stage is the triggered, tunnel-vision, limited-choice, heavy, guilt and shame-laden stage. This stage is filled with characters who have defensive postures with hunched over psyches, bodies hollowed out from shallow or no breath, looking thru polarized tunnel vision and shadow-world feelings of a hostage state. If this is you, chances are you'll enter your money space already feeling challenged, which will reflectively create challenged finances. Instead, click your fingers! Or splash water on your face! Or jump up and down! Or stand in your superheroine or hero pose! Physically connect with your shift to change this picture! Then, breathe and fill your body with air. Ground out into your center. Bring your awareness of your money space up several notches so you're in a better position of attitude for your psyche and your money. There. That's better!

At the Edge. When you walk to your physical money area and arrive at the edge of your money space (let yourself feel that energy bubble around where you work your money), before you do anything, STOP. At the edge of your money space, BREATHE. As you're breathing, let your body open up by rolling your shoulders back and open up your chest. Then, stretch your hands and arms out and up to the sky, reaching, then fan those arms out like wings, feeling large. Maybe turn, opening up your space. Maybe stretch. As you do all this, it's a great time to be talking with yourself about how powerful and valuable you are in your own money space. No more hunkering in or hunching over in your money space like a shriveled ball!

Embrace and Invoke the Space. Then, don't rush into your money space quite yet. Stand there for a few moments, perhaps with arms wide, and invoke visualizations of your money space filling with white light, with higher vibrational energy, good energy. As the space fills with white light or gold light, consciously call in your Money Guides, Money Angels or Money Team. You are not working with your money alone. They are with you. Call them in. Hopefully, by now, you'll feel a few tingles, a bit of a lift, a confirmation that the space you're creating feels good.

Coming to Center in Your Sacred Money Space. As you move into your Sacred Money Space, sitting down, ask your Higher Power or The Universe that you are supported, guided and protected in your money process. Ask for everything to line up better than you can imagine. Be in your chair for a few moments while you feel your body: feet on the floor, bend in your knees, weight of legs and butt in your chair, your spine holding you up, your diaphragm and lungs breathing, your shoulders rolled back. Lean back and take it in. Feel yourself come to center in as calm and grounded energy as possible. No need to force, allow it all to settle.

Music, Candles and Sage Can Lift Your Space. Sometimes, lighting a candle (don't set paperwork on fire) and turning on music will help you feel good. If you want, clear your area with sage (information below).

Commence with Numbers and Money. Once you've created this space, you've created a foundation to welcome in your numbers and your money. You are officially creating your Sacred Money Cere-money. Allow yourself to be guided (intuiting), what your best logistical tasks are. You might find yourself changing up your routine or coming up with new structural financial ideas that are helpful. As you work your Masculine Money IQ logical process with money (important), be sure to check in with yourself about your Feminine Money EQ process (important) to see how you're feeling about what you're doing. Let the IQ and the EQ connect, integrate. Don't be too quick to brush what you are feeling under the rug. Embrace yourself.

Do your breathwork. Hold yourself with presence in your space. Use the tools I've already given you to the best of your ability. Allow yourself to co-create your foundational Sacred Money Space through time and with process.

Pauses During Your Money Process. It's important to take pauses during your money process and come up for air. Spot check yourself. Maybe get up and walk around and stretch. Tune in and marvel at the little miracles you're already creating. When things work well, celebrate, have gratitude, anchor in the good stuff. If things aren't going well, coach yourself through it with your tools. Lean back, enjoy the process. Laugh a little.

Close Out Your Sacred Money Space. Congratulations, you've officially moved through your first Sacred Money Cere-money with yourself. And as is important with all ceremonies, when you are complete, be sure to physically close out your books and give all of it a sacred blessing. Give thanks to the money, the help, the support, the guidance and the protection. Ask for the continued grace of healthy money to continue with you.

Now that I have shown you a blueprint for co-creating your Sacred Money Space, I hope your money space and your money processes are illuminated in a new way. For those of you already engaged with a conscious or spiritual practice, do you see how you may *integrate* your existing practice into your money space? Please, no more of the separation between the "money work over here" and "spiritual space over there." *Combine* your Masculine Money IQ tasks with your Feminine Money EQ skills and tools. The first will give your money space a structure, logic and a backbone. The second will fill the space with the voluptuous energy you need to lift up your money relationship!

One of the most responsive stories I can tell you about creating Sacred Money Space is about a construction owner in Albuquerque, New Mexico. This was a man who sat down and took care of his money in a no-bones-about-it, logical, task-oriented way. His work with money was all left brain. When I asked him, "Who is in the space with you?" He humorously had no idea what I was talking about. I said, "You know, Divine Guidance. Who is in your space with you?" When he opened to the intuitive aspect of himself and tuned in, we both realized that his Goddess was always there working with him in his money space. He'd never thought about that, and he'd never made any attempt to connect with her. From then on, whenever he worked with his money, he lit a candle giving honor to his Divine Goddess and spent more time in each of his business-money bookkeeping sessions tuning into his intuitive nature. Through that summer, his business unexplainably tripled. By the end of the summer, he had more business than he could handle and was hiring more contractors. This is a great example of the power in balancing both Feminine Money EQ and Masculine Money IQ, integrating both in the same space.

As we wrap up this Sacred Money Space creation, for those of you who are new to this process, it takes practice. Over time you'll begin to feel the energy of a supportive, emotionally intelligent foundation and you'll wonder how you went without it! You'll make new discoveries and adjust this practice to suit your needs and taste.

Consciously co-creating Sacred Money Space is what I've used and my clients have used to foundationally improve our money relationships and finances over a period of time. For those of you who want the practical punch list of how to work with elements in creating your Sacred Money Space, please check out the list below. Highlight and work with the ones that are right for you:

Elements to Create Your Sacred Money Space

- *Spritz aromatherapy or sage your working money space* with California White Sage, Southwestern Black Sage, Palo Santo, Sweetgrass or the energetic clearing agent of your choice. If you are sensitive to smoke, you could spritz with an aromatherapy combination of mint, rosemary, lemon or eucalyptus. Spritzing and especially saging will help you clear the old money residues (low vibrational or toxic energy) from your space and allow you to experience higher resonances in relationship with your money. Some of my clients have had positive money shifts just by doing this.

- *Light a designated money candle or incense* with intentions of improving your money relationship or specific financial situation. Intentional candle magic (noting the candle color) and incense (noting the type of incense) is powerful, especially combined with money practices. Please be clear about your intentions and don't set any paperwork on fire.

- *Call in your Designated Money Team* to support, guide and protect you with your money play/work in your money space. In the last chapter, we introduced you to your Money Guide / Team. I highly recommend that you call in your guides and team to your Sacred Money Space and your Monthly Money Game Planning for financial support, guidance and protection. You may even ask them for specific help. You'll find that their presence will help you with intuitive guidance on financial strategies.

  ○ *ADVANCED: Animal or Symbolic Totems for Money.* Not always, but frequently, I find clients missing energy gaps in their money pictures that animal totems or power money symbols can help with. In this practice allow yourself to be guided to or chosen by the animal totem or money symbol that appears. Then, picture that totem in and around your energy and your money energy to provide the healing and programming work that needs to be done with the numbers and money. Sometimes, it's a good idea to print images of these totems or symbols and place them in financial files, wallets or purses. Make sure the printed images have clean energy and change as needed.

- *Imagine yourself and your money space filled with light.* To help lift your space, imagine yourself, your money and your money space filled with white light, gold light, or the color of light of your choice. Light is vibrational. Money responds to energy. Lighted energy helps improve your money space and your money programming. Uplift the space.

  - *ADVANCED: Programming Money and Numbers with White Light.* I've found that regularly infusing or programming money and numbers in white light guides numbers to naturally line up and work out, even if you can't figure out logically how things are going to financially work. White light also provides an added level of protection, creating a security buffer zone from identity theft and hacking. All you have to do is picture the numbers, the money, in all of your accounts, receivables, payables and financial vehicles completely filled with white light. I like to add an instruction to my Money Team during this white lighting process about protecting, supporting and guiding the numbers for better than expected outcomes.

  - *ADVANCED: Programming Money and Numbers with Gold Light.* I've found that if an individual has experienced serious trauma, especially affecting the money and numbers, gold light is a deep healing energy for the hurt, pain or wound energy that becomes infused through the numbers. Gold light says to numbers, "It's okay to heal. To get back up. To walk again. To become whole. You're going to be okay. You're safe." Use the instructions in white lighting (above) for gold lighting.

- *Intuitively tune and say a prayer, mantra or speak your money intentions* before you begin working with your Monthly

Money Game Plan. Before you turn on computers, open your phone, open files or open checkbooks, take a few moments with your presence practice, breathe and tune in. Feel your presence and the presence in the room with your money. Allow yourself to come into alignment with your money space and vice versa. Allow yourself to receive any intuition that might be flowing to serve you in your money space. Speak the prayer, mantra or intention that you feel guided in. Allow yourself to be guided in the driver's seat of your money life.

○ *ADVANCED: Emotion Medicine with Money.* As I mentioned before in the "What do you need?" segment of the last chapter, sometimes your body, psyche and money want to feel a certain feeling infused through you and your money space. Be sure to check in semi-regularly and ask your body, your money, what type of emotion medicine you might be needing in your money space. On that note, most of us have a very unique vibration with our money, so your exploration in this area might turn up the sacred energy emotion that is your authentic money-emotion. This is the energy that your money works best in.

• *Play higher vibrational music* in your money space to lift your emotions and energies while you work with money. For example, this could be whale music, Mozart, Deva Premal's mantra music, Reiki music, your favorite playlist, meditation music or something that helps you feel good.

• *Clean Out Your Purse and Wallet. Or Heck, Buy New Ones!* If you're having problems with your money and you're hauling around a nasty old purse and/or wallet, chances are the low vibrational energy in your money vessel is gumming up the water works. Get a new purse or wallet, making sure that you sage it and energetically clear it to make it your own. Also, make sure you sage and energetically clear all the items that are going into your purse or wallet. Be sure to bless your purse and wallet with your new money energy. Your purse and wallet are your mobile sacred money altars, pinnacles of your exchange space. Treat them with respect!

- *Energy Medicine with Money. The Popular Favorites.* And, of course, we have to include the popular favorites. If these are a match for when you need them, please work with your gratitude practice, your Law of Attraction practice, your visioning practice and your abundance or manifestation practice in your Sacred Money Space. Keep in mind that sometimes these practices are overused or used too generally, but they are still pertinent and a powerful part of the money picture. Work with as needed.

  o *ADVANCED: Energy Medicine with Money.* All kinds of healing modalities are available to us these days. Reiki. Healing Hands. Tapping. Acupressure. Chakra Meditations. Jin Shin Jyutsu. EMDR. Hand Mudras. And the list goes on. With this plethora of modalities, please be discerning about what you bring into your money space. Make sure you feel the intuitive tug and guidance that the energy medicine modality you feel drawn to for your money is right for you in your money space with right timing. And if it is, then bring that modality into your space and work with it for as long as it's pertinent.

- *Color and inspiration!* In softening your money space to improve your sense of safety, security, inspiration and environmental improvement, hang up art, create color and texture, post inspirational signage or add a vase of fresh cut flowers.

These elements are suggestions to help you create your most Sacred Money Space as you see fit by combining Feminine Money elements into the Masculine Money space, encouraging you to creatively build your vessel where you will feel best in working with your money!

Old Furniture Budget
or New Furniture Sacred Money Vessel

We have arrived at our moment of truth: What is happening *inside* your Sacred Money Vessel with your Monthly Money Game Plan? If you are squirming uncomfortably, still wondering why you have to go through a torturous financial incantation once a month, let's give you a new viewfinder. I'll cut to the chase and say, the entire point of working with your Monthly Money Game Plan is not to go through an empty ritual of numbers-keeping laden with dread, triggers, guilt or shame. Instead, it's an opportunity for you to actively co-create your financial goals and dreams in your own step-by-step process by arranging your financial furniture in the way that works for you. Here, you'll powerfully raise your emotional resilience of your Feminine Money EQ and match it in logistical dance with your Masculine Money IQ.

Your Monthly Money Game Plan is your opportunity to actively tune with your money relationship, locating what you feel strong with in your money picture and what you don't. Learning this landscape will help you know where to stand in stability and lean with your Somatic Money healing tools to engage greater resilience where it counts. Now, with the tools, concepts and stories I've provided, you have an entire toolkit to foundationally use right in the middle of your Sacred Money Vessel with your Monthly Money Game Plan. Instead of cowering with the vulnerable mantel of the household finances, you may now work this space with greater awareness, skill and even panache. It's time to breathe life into the tired rag of your budget and infuse your Monthly Money Game Plan in your Sacred Money Vessel with the conscious power of mythmaking (your conscious Money Story) with your Heroine's/Hero's Journey.

As we move forward to share this process with you, for practicality sake, we're going to begin from the most basic level and lean towards the more advanced levels. With these descriptions below, please locate where you are already in process with your money picture and then pick up the pace that works best for you. I am not interested in you forcing the issue. I am interested in you systematically supporting yourself in a step-by-step unfolding of process as your inner money picture beneficially takes shape.

Co-Creating in Your Sacred Money Vessel

To set the stage, you have all your tools from the previous chapters, you've already selected your Money Space and you're taking steps to improve this space into your Sacred Money Space. You're doing what you can to beneficially lift and leverage your money relationship! Here we go with the next steps at the confluence of your money life. Woot!

Exploration and Excavation. At the ground floor, we're going to begin with a little bit of exploration before we have you take any practical financial steps. This is the spot where I gently visit with clients about why or how they have no visible Monthly Money Game Plan. And I'm not talking about a guilt or shame conversation. I'm talking about a genuine, "Please, tell me what is going on here. What does this look like to you? How does it feel? What are you experiencing with the budget space? What challenges or road-blocks might be coming up for you?" Be sure to use your Somatic Money Presence Practice and emotionally process in this space. I also suggest you write your exploration down in a journal, share it with a therapist or share it with a trusted friend. *Verbalizing this space is powerful* in creating awareness and release. I have watched person after person catapult into much healthier money relationships when they excavate this roadblock and allow themselves to be in their money pictures in brand new ways. Let's just put it this way, in rather indelicate terms.

The emotional residue built up at this spot in our collective financial culture is like an overfilled septic tank keeping people from their empowered Monthly Money Game Plan. Symbolically, I've even had clients clear backed-up septic tanks or sewer lines while doing this work! It's a real thing that as we purge the toxic and stuck emotional energy, the more financial clarity there is in our personal lives and our culture. It's time for you to climb out of the septic tank and grow financial flowers with the fertilizer. You don't have to buy into the old emotional hostage space any longer.

Watch for Pitfalls in the Money IQ and Money EQ Set Up. Once you excavate and identify your initial potential emotional baggage and blocks with your Monthly Money Game Plan, and you feel some of the baggage lift, it's time to more specifically plot your financial adventure. In doing so, it's key that you be aware of these elemental building blocks and pitfalls so that you may stay focused during your process. Here they are:

- **Collect Your Financial Data Ahead of Time.** There is nothing worse than getting into a money groove than having to break your rhythm to run around and find that piece of paper or account information. **Pro Tip:** First locate as much of your account data as possible.

- **Boundaries and Building Your Attention Span.** Is it easy to get distracted by other things? Drama in the household? Drama on the internet? A thousand other things that "need" to be done? Feel free to set up some compassionate and kick ass boundaries with yourself and others in the household. Then, when it comes to real attention, is it that you just have a hard time focusing on numbers period? Whatever your attention dilemma is, I encourage you to bring your attention-building skills or modalities into this space. Combine your attention-building techniques *with* your money. Begin with easily attainable goals of time periods and portions of bookkeeping projects so that you may achieve bite-sized pieces into your platform for confidence building.

- **Embrace Your Financial Wounds, Triggers or PTSD.** Remember, your Monthly Money Game Plan is the vulnerable confluence of your emotion meeting with your financial logistics. This means that you might hit places in your financial terrain where you trigger, feel wounding or even PTSD. Chances are, that if you haven't worked with your bookkeeping, you've built up emotional residue within your numbers that is going to need some extra TLC. Let's be clear — there is no shame in triggering with your wound work in the middle of your money, your numbers. That's normal. So, please don't run away, shut down or get defensive (fight-flight-freeze survival triggers). Have your Somatic Money Presence Practice ready so that if you hit rough emotional terrain, you may lean back and stop, breathe, come into awareness and center yourself again into grounded space. It is a two steps forward and one step back process that eventually leads to breakthroughs. You got this! (Bringing your other healing therapies or modalities that are working for you into this space is recommended.)

- **Pay Extra Attention to a Safe and Secure Space.** For those of you who are sensitive or in trauma recovery, being clear about feeling safe and secure in your money space is important. Whatever you need to do (within reason) to help yourself achieve a safe and secure money space is in your best interest.

- **Clarify Your Digital Space and Your Non-Digital Space with Money.** We seem to be reaching regular new highs of digital absorption in our lives. As you work with your money and numbers in your Monthly Money Game Plan, I want you to be clear about how you experience your money relationship when you're on-line, especially connected into network software, versus when you're not. Sometimes the digital input creates a feeling of overwhelm or "too much input in one spot." Being aware of this will help you modify when and how you work with your money using both your digital connections and analog space for your best financial outcomes. Money relationship vibrates differently in technical space versus analog space and depending upon how sensitive you are, this can affect financial interactions.

These are the best highlights I can call out in preparation for creating your Sacred Money Vessel for your Monthly Money Game Plan. Even if I've not named your unique combination of what your challenges are, they are no less valid. I hope this outline provides ideas to level up your money relationship and step into the adventure of your Heroine's/Hero's Journey with your activated money myth-making! (Your consciously activated Money Story.)

Creative Masculine Money IQ for Your Monthly Money Game Plan. Now, let's bring your foundational Feminine Money EQ into pairing with your Masculine Money IQ. The first question is, what *form* do you want your Monthly Money Game Plan to take because you get to create in the style that you want! If the thought of an Excel spreadsheet gives you the jitters, please review these options to begin and build your journey.

- **Old Fashioned Pen and White Sheet of Paper.** Sometimes, we make things more complicated than they need to be. If you're not ready for Excel spreadsheets or personal financial software, this is a great way to begin. Every month, sit down with pen and a blank sheet of paper and pen out your monthly numbers, dating your entries chronologically so that you may see when your income arrives and the amount, along with each billing account and its due date with amount. As you make your entries, notice which ones are easeful and connected for you and which ones are painful, triggering or heavy. This is how you begin to take stock of the energy and emotional flow of your Monthly Money Game Plan.

Pro Tip: As you take stock and get clear about how your body and emotions are responding, this is exactly the space where you implement your Somatic Money Presence Practice and become aware of the emotional direction you want to create in your financial experience. For instance, if I find myself overly triggering about certain finances, I stop and work the practice and get clear about what I'm holding, what I might need (emotionally and energetically), and the shift I'd like to create. The brilliance of initially building your Monthly Money Game Plan in your analog space is that you may do so without interference from the digital world. This step will give you a slowed-down context of what is truly happening inside your money relationship between your Feminine Money EQ responsiveness and your Masculine Money IQ logistics. I've found that this slowed-down step gives us a visceral, physical, awakened connection with our money exchanges that we might not have otherwise. This is the brilliance of building your emotional resiliency and filling your Somatic Money vessel in action! Once you feel better and stable with your numbers and your financial picture, then feel free to move into working with a Word Doc or an Excel spreadsheet or financial software. This is how you may gradually, methodically, securely build out your financial picture. You may always have this analog tool to fall back on when the going gets tough. Note: This is exactly where I began and gained footing in my financial recovery.

- **Animate with Markers, Colors and Stickers.** If you're a creative. If you need a lift. If you need to break up your money monotony, feel free to bring in the color, the stickers, the markers to liven up your Monthly Money Game Plan. Sure, it might sound crazy, but this power of expression will add to activating your voice and value with your money relationship. Animate what you're feeling and what you want to create.

Pro Tip: I once gave an optometrist, who was having a hard time voicing her money relationship, the assignment of, "Please draw me a picture of what your money relationship looks or feels like for you." Her image was powerful, showing us that she had frozen in time in a non-verbalized state in front of her father about her value. Once she revealed this to herself through her drawing and spoke about it, she began taking powerful steps in voicing and making financial decisions to move forward in her life. Do not underestimate the power of art to express your financial life and reveal what is important to you. Color away!

- **Step It Up with A Digital Document Like Word Doc.** Once you get tired of handwriting your Monthly Money Game Plan, and you're ready to expand, it's time to shift your monthly information to a digital document format like Word Doc. This is where you not only account for your monthly income and expenses, you also begin to build out your money picture of your assets and liabilities. Type in goals or dreams. Do your monthly tallies at the front of the document and then add your mortgage/rent with balance and equity, car payments with balances and equity, credit card debt balances, etc. If you have debt, this is a great place to track your debt balances and payment plan. Basically, as you realize the layers of your financial life, add them into the picture here along with your Somatic Money Presence Practice checks. If you feel you need logistical strategy support, a money management book or videos, a visit with a budgetologist or an accountant is a good idea to give you the Masculine Money IQ picture that is right for you.

Pro Tip: This process might come as a gradual awakening for you with all the layers of your money life. Don't be shy in your exploration! This is your mythmaking with money (building your new Money Story) and claiming your financial life. Each one of these Monthly Money Game Plan documents becomes a living, breathing financial journal entry of your path. Embrace it!

- **Excel Spreadsheets and Personal Financial Software.** Once you move your Monthly Money Game Plan into your personal digital documents, and you want to move into something more structured or logistically guided, then you'll want to set up your Excel spreadsheets or work with personal finance software. All of this is a matter of personal preference as to what is going to support you the best in your process. Personally, I like my combo of my financials in a monthly Word Doc along with my Excel spreadsheets. I know others who are totally committed to the functionality and accountability of personal financial software that guides them in their process. And yet, others are happy as clams writing their numbers down analog style. Please do what works best for you.

Pro Tip: If you are totally committed to the digital world of your money picture and you follow our financial program to a "T", yet, your money is not working out, you might need a change. I suggest you step back from your digital space, and for several months, write out your financial line items so you may experientially feel what is happening through your body. This may give you glimmers of what is truly happening inside your financial life.

We did it! We brought tools from the earlier chapters in the book and set them up as a foundation to support you in building and working with your Monthly Money Game Plan in your Sacred Money Vessel housed in your Sacred Money Space. Step-by-step, we showed you how to integrate your Masculine Money IQ process with your Feminine Money EQ process. From here, you'll continue to work this process in its wash, rinse, repeat style. This is your opportunity to continue to learn your layers, go deep, claim your healing with money. It's all yours and you got this!

Client Money Story - How a Single Mom Worked Her Somatic Money Program for Long Term Results

Out of all my clients who have worked with Somatic Money, it's Jessica, a single mom in California, who is the most brilliantly diligent body-based money trainer with her money relationship that I've ever seen. She's the one who kept working the tools and working the tools even before I knew how to name and verbalize the cross-training in Somatic Money. This is what she did in her money life.

Through the basis of the Somatic Money Presence Practice, she was initially able to slow down, breathe and get present in her body at her financial exchange spaces, no matter how passionate she felt about the money event that was happening. She used the presence practice to allow herself to mentally and emotionally process what she was experiencing in real time with money, even if was during a vehicle repair for her Jeep or figuring out child support with her ex or providing a happy birthday for her daughters. Jessica used her presence practice as an integrated tool in her life. This is how she focused on and reined in her financial triggers that were creating financial havoc.

Once she got a handle on her triggers, she shifted her attention and began cultivating her physical money space more consciously in her home with her Monthly Money Game Plan. After several months of achieving presence work with her vulnerable money picture, she noticed her money languaging was holding her back. That's when she did her money languaging process (Chapter Nine) where she located her authentic money language and her financial life unhinged for her in a good way.

She said to me, "The more I used the Somatic Money Presence Practice in my daily finances and life along with intent-filled money language, the more I was able to clear unneeded aspects from my life that no longer served me. I truly released myself out of old roles and old contracts and this was cathartic. Once these old patterns and contracts began to dissolve, I felt the wave of new energy flowing through me with a higher vibration and a sense of excitement returning. I found a job and within three months I was promoted, three months after that I was promoted again and three months after that I was promoted again and six months after that I was promoted again! Most of those promotions came with raises. I am now the Regional Operations Manager and I am independently making my own money because I diligently invested in my self-development. In a year's time I moved the needle on my credit score from 500 to 700, paid off a substantial amount of debt and was able to emotionally handle a large dental bill for my daughter. This all gives me a sense of pure joy through my entire body! These were the tools I needed during the time of my pre-divorce, but I am so grateful to have them now. What a game-changer!"

Spot Check

Congratulations! You've made it through all of Part Two of Somatic Money! This is what we're doing to build your foundational tools:

- You are strengthening your **presence and awareness** in your money life with your **Somatic Money Presence Practice** by slowing down, breathing, coming to center during your financial transactions, placing you at the heart of your **interactive experiences** with money relationship.

- This fills your internal vessel with greater **emotional resiliency,** giving you support in cultivating your emotional tracking and processing for better emotional choices, boundaries and ownership with money. This helps **reduce your money triggers**, giving you greater ability to develop your **emotional responsibility and accountability,** especially where you feel vulnerable.

- Which means that you're identifying your emotional and spiritual masking so that you may function more clearly in your **Authentic Money Blueprint** and less in your shadow money contracts.

- Especially making it possible to **strengthen and activate your Monthly Money Game Plan** in your **Sacred Money Vessel and Space.**

All of this leads to better financial choices, decisions and better money relationships.

If I could hand out an award's certificate to you, I would! Walking through this landscape is no small feat. And you are still here, working your process in the true courageousness of an adventuring heroine or hero!

About One Month. The activities in Chapter Seven, building your Monthly Money Game Plan in your Sacred Money Vessel in the designated positive money environment of your Sacred Money Space takes about a month. Again, it's a matter of building your Sacred Money Space and practices in an integrated way that works for you along a timeline that works for you. Pace yourself.

When you're ready, let's move on to Part Three. We have some excavations to do. Let's go!

Part Three:
Excavating Your
Financial Anthropology

Transform Your Inner Money Stories
to Create Your Outer Financial Reality

Shift Gears for Part Three
of the Somatic Money Workshop

Get ready to shift gears! While Part Two of Somatic Money was a rapid succession of steps and practices that built into a cohesive foundational process, Part Three is a new gear setting. Although you will be using the foundation from Chapters Two through Seven for the remainder of this book, it is now time to shift into the slowed-down depths of excavating your Money Story, language and intent. Like before, feel free to walk through Part Three of this book at the unfolding and methodical pace that works for you. No need to rush. As ignition for your excavations here, be sure to bring along into Part Three what you already learned in Part Two about your personal money life.

CHAPTER EIGHT

Your Big Dig: Claiming Your Mythmaking with Money

The Financial Power of Voicing Your Money Stories

Five hundred years ago, the Iroquois Native American Indian Nation wrote into their constitution the belief, "In every deliberation, we must consider the impact of our decisions on the next seven generations." Seven generations. Keep that in mind. (Reference from Indigenous Corporate Training, City Year.)

Today, the consciousness community semi-regularly adopts this belief as a framework that the consciousness work we do in this lifetime affects our family line seven generations forward and seven generations behind us, from an energetic and emotional intelligence perspective. The bridge between is the mutable information of our generational lineage, stored in our bodies, layered in the coding of our DNA and light field (Hurley, Dan, Discover Magazine, 2015). This is the lighted information each of us viscerally carries as our mythmaking power and we bring it to life every day. Our job is to tune our awareness so we may learn and understand the deeper stories, buried in our bodies, holding the rudders that direct the greater mythmaking of our lives.

As a Somatic Money coach, I deeply listen to my clients' modern-day Money Stories, so that we may piece together their personal mythmaking with money. This is about tracing their past into their present and divining the future. What I regularly find is that their DNA's cellular coding, even with money relationship, has generational roots. In other words, the Money Stories, money language and money intent you tell yourself today about your money relationship more than likely holds epigenetic coding deep in the cellular layers of your body. This generational coding of your money life, telling your Money Stories, directing your mythmaking is your financial anthropology.

Why is this important? Your money life is not happening at or to you from the outside in; you are creating it from the inside out. The conscious inner Money Stories you tell yourself, especially the unconscious ones that bubble through from your depths, form the powerful direction of your money agreements and attract particular money partnerships, indicating your specific financial direction. This is the powerful magnetic force of your financial mythmaking!

If you are concerned about where your money ship is taking you, the good news is that change is possible. The beautiful magic of excavating your financial anthropology for your telltale Money Stories that build your collective greater mythmaking is that the more you dig, the more you learn. The more you learn, the more you lay your hands on your deep internal Money Stories so that you may rewrite them in healthier, better, more constructive ways to serve you. The seven generations of layered Money Stories living inside you are mutable!

So, are you ready to begin your Big Dig? Your financial anthropology dig? I hope you are! The name Big Dig comes from Boston's decade-plus inner-city highway restructuring project that started in the 1990s. It's likely that your dig won't take nearly as long and will definitely be under budget while unearthing timely gems. To help you get ready for your Big Dig, here are the foundational tools you'll be working with:

Tools for Your Financial Anthropology Dig

1. **Voice** for activation.

2. **Awareness** to engage with your **Money Story data.**

3. Your **Somatic Money Presence Practice** from Part Two of this book.

4. **Data** you've already excavated from Part Two of this book.

5. **Excavation energy** to dig out your **Money Stories.**

6. A **pen and notebook** to track.

See? You already have everything you need for your Big Dig. I would also like to give you several **perceptual options for framing your excavation.** You may go about this work through a general viewfinder of finding whatever wants to be found. If you feel you need focus, you may select your current Compelling Money Issue (see the steps below) to give your excavation quest a certain focus. That will help bring patterns excavated from the past into clarity with certain financial issues or patterning. And, most definitely, you'll also find the data and pattern tracking you've already created through your Heroine's/Hero's Journey will meet up with your personal Money Story excavations that you do here. Everything is connected. On that note, let's give you some foundational prep work.

Voice: Break Generational Codes of Silence in Your Big Dig.

Your voice is one of your precious and powerful sovereign birthrights. For a few moments, I'd love for you to hold the palm of your hand to your entire throat, and then hum. Feel the vibration in your throat box. Feel the vibration in your body. This vibration you hear and feel is uniquely yours, your sacred energetic imprint brought to life, vibrating through your entire body and surrounding energy field. Your sound belongs to no one else but you. Your vibration is your authentic empowerment.

Your voiced empowerment can do things, powerfully important and special things. Your voiced empowerment can break generational taboos, shattering the silence that you've held for lifetimes. It can transform the emotional hostage state of a family's financial lineage into liberating expression. It can help you claim what is rightfully yours. Your voice, supported by all that you learned to practice in Part Two of this book, is your pathway through. When you slow down, breathe and become present in your core, especially with your vulnerability, you are anchoring your voice's support system, your empowered platform of expression, as a pathway through your money life. You will need this dynamic every step of the way through the rest of this book and into your new money life. Why?

You are going to stand toe-to-toe with two powerful shadow forces in your money life that have been married for centuries in our greater genealogical coding. One shadow force, as mentioned in Part Two, is the code of silence, especially relating to money; this code has soaked through the generations of our culture. This code of silence locks us into our financial boxes because others have likely taught you, taught us, that "talking about personal money is not correct or polite." This simply is not true. Talking about money, especially speaking your money truth to yourself and trusted others, is one of the most powerful practices I know to liberate you from your old money box.

The second shadow force, as we covered in Part Two, is the code that says vulnerability is a weakness, and you don't dare show it – especially with money. This is also not true. Remember, embracing your vulnerability is embracing your connective strength, so embracing your money vulnerability is embracing your personal connective financial strength. When you break your personal money silence by speaking your financial truth while embracing your money vulnerability, you are shattering two combined untruths about your money relationship. This magnificent paradigm-busting pathway through to financial redemption means:

Your empowered voice of identity
while embracing your connective money vulnerability
is your financially expressed liberation.

If I am inspiring you, that's fantastic! If I am scaring the crap out of you, that's perfectly understandable because we're in new territory. Keep in mind, this breakthrough movement happens in your house of Money Value, directly relating to your self-value and self-worth. It's here that your sense of strengthened identity of who you are as you journey through your excavations is one of your greatest gifts in this mythmaking work. As an incentive I'd like to share this with you: When I work with clients and consultees in this step of voicing vulnerable money truth through the telling of their Money Stories, a high percentage of participants say, sometimes with tears of emotion in their voices, "Dana, I have never voiced my Money Story to anyone. I didn't know that was in me. I so needed to speak it, and now I feel so much better!" When you to speak your money truth, no matter how uncomfortable or possibly scary, it's a gift of liberation!

This block between our verbal financial frozenness and finally thawing our throat box to tell our Money Stories is the cultural financial setting we all live in. Within our culture's financial stigma of silence and blocked vulnerability, rarely, if ever, are we encouraged to create a safe, secure and supported space to unlock our Money Stories. That is the paradox of living in a predominately capitalistic culture while remaining financially mute and un-vulnerable about our personal money relationships. This imbalance of pulsing capitalism while we experience personal mute financial states, creates our frozen un-expressions and financial silence that become our versions of financial self-hostage-taking. This silenced space, unfortunately, builds up energetic and emotional charges within our bodies, resulting in dysfunctional and even damaging financial effects.

Without an outlet or some form of expression, this financial charge finds a way to express itself. How? Oh, let us count the ways! Lack of expression accrues emotional baggage that forms into weight, including debt. This pattern also creates stress that charges up the fight-flight-freeze trigger system in the body, making it more difficult to create healthy financial decisions. Banking emotional charges in the body can eventually explode into financial self-sabotage and relationship damage. An unexpressed financial charge can channel as insidious inner chess of financial manipulation and power plays, breaking trust. You name it, I've seen all kinds of patterned shadow world financial shenanigans, all driven by the cost of unvoiced, unexpressed money relationship. Long story short, *suppressed money voice is unhealthy and creates profound financial and health costs.* It's time to culturally break this financial enigma that is costing so many so much.

You might have no idea what is locked in your financial story vault because of the generational financial silence in your lineage. That's okay because you now know the excavations of Money Stories are worth it in your money myth-claiming. This is a way for you to facilitate unearthing unconscious emotion to help remove the baggage of unwanted debt. It's a way to free yourself from inner financial manipulations, giving you access to solving the noodle bowls of your financial messes. And Money Story excavations open the pathway out of emotional financial hostage states, giving you access to breaking through your glass ceilings. Remember, the vibration of your voice with presence uncovers the uncoverable. It retrieves the irretrievable. And then it releases, transforms and shifts the impossible into the possible, revealing what needs to be seen, heard and felt. It provides clarity on a new discerning truth – a freshly redeemed path. You have Money Stories to uncover and voice!

You are embarking on a unique activity in your Big Dig of uncovering Money Stories to claim your mythmaking that probably hasn't been done for generations in your family. By becoming aware of your Money Stories and financial anthropology, you are igniting your torch of voice, backed by your presence practice. You are intrepidly breaking codes of familial lineage silence to stand in solidarity with financial vulnerability. Imagine how your presence of voice, your unique vibration, is singularly slicing through the silent money layers of the generational coding in your family. Your actions here are profound! Heroine's and Hero's Journey profound!

About Your Big Dig and Excavating Money Story.

What is Money Story? Money Story engages how you internally visit with yourself and others, at any given time during the day, about your financial relationship. This is your mental money chatter that glibly tumbles over your tongue, both consciously and unconsciously about your financial interactions. Money Story is the deeply spoken and unspoken financial dialogue you keep with your intimate partnerships and family, as informed by seven generations of familial lineage programming in your body. Money Story is the financial experience and events you cultivate in your life and how you dialogue and define with them, attaching meaning in your life. If your belief system allows you to go there, Money Story is also the irrational sensations or patterns you have about money that might not be from this lifetime; your Money Stories might be bleeding through from echoes and imprints of past lifetimes. Money Story is the emotional data you keep with your Monthly Money Game Plan, your wallet, your income and expenses. This dynamic weave of story in the numbers, and the numbers in the story, boldly and intricately traces the pulse of your financial life.

Even though the wealth of informative Money Story is resting right below the surface of our lives, most days, when we're interacting with our money, we're reviewing it in the here and now. We rarely look at our money through the longer scope of how our families, our forefathers and foremothers are affecting the dollars in our wallets. This generational long view of financial anthropology holds the layers of our family's financial stories, mixed with our own, much like our bodies hold the hereditary markers of genetic coding: it's all right there, ready to be connected.

What does this look like as a real-life example? Let's say you're expecting your employer to digitally deposit your paycheck into your bank account on a certain date every pay period. No big deal, right? But, oops. Due to a glitch, the accounting department didn't get the programming right. Or your bank's computers went down. Or someone accidentally changed your hours to zero. You check your account and the money's not there. You can feel everything unravel, from nauseousness in your stomach to your heart beating fast, to a catch in your breath.

In your head, you begin to hear, "This always happens. Just when I need it all to line up just right, it doesn't work." And along with your thoughts, you hear the echoes of your mother, emotionally reverberating through your body, about how "Our family isn't lucky and we just need to lump it." And how "We have to work harder than everyone else to get ahead, and even then, we might not." I suspect, if we interviewed your mother, she'd say that this was something she heard as a child as her father spoke to his wife about financial deals souring.

This example is a Money Story, a past money program from a family line hooked to a money event today. When you're immersed in it, you think the situation is happening at you and to you, and you're an innocent victim. In reality, you're the one attracting, creating and contributing to the entire situation because of the rich magnetic data you're carrying around in your body about your Money Stories in your mythmaking from your familial lineage. How do you turn it around? Use these steps:

1. **Engage your Somatic Money Presence Practice** of slowing down, breathing and getting present in your body with your money vulnerability so that you may begin to get some perspective on your present-day money drama situation. No matter how real the situation seems, keep in mind that it's part of a larger, older and longer story.

2. **Identify Your Compelling Money Issue (or Dream) as Your Viewfinder.** This is where I'd like you to take the present-day money drama (like the one above), that seems so real, and cast it as your Compelling Money Issue. I'm going to ask you to disengage from the heat of the emotion (after you've done your presence work and dropped the trigger in size), and step away from your interior spot. I'd like you to begin to see the drama pattern of the story as your viewfinder. You are going to be looking for, with this viewfinder, the hints, clues and similar patterning in your Money Story excavations. (I.E. you're using the patterning from current money situations to illuminate past familial lineage patterns with money and vice versa. What's the pattern of the imprint?)

3. **Heroine's/Hero's Journey.** Then, be aware that by identifying your past and current patterned imprints with money, you are placing yourself on the map, the cycle, of your own Heroine's/Hero's Journey. Through excavating historic Money Stories in your family, through the viewfinder of the pattern of your Compelling Money Issue, you're going to be able to see the greater patterning. This is HUGE. This is your "super suit, super power, I'm leveraging my mythmaking" time! While you're in process, what you're looking for is the turning-point places of vulnerability where it's important to be present with the dragon in the shadows — this is where you reclaim your financial empowerment. Keep in mind, you might be the first person in generations in your family that has ever considered this, let alone done anything about it. So ... did I say how huge this is? HUGE! Good for you for having the courage to do this! I'm so proud of you!

As you head into your Big Dig, here are a few pro tips to help you set the stage to make the process more supported and accessible.

Pro Tips to Engage Your Big Dig.

The Big Dig of your money excavation will give you permission to identify your Money Story and then break from the pre-written money fates that have held you, loosening the ancestral financial hold that is no longer working for you. It's time to unhinge the lock and rattle loose the silent stigma of your family's personal financial stories. Before you do, please check-in briefly with these tips to set the stage.

Pro Tip 1: Self-Care. Whether you're a pro or you have never excavated and inventoried Money Story before, the emotional and energy releases that you might experience have the power to create deep shifts that will most likely affect your cellular code. Be sure to use the self-care listing at the end of this book in the Resource Chapter to support you and your body. If you arrive at resistance in the work, it's best to not push through. Allow your body to naturally sort itself before resuming the excavation.

Pro Tip 2: Choose Your Sacred Space. Your Big Dig might feel vulnerable and your money relationship practices are sacred. It makes sense to work your Big Dig from a secure and sacred space. I mention this because I've had clients try this work, literally, in the middle of the highway of their lives, making it more painful than necessary. Get off the freeway of life and please give yourself the space and time this process deserves. Locate a Big Dig space in your home, in nature where you love to meditate, or a retreat space where you know you will be safe and secure. If you've never allowed your sacred relationship with money to be this important, this step alone might shift your money life.

Pro Tip 3: Feel the Shift in Your Body. Track your awareness of how you feel in your body through your Big Dig process. As you un-earth your Money Story nuggets, systematically check in with your-self. Yes, this is exactly where engaging the growing strength of your presence practice is ever more critical. Check in with your Money Stories through slowing down, breathing, centering and being aware of your Somatic Money vulnerability. How is your body responding and shifting? How are you feeling in specific locations of your body?

Sure, you can mentally go through the motions of your Big Dig and stay in your head. The real power of shift occurs when you think about your Money Stories and then feel twinges in your throat, shifts in your breathing and heartbeat, rolls in your stomach, or tingles in your spine, hips and legs. These body responses are signals that you're engaging your core, your deep layers of cellular coding, and creating energy releases, emotional releases and coding shifts. This is the gift!

Pro Tip 4: Extend the Telling. Excavating your Money Story with your internal self in sacred space is one thing. Voicing it to another soul in co-creative vibration is entirely another. Do you know how many of us get to tell our sacred vulnerable Money Stories to trusted others? Not many. We rarely think to do it, and if we do, few of us believe it's possible. Yet, unlocking our money lives hinges on therapeutically voicing our vulnerable money truths lying fertile in our Money Stories. When you are ready, take the time to practice speaking your money truth out loud to a trusted other in a secure and sacred space.

Pro Tip 5: Track and Notate Your Data. By tracking and taking notes in your journal of how you and your body are responding to your Big Dig will help you clarify where you are in your Heroine's/Hero's Journey. Everything you collect – body responses, memories, dreams, current incidences, triggers, mental money tapes, deeper patterning –is relevant. As you uncover your Big Dig, watch how your initial work serves as the breadcrumbs into your deeper Money Stories.

Pro Tip 6: Tracking Data from Previous Chapters. Of course, any of the excavations you've already done in previous chapters are important and connective to your Big Dig work here. You might have already excavated a considerable amount of information. Here is where you may put more of the collective pieces together.

It's Time for Your Big Dig!

It's time to roll up your sleeves, get out your shovel and begin your dig! Keep in mind that the excavation list below is extensive. To avoid overwhelm, please allow yourself to skim the list and be intuitively drawn to the topics that best fit with your Big Dig.

Take it a step at a time.

Here we go!

Family of Origin Environment and Primary Influencers. The first major stop during your Big Dig is, of course, excavating your money environment from your home of origin. The formative time of your childhood, tween years and teen years significantly shape your money relationship, consciously and subconsciously. I begin the majority of financial excavation interviews with my clients right here. Whether you grew up with your biological parents and siblings, you were adopted, you grew up in a single-parent home, a same-sex parent home or you grew up in the foster care system, your home of origin money excavation is essential to your Big Dig.

- What are you looking for? When I interview my clients about their homes of origin, I usually start with questions like:

- What was your mother's relationship with money while you were growing up? What did you see, hear and feel about money through her? What did you consciously and subconsciously internalize and absorb about money relationship through her presence?

- Answer these same questions in light of your relationship with your father or any other parent-figure.

- If you had/have same-sex parents, please do the same for both of your dads or both of your moms.

- If you had/have step-parents, please include an inventory about how your step-mother, step-father or parents' girlfriends or boyfriends affected your money relationship.

- If you did not grow up with your biological parents, then identify your primary money relationship influencers.

- Also answer these questions in regards to any significant sibling relationship or how the sibling-parent relationship affected money dynamics in your household. Here, we are looking at group financial dynamics and household roles. What role did you play in the family and how does that affect your money relationship today?

- How was money handled in the household and how did that impact you?

- Then, describe the money environment. Too much? Too little? Stable? Unstable? Enough? Not enough? Silent? Expressive? Confused? Clear? Explosive? Passive-aggressive? Hidden? Out-in-the-open? Taken care of? Survivalism? Other? Peel back the onion layers and allow yourself to be emotionally honest with what you see, hear and feel. ***You do not have to give free passes to family members because this is your excavation.***

During this excavation, you're looking for the obvious. Begin there. And then, as you recall and document data, if you notice threads spiraling off, follow them. No breadcrumb is insignificant. They all add up.

As you do your excavation, use your presence practice to help you be aware, track and shift. Connect the dots between your Big Dig and the data you've already collected from your practice in the earlier chapters of this book. You might begin to see patterning between here and your Heroine's/Hero's Journey. Remember, the literal and metaphorical pieces of your financial puzzle will illuminate and fall into place.

People of Influence. Close on the heels of your family of origin money relationships are your people of influence relationships outside the family, especially as you move out into the world with your money experiences. Usually, one or two people most profoundly affect our money relationships outside of our immediate family, especially at pivotal points in life. They can be teachers, community leaders, church figures, employers, colleagues, partners, team leaders or famous figureheads. Outside of family, who has affected or affects your Money Story the most?

Coming of Age with Money. Next, explore the money relationship experiences you were immersed in when you left home. Recall as you gained your first footing with finances and money relationship beyond the home where you grew up. What was the environment like? What was your attitude? What was your skill level? How did you apply what you knew to your situations? What events happened?

Adulthood Life Money Experiences in Stages. From there, pay attention to how the layers of experience with money relationship developed through your adult life. How did you grow and change with your money relationship and finances? What old patterns stayed with you that helped or hindered your money relationship? What new skills, experiences, tools and ideas helped you grow out of your old space and into your new space? If this is too overwhelming to review the full scope of your money life, perhaps break it down into decades or life stages: emancipation from your home of origin into work life or college, young professional life, first car purchase, marriage, first home purchase, established professional life, children/raising a family, empty-nesting, divorce, loss/death, retirement, life reinvention. Look at your money relationship within each life stage and notice patterns, growth or anchor-weights.

Familial Lineage Money. Remember how I mentioned that the DNA coding in our bodies is informing us from seven generations behind us and ahead of us in our family line? Notice how I mention that money is affected by our unconscious? This is the connection where the familial lineage coding of your money relationship is hidden in the coding of your subconscious and unconscious money layers of your body!

That means it is now crucial for you to look at and retrieve any information about your generational financial history with money relationship. Please excavate whatever you can about your grand-parents' financial history or money relationship, and even significant aunts and uncles who might have directly impacted your money relationship. Go as far back in the family lines as you can without straining yourself.

Of note, when I am working with vibrational energy deep within clients' cellular codes, many times we unearth financial belief systems and money relationship decisions made generations ago that have never been questioned, voiced or changed. Remember, questioning financial authority has been taboo for centuries. That means, for ex-ample, a financial survival decision your great-great-grandmother or grandfather made back in the 1800s or even late 1700s about how she or he was going to show up with money might still be embedded in the familial code today!

I've literally heard great-grandmothers, several times removed, crow down the family line, "Good girls aren't seen with money! It's not polite!" Or the enslaved ancestors to African Americans boom, "It's dangerous to be seen with money. Money on a person kills." Or generations ago from European family lines that says, "Tsk! Peas-ants aren't allowed to have money in front of the king." I know these financial beliefs and programs seem preposterous today, but they were very real a century and a half ago or more. You never know what money program in the DNA coding of your body is still spinning, unquestioned, from your generational lineage. So, enter-tain and allow yourself to unearth the irrational. Then honor, release and rewrite that code to emancipate yourself, even your family from untrue money programs!

Cultural or Heritage Money. In America's immigrant melting pot, we've created the socioeconomics of micro-economies saturated with diversity, ethnicity, culture and heritage that richly inform our money relationship. The epigenetic coding each of us carries from our communities, both constructive and sometimes destructive, regularly defines our financial lives. Now it's time to broaden your money relationship scope from looking at your immediate life and your extended family to the broader and deeper surrounding of your ethnic community that also shapes your money relationship. Your money relationship is steeped in the fertile ground of your community's culture and heritage, such as:

- How do your religious and spiritual beliefs and practices affect your finances?

- How does your nationality and skin tone affect financial experiences?

- How does your sexual orientation and partnering (male, female, LGBTQ) affect your financial role and experiences?

- How does your cultural identity indicate your Money Story?

- How does your education or professional experience inform the money life of you, your family and your community?

- How does the culture of your professional identity or career affect your money relationship.

The financial energy held in cultural vessels is subtle, yet powerful, and informs Money Story like trees in a forest. When you're in the trees, it's hard to see them. When you step back, the leaves, limbs, bird songs and ground foliage make a whole lot more sense. Try taking a few paces back, and then refocus and locate what you see, feel and hear. For example, here is a brief sketch of generalized cultural Money Story I've witnessed through my coaching practice. Although this is written in first person, the voice is actually multiple voices telling one similar story, grouped as one voice:

"The Midwestern home I grew up in was Catholic and my father was the breadwinner whose financial decisions for us were final. I did not understand then how much the religious, financial and male-female roles affected me, mixing and creating tension in our home. Now, I'm a single mom, responsible for creating and managing our household income, and doing so successfully. Looking back, I can see how much I've grown and broken through the confusions, the limitations, the anchor-weights of religious roles, gender roles and financial roles."

Past Lifetimes and Sacred Ancient Site Money Relationship. For those of you who are logical and literal with your money, this portion of the excavation might not be for you. But, as always, I ask that you be curious. For those of you who are experiencing irrational money events in your life that make no sense, there is a strong likelihood those events are connected to past lifetimes, especially at sacred ancient sites. This portion of the excavation is for you.

In my coaching practice, where traditional money management techniques fall short for clients with looping irrational and sticky money issues, these two esoteric topics of past lifetimes and sacred ancient sites are often the key to unlocking a patterned financial mess. If your belief system allows that we experience multiple lifetimes, we can open the door to the idea that your DNA coding informing your money relationship is unfinished business from other multiple lifetimes. The information from those lifetimes might be vibrating in your light field, informing your cellular DNA, which informs your life, including your Money Story. So, how do you consciously get your hands on past lifetime Money Story, especially if you've buried it in the subconscious and unconscious? Here are your tools to access those past lifetime Money Story memories:

• Dream work

- Hypnotherapy

- An irrational draw to past times, in certain foreign lands, to specific historical events or locations.

- Irrational draws to certain people in your life with whom you wouldn't normally want to connect.

- Synchronistic events today that deliver messages, songs, signs, media resources and conversations that all point toward one past lifetime location.

During Money Story excavations with clients in session, we've traced past lifetimes affecting money relationship today back to the era of Genghis Kahn and his great conquests where fighting and death shaped a current money life. Back to the ancient times of Egypt in the rich period of the Essenes, where oath-taking of spiritual purity informed what money meant. Back to the spiritual wealth of Atlantis before its cracking and sinking, and even during its destruction, defining sacrifice and vibrating as financial information today. Back to the feudal times of Europe that entrenched a caste system of peasants, knights, lords, kings and queens, cementing into place a glass ceiling. Back to the honor and loyalty of living in an indigenous tribe roaming North America where word and bond meant life and death, even today. These are just a few of the locations and historical times, defining lives and agreements that my clients have gravitated towards and unearthed. Once they did, it helped unlock them from an irrational money pattern that had been destructively informing their money life. When the past and present are superimposed together, they inform and transform what looks like irrational money patterns into incredible financial sense-making. Locate the agreements you made centuries ago in specific past lifetime events and you may find the key that can unlock your money life today!

Now that I've introduced the power of past lifetimes in your Money Story excavation, it bears mentioning that the sacred ancient sites located around our world are powerhouses for holding past lifetime soul agreements, including money agreements. Most of the excavations I've experienced and my clients have experienced lead like magnets to sacred ancient sites around the world. Why is this? Our ancestors built sacred ancient sites upon locations where the powerful magnetics of earthly ley lines converge. Ley lines are a lot like Earth's version of acupressure points and meridians. They are the locations where Earth energy flows and converges, especially magnetically. Ancient peoples on our planet were drawn to place their most revered sites of worship and ceremony at these locations, amplifying their power of prayer and ceremony. At the same time, when they invoked Earth energies and the power of the Gods at these locations for community, it created great impact and a solidifying effect on personal agreements.

Think about it like this – the power of prayer amplified by hundreds, if not thousands, of people at a fervent level, amplified by the increased magnetic crossroads. Anything you held in a past lifetime at these events as an intent in your body at these locations would be imprinted into your DNA coding. This power transcended down through lifetimes. Our imprints from places like Easter Island, Angkor Wat, Notre Dame, The Pyramids and The Sphynx, Queztelcoatl and so many more still ricochet in our bodies, when triggered, like vibrating beacons. So, in your Money Story excavation, what are the money agreement imprints still vibrating in your body from sacred ancient sites? If you need help shaking the sacred ancient site tree, a great resource is Graham Hancock and Santha Faiia's book *Heaven's Mirror: Quest for the Lost Civilization.*

Personal Financial Trauma and National Historic Money Trauma. Here, we are re-engaging the conversation from Chapter Four about Money Triggers and trauma in this Money Story excavation. The conversational money relationship patterns in our traditional houses of finance – financial planning, bookkeeping, accounting and strategy – promote sterile and semi-sterile financial conversations. As I've mentioned earlier in this book, these conversations require predominately factual data (Masculine Money IQ) to get to the logistics of money management. Although this is a critical aspect of money, it's not the only one. As my coaching practice has deepened, I've found this sterile money talk, without an avenue of Feminine Money EQ voicing, is disturbing and damaging. When we are not able to discuss the true emotionally intelligent nature of the root of our money messes, then we're covering up and delaying inevitable financial crises.

When I encourage my clients to voice how they are feeling and what they are hearing, seeing and more deeply knowing in the knotted noodle bowl of their money picture, even in the middle of a sterile money conversation, the flow of words regularly connects to previously experienced trauma. Trauma is the somatic dynamic of the repeating internal disconnects that we experience in our body and our psyche through previous emotional, mental or physically disruptive, and very likely painful, events in our lives. The disconnect is the body's way of protecting us from further pain or damage. Unfortunately, these traumatic patterns of internal disconnects keep us from healthy mental, emotional and physical lives, which I have found through my coaching work, also hinders the development of healthy and successful money relationship. Addressing the hidden minefields of trauma, especially locating them in this Big Dig, will help you identify the roots to the money messes that you've created in your life. Hint, the vulnerable journey work that you're already addressing in your financial Heroine's/Hero's Journey is exactly the landscape of healing hidden trauma. You're already there!

In taking a closer look, how does trauma affect your money relationship? It works like this: As we hold the trauma, the internal disconnect, from previous disruptive events in our lives, we're affecting the cellular coding in our bodies. The unreleased tension from trauma, its energy informs our survival instincts, psychology, belief systems and emotions. This unreleased trauma also directly informs, in deep nonverbal ways, how we relate with and handle our money relationship. So, this unrealized, unembraced, unhealed, unspoken trauma, unreleased from the body, can hold us in its aftermath, directing the very traffic of money relationship, holding us financially hostage to its patterning.

If you haven't already made the trauma-money connection, part of your Money Story excavation is to shine the light of your awareness into how these trauma areas might impact your money life. As uncomfortable or painful as it might be, gently considering these topics might be a powerful personal and financial lifeline you send to yourself. Please look at these potential trauma-creating events that might be affecting your money relationship:

- Out-of-control life events impacting your physical, emotional, mental and psychological self in the form of tragic accidents or circumstances.

- Geophysical events such as natural disasters and storms, including forest fires, hurricanes, floods, earthquakes, mudslides and tornadoes.

- Socioeconomic events like The Great Depression, segregation and the Civil Rights movement, the Holocaust, inequality and the women's rights movement, the rise of legal rights for sexual orientation, riots, protests past and present and McCarthyism – to name a few.

- Wars like World War I, World War II, the Vietnam War, the Korean War, Desert Storm, the conflict in Afghanistan and Iraq.

- Divorce, moves, job changes or job losses.

- Financial neglect, trauma or abuse.

- Physical, mental, and/or emotional neglect, trauma or abuse.

I understand that these might be uncomfortable topics to look at, consider and talk about, especially if you have not previously explored them. As I've mentioned in previous warnings in this book, if you have not already excavated your personal trauma work, please seek professional help for support and don't go it alone. If you feel you have enough of a foundation to explore Money Story excavation in trauma, please identify the trauma areas that have impacted your life. Look at how these experiences and events might still be lodged in your body energetically. From there, you may open up a gentle awareness of how these energies in your body are informing how you relate and respond to your money relationship. By all means, please work with your Somatic Money Presence Practice to support you in this process by slowing down, breathing and becoming present in your core, to help you begin to move any energy that wants to release.

For right now, you don't need to know all the answers. You don't even need to know the details. You do need to identify events and their potential connections enough to keep the door open to your money relationship.

The Importance of Financial Cultural Identity in Light of Trauma and/or Privilege as Experienced with the Institutionalized Financial System. I am engaging this financial cultural conversation because of the results I have found in my Somatic Money research that shows how important a strong self-identity is (Money Value) for the cultivation of an empowered personal money relationship. This includes and is especially related to our financial cultural self-identities through the experiential viewfinders of what our generational cultures tell us about our personal experiences of gender, race and sexual orientation in the workplace, shaping our relationships with money. For some of us, these experiential viewfinders might give us financial privilege, status and access. For others, these experiential viewfinders might cause us harm, challenges and blocked career pathways resulting in cultural financial trauma as we experience other's prejudice and/or privilege used against us. For many of us, we are in the middle of this continuum, experiencing the nuanced double-entendres of financial cultural access and financial cultural trauma as we negotiate the varying landscapes of our careers. If we are to rip the veil back and speak honestly, what are we talking about here? We're talking about the root, the residue, of White Colonialism causing the out-of-balance toxic masculine and toxic feminine that favors a white male patriarchal system in our socioeconomic structure and especially in the financial services sectors (banking, investments, accounting and so forth). This system still financially favors some while limiting and punishing others, simply because of gender, race, sexual orientation and/or otherness.

Yes, these are challenging, yet very important issues to talk about. I have deeply wrestled with the questions of whether I should include introductions to cultural financial trauma and privilege here, and if so, how? What I came to understand is that no matter how much these issues are whitewashed out of mainstream money management books and not spoken about, these experiences are vitally woven through the collective financial fabric of our lives, our bodies. I determined that financial culturalism, with its greatness and its shadows, is a somatic experience and therefore, it *is* important to talk about, especially here.

In my quest to explore and create a legitimate framework for excavation and discussion, this small segment unfolded into a chapter. Then, the chapter erupted into a 3-in-1 chapter that spilled over into an outline for the better part of a book. So, no matter how I try, I cannot encompass here what needs to be covered. We'll be exploring this work in greater depth during a future Somatic Money book. However, we're still going to do something here and now. A very big something. We're going to begin the conversation, no matter how imperfect or uncomfortable.

Before we begin, on a quick cultural note. I apologize ahead of time to my readers of diversity for this initial sterile language (for definition purposes only) and any potential white/cultural blindness that I might exhibit in writing about these sensitive topics. I am open to hearing your suggestions and feedback for improvement. Then, for my white, straight, binary gender readers, and especially men, please know that I encourage you to be here and stay here. Your presence is welcome, and frankly, required, if we're going to make needed financial cultural changes in our communities. We need your participation. That said, I'll be writing from a perspective of candid exploration, leaving out as much cultural blaming, shaming and guilting as possible. We need everyone here to have this conversation if we're going to move forward into constructive changes so that we may be able to develop greater strength and health in our financial cultures.

Here is the initial outline of the self-empowering and self-accountable Somatic Money model that I arrived at, focused in light of our individual cultural financial identities. In full transparency, all other practices in this book have been used in individual and group coaching, while this model I'm presenting here is new and untested. I've used everything I know about Somatic Money to beneficially create this new model and I'd love to hear from you about how it works or doesn't work.

To stay on task, we begin our excavation of financial cultural identities from the simple leverage of *a sliding scale model that depends upon your ability to name <u>both</u> your self-empowered or disempowered financial identity and your self-accountability with your financial privilege and/or prejudice.* If you initially feel the push-pull of opposing emotions or sensations that give you combinations of self-inflation, deflation, stings, self-righteousness, pride, shame, blame or guilt — congratulations, you're on the mat! You made it to the right spot which is the hot spot. My hope is the simplicity of the model brings out the *complexity* of your cultural financial identities and experiences so that you may begin to have greater awareness for yourself and for those around you.

Now that I've outlined the method, let's break it down into doable steps. First, do your Somatic Money Presence Practice and come into your core stability and presence. Then, check in with your sliding scale of empowerment and ask yourself, *"How disempowered to empowered do I feel about my cultural financial identity?"* This takes into account your empowered checks with your race/ethnicity in your family and in your workspace; your gender in your family and in your workspace; your identity of sexual orientation in your family and in your workspace. Although I haven't mentioned it before, I believe your identity with age also matters here as well as any other identity factors that you experience through your family and your surrounding working environment that are important to you. Allow yourself to feel or see the varying nuances of each of these aspects of your identity and your somatic experience with each one. Notice the emotions, thoughts, memories, scripts and body responses you experience. Once you complete the exercise, you're going to understand, if you hadn't already, where and how you feel empowered, enlightened, illuminated with your sense of identity in healthy, conscious and constructive ways. You're also going to be much more aware of where and how you feel disempowered (or other challenging emotions) with your sense of identity. This excavation is going to give you a better idea of where you're already stable and solid, or where you've already done your healing work with your empowered cultural financial identity. It's also going to show you where you might need healing, support, development or help in areas of your cultural financial identity where you might feel wounded, traumatized, unsupported or undeveloped. This is where I encourage you to seek support with resources, specialists, therapists in these potential trauma or wound zones. Be sure to refer to the Resources Chapter in the back of this book.

The empowered identity check we just did focuses on how you are seen and heard in value with yourself and others in your family and workspace when it comes to your cultural financial identity. The home for this, in your body, is in your throat chakra (nose, ears, mouth, throat), supported by your solar plexus, empowerment, in the stomach region. Also, further supported in your pelvis, hips and legs.

Usually, with throat chakra value and identity work, the excavation stops there. But we're going to continue to another aspect of throat chakra value work and that is *"How do you see and hear others?"* In other words, how good are you at listening? Witnessing? Observing? And when you listen and observe, what filters are you looking through? Are you looking with eyes and ears of appreciation, compassion, gratitude? Are you looking with eyes and ears of detail, discernment, empathy? Are you looking with eyes and ears of judgement, criticalness, fear? When you witness the world around you, what's your filter? How does your filter change, depending on your emotional state, environment or situation? This sets the stage for how you wield any potential privilege or prejudice in relationship with the people in your life, including your financial privilege or prejudice.

Now, no matter what results you experienced with your empowered self-identity checks in the last exercise, we're beginning from a fresh space. So, shake out your body, move around, stretch and recalibrate. Once you feel like you're clear, we're going to begin with a similar check, but now we'll be working with how you see/observe and hear/listen to the people around you. Again, I'd like you to engage your Somatic Money Presence Practice and allow yourself to come back into your calm core with some breathwork. Once you do, I'd like you to put yourself in the shoes of those around you. *When it comes to ethnicities, cultures, racial tones of people other than your own, especially in your family and work environment, are you seeing and hearing these individuals with compassion or tones of judgement and/ or prejudice?* How you hear and see others in your surrounding world is going to take a strong sense of self-honesty and self-accountability on your part. You are going to want to re-engage this same question about gender, sexual orientation and age. Then, here's the next step. Once you identify how you are seeing and hearing others, ask yourself, *"What, if any privilege, am I wielding in the financial and/ or working relationships that I have?"* Again, this is going to take a strong sense of self-honesty and self-accountability on your part. Then, for the last question, *"Is it possible, even if I'm doing it innocently or blindly, that I might be using my prejudice and/or privilege to harm others?"* Again, this is going to take a sense of strong self-honesty and self-accountability on your part.

Depending upon what you find, if you have a sense of prejudice or privilege that you haven't come to terms with, especially if it's epigenetically encoded through your family's genealogy, this is your opportunity to do your work and engage your own healing. This is a great place to engage sensitivity training in areas of race, gender, sexual orientation and/or age. Also, if you've never learned about privilege, especially white privilege, this is a great time to engage this topic and learn to identify your privilege, your blind spots, and the steps you can do in your environment to make constructive changes. Last, if you find yourself buying into or emotionally caving into guilt or shame, that's your indicator that you probably need to learn about your fragility, as in white fragility, male fragility or homophobia. Last, as you learn about your prejudice and/or privilege, and as you're ready, it is also your job to take a next step and ask, *"How may I make constructive changes (not rescuer's complex) to help and/or leave the door open to empower another individual's cultural financial identity experience."* Here's the beauty in bridging this process. No matter how uncomfortable, scary or vulnerable this might feel to you, when you become open to where you've been culturally blind and/or deaf, and you embrace the vulnerable reality of your internal emotional space, you open the doorway to possibilities. Possibilities of healing internal aspects of yourself while you engage greater possibilities and potentials for others.

Overall, here's the nuanced complexity of this modeling that I'd like to point out. None of us are going to fit, lock-stock-and-barrel, into one box. We're very diverse and complex creatures, so these checks may turn up varying tones, colors and hues of your nuanced cultural financial identity empowerment and/or disempowerment, along with your cultural financial prejudices and privileges. That knowledge alone might help give you greater leverage and relief in your life while you provide beautiful leverage and relief for others. My intent and hope is that this is a model that mutually lifts people up.

If you find yourself in resistance here to your prejudice and privilege checks, I'd like to share with you a patterning sequence that I've found in Somatic Money. It begins with the emotional energy of judgement as a sense of self-protection or self-defense. Emotional judgement is your inner fear switch saying, "I don't feel safe and I need protection and I'm going to use the shield of judgement to help me feel safe." This is connected to your internal fear and scarcity switch about being enough and having enough. (Remember your biological triggers in Chapter Four?) When we buy into this internal trigger, landing us in the self-protective judgement fields of prejudice and/or privilege, we are in disconnect — from ourselves and one another. It's this disconnect, out of an illusion of fear and scarcity, that keeps us from truly getting to know one another as humans and seeing the humanity in one another. This is where our internal work begins, at the location of bridging the divide of our cultural financial wounds through deaf and blind prejudice and privilege to consciously implement empowered cultural financial identity in tandem with honest and constructive self-checks.

* * *

Congratulations for journeying through the amazing landscape of your Big Dig for the first time! Here are a few post-excavation concepts worth reviewing.

The Magic of Money Story: The Journey *IS* the Healing.

Money Story is a funny beast. Sometimes, it's elusive and no matter what you do to tweak it out of the shadows, it will not allow itself to be found until it's ready. Other times, Money Story will smack you over the head, demanding to be seen and heard as it howls its adventures to you with, "It's time to know this truth!" Then, there's the Money Story that won't tell, but will take you with it, traversing over mountains, through deserts, slogging in swamps, thwack-sacking through jungles so that you receive every ounce of its foliage, its detail. Most of all, when you go looking for Money Story, it will eventually unfold around you, through you, not in the way you hoped, but in the way it happens.

What you need to know about Money Story, is that while your journey unfolds in the surface of your consciousness, deep within you, changes are tugging at the cellular coding of your DNA — much like adventure. The stories that you lay bare on the surface might have the equivalent of putting one toe-hold after another into the mountainside with the weight of a backpack on your shoulders, as you climb your way to the mountain meadow near the elk herd, listening to the freedom and power of their bugling. The stories you reveal might have the depth charge equivalent of you swimming in the ocean of your truth, sounding off with the whales. Sometimes, these stories might have the equivalent of you swaying through the murkiness of your unknown swamp, with gators eyeing you and snakes falling from cypress out of the Spanish moss.

The stories you lay your hands on are alive as patterns in the deep coils of your DNA and RNA – the caves of your psyche. Here in the depths, your inner and outer worlds and your past-present-future worlds, could not be more intrinsically connected. In the mists where the two worlds of physicality and vibrational illumination cross over and intermingle in dancing spirals of illuminated cells, that's where your Money Story, your deep Money Story, comes to life.

The magic is that as you journeyed, with your excavation, through the depths of your cellular code, in all the glory or gloom, triumph or nightmare, you naturally released old story, old ghosts, old patterns and old triggers. They left you and along with it, their power in your life. You released trails of magnificent phantoms you no longer need. As these phantoms left, their exhalation of exit created space. This space is the room in your cells for your body's psyche to breathe. This breathing room gives you redemption, empowerment, healing and the space to consider the new dream of your authentic self, authentic patterns. It's what the shamans teach us: that we truly dream our world into being through the inhale-exhale of cellular light. It's up to you to dream your new money code, your new Money Story. And it's already begun in your cellular code with new patterns, new love and energy.

If, however, you notice that something big has begun to reveal itself or shift within you, but not release yet, then you're working with a larger, more complex and deeply anchored pattern that will require more process. The best word to describe these patterns is "sticky." This sticky energy is somewhat insidious and frustrating, making you feel like you're trapped inside a Money Story loop that is a lot like the movie *Groundhog Day*. No matter what you do, you can't seem to get yourself out of the financial dynamic or un-anchor the energy from your body. Of note, your outside actions to strong-arm this repeating pattern into submission will most likely not help; however, your inner actions to unhook, rewrite and release energy will eventually create shift.

These sticky patterns might take time, patience, persistence and require more conscious recoding or healing work on your part. In this area of the journey, the best you can do is to practice a presence process of:

1.   Excavating your Money Story as we've described here.

2.   Being aware and practicing your slow down, breathing, centering and becoming present in your body at the location of your vulnerability where the Money Story exists.

3.   Keeping an attitude of presence without "fixing" it. An attitude of "I might not know exactly what is going on here, but that is okay. I'm holding presence and allowing my body, my psyche, to sort it out, releasing what needs to be released so..."

4. Anticipating the arrival of a new, higher, better, more light-filled pattern into the space you've created.

This key pivot of holding presence in your body at the location of the old residual pattern allows release, reconfiguration and healing to take place – even if you don't "know." The intent of holding space for a new pattern of light in the body to come alive (reprogramming) is the key part of the equation, bringing a breath of fresh air to your cellular code and creating your new money programming.

Taking action might be a part of this process. Once you've excavated Money Story and shifted energy, creating space for your new money coding or your Authentic Money Blueprint, please pay close attention. Be on alert for new conscious choices that appear for you, sometimes as new perceptual framing, sometimes as actual physical connections. Here, your action will be required. You might be required to make conscious and courageous action to do what I call, ***"make a new choice about an old thing."*** It might be straightforward, fast and smooth, like letting go of old work overnight that you no longer like and stepping into better paying new work that you love. It might be uncomfortable, messy and not completely clear, like setting boundaries with a relationship that took advantage of you. It might be a naturally emergent unfolding like a missing resource appearing that you need to finish an important project. Whatever it is, this new space that your Money Story excavation created is an opportunity for you to make new choices. This is the Universe saying, "So, you want to make a change? You want to make a new choice? Here is your opportunity." It's up to you to step up to the plate.

Release Your Polarized Money Story Elements for Empowered Integration.

If I've learned one thing about Money Story, it's that every individual on the planet holds a Money Story as unique as the proverbial snowflake. Although we might share similar patterns in our Money

Stories, like the fractal geometry of the unerring six-pointed snow crystal, no two Money Stories are alike.

I hope you take this insight to heart, accepting the inspiration that no matter the nature of your Money Story, it matters because it's authentically yours and brilliantly unique. Allowing your Money Story to shine in your life creates the pathway for you to learn and understand your money relationship landscape. Your Money Story might range from good, bad, wonderful, messy, logical, uncomfortable, colorful, boring, different or pie-in-the-sky – you name it, all of it is important.

Let me repeat that: your *entire* Money Story is important. That means in celebrating your authentic Money Stories, you absolutely cannot play favorites with your data collection. You cannot love some of the story and it's information and cast aside parts you don't like or that makes you feel uncomfortable. The moment you allow your self-critical eye, in an act of self-protection, to parse judgment between the data you like and dislike, you have just created confusion in your Money Story and you have lost your money game. You've stepped off the path of your Heroine's/Hero's Journey. Being your own best friend is the way through, as you courageously hold yourself in your presence practice with unconditional love to dig out your financial skeletons, both the ones you like and dislike. I guarantee that if you're willing to do this, it will serve you well and literally pay off in your bank account.

The cousin to playing favorites with your data is the trap of sugar-coating your Money Stories with positive thinking or giving the players in your Money Stories, including yourself, a free pass, even if they or you don't deserve it. Although positive thinking and free passes with forgiveness can occasionally serve constructive purposes, they only do so when they aren't used as a crutch. I'm encouraging you to break a terrible habit we've conjured in the spiritual and consciousness community, the self-growth community, possibly the Christian community, and maybe even in therapy services. It's that habit of only looking at and embracing the labeled good while covering up our labeled bad while we sugar-coat the "bad" with positive thinking. Frankly, calling things for what they are is so much more empowering and freeing. Sugar-coating your Money Story process with positive thinking, like frosting your flakes, only prolongs the inevitable crisis of your self-truth, which will eventually land in a sugar crash.

From an emotional and energy dynamic, embracing your "good" Money Stories while vilifying, rejecting and covering up your "bad" Money Stories is like running toward your light while being chased by your shadow. Or like cranking out laps on a hamster wheel until dropping off, exhausted. I'm encouraging you to courageously leap off your hamster wheel and authentically embrace both your good and bad Money Stories for something new — *a move from polarized Money Story landscapes to your integrated one.* How?

To start, acknowledge that your polarized self-tellings of your Money Story, the severe swings from good to bad and light to dark, spinning breathless on the mental hamster wheel of your mind, do one thing: they protect you from the truth of your money wounds and subsequent empowerment that lie in the middle. What does this look like in real life? An example I can share with you is from one of my clients in the Midwest who owns a salon. During our work together, she mentioned an intense drama playing out with one of her employees that was giving her fits. She framed herself into her own Money Story as "I can either be the nasty bitch (bad, villain) who calls my employee out on her stuff, or I can be the kind employer (good, victim) who 'makes nice' with her." She kept rotating between these two scenarios looking for her "rescue." (Karpman Drama Triangle.) My client was painting herself into two polarized corners of the "bad person" who doesn't win or the "good person" who also doesn't win while waiting for the rescue and she couldn't find her way out. What did I ask her to do? Once she laid out her Money Story and we identified the two polarized positions, releasing the drama out of her system. Then, I asked her to locate her authentic and empowered truth, that integrated place in the middle of her body. And for her, that came down to embracing her "empowered leadership with constructively communicated boundaries while releasing what others thought about her."

When you're able to vulnerably let go of the shields of your good and bad money labels, courageously holding space in breath and presence with the vulnerable unknown of what is in the middle, you step into the space of integrating your light and shadow worlds in the roots of your body, giving you more empowered solutions. This integration is the practice of being present, without judgment, with what is uncomfortably emerging. It's a space of acceptance and acknowledgment without defeat or celebration that allows what is without forcing your will. This is powerful healing stuff that alchemically transforms our lives for the better, while it's also another clear aspect of your financial Heroine's/Hero's Journey.

Even though I'm writing about this vulnerable integration practice with a certain amount of grace, I can assure you that I, along with so many other worthy souls, find this vulnerability presence practice one of the most challenging. This somatic integration of light and shadow is about learning your personal truth and your soul's true north no matter the discomfort. No one can do it for you or name it for you, yet we can stand in solidarity with you as you grow. While it's a process that is never over, it's one that powerfully serves and deeply rewards. If you feel overwhelmed by these initial Money Story ideas, take a few breaths and let yourself know, "It's okay." We're making introductions and planting seeds. You do not have to do this all at once.

Dropping the Drama.

If you notice, I'm gently and firmly walking you through the back door of shedding your Money Story drama. Yes, I know who you are with your adrenaline-spiked, polarized swinging, finger-pointing, helpless feeling, word tirades of your Money Story drama. Yes, I know the game you play with yourself because I've played it right along with you, and hundreds of others have told me about their money dramas too! With some humor, love and a reminder that this Somatic Money zone is Switzerland (a peaceful money zone), I ask that you start to shed your money drama *after* the telling. Sure, re-joice in the succulent juices of drama and *then let... it... go.* Drop the shield. Pull the plug. It's time to release buying into your Money Story drama because it literally costs you so much! It costs you emotion, energy and even dollars and cents.

When you gradually stop buying into your Money Story drama of "then he did this and then she did this and then that happened and then point-blame-point-blame and money money money," then you'll begin to release attachments. As you release attachments, a kind of magic will unfold. You'll see better, greater, more full potentials in the field before you. This magic takes shape as you shift from your singularly clenched and invested position of possessing the drama of your polarized good/bad Money Story labels, to letting go into the integrated presence practice of light and shadow with the field of your multiple higher potentials.

This subtle, yet powerful shift of moving from *Money Stories practiced in polarized drama versus Money Stories practiced in presence, release from attachment and then integration* moves the clarity of your money life from happening "out there" to "in here." It shifts from the illusion of financial events and elements happening to you and at you, holding you in suspended animation, to putting yourself internally at the helm of your financial ship.

For example, I've witnessed individuals, nearly in diatribe, al-most without breath and while disembodied, pointing to the deluge of events that seem so monster-real about how their money life is happening at them and to them. If this is an emotional state that you catch yourself in, it's time to tell yourself to breathe. Roll those shoulders back. Let yourself come back down into your core with some calm. Using your presence practice of slowing down, breathing and becoming present will help you integrate, recognize and acknowledge that these are external financial events being created from the inside out – no matter how real they seem. While you reclaim your breath and presence, it's your opportunity to shift internally and create an environment that will lose the energetic blame labeling. You will experience these events internally in the power of the here and now, embracing your internal responses with shadow and light.

From here, you'll be able to name your truth about who you are, how you feel, what choices you have and what you want to do. Your Money Story drama will continually create a polarized supercharge, cranking out your hamster wheel as long as you let it. So, gradually use your practice, diffusing the charge, anchoring yourself into your core with integration, so that you may perceive your transformed framework and greater field of potential in your multi-aspected Money Story.

The following story illustrates Somatic Money Presence Practice work in action, as clients learn to voice their Money Stories.

Client Money Story - How Embracing and Voicing Money Story Alleviated Layers of Emotional Financial Residue for an Immigration Attorney

When I met and began working with an immigration attorney in Glenwood Springs, Colorado, she knew something was deeply wrong in her financial life. She was making money and had a strong practice, but managing her money picture in that practice was her bane. She knew she needed to logistically work with her numbers in her personal and professional life, but no matter what she did or how hard she tried, she could not lay her hands on her financial books.

What we directly learned at the front of her Somatic Money Mapping is that she had been stuffing away her emotional intelligence about money, her Feminine Money aspect, and had solely focused only on her Masculine Money (the logistics and logic). What this means is that she had layers and layers of Money Story in her money bucket that she was ignoring and actively avoiding out of cultural and professional patterning. These avoided and ignored emotional layers were the block keeping her from getting to her money logistics – from balancing her books and making financial decisions about invoicing clients and paying her bills. Quite literally, the stuffed emotion was layered like geology inside her body, keeping her from the very thing she needed to do: structure and balance her books. Her banked emotional past was blocking her financial logistical present and future.

At the outset, I showed her how to give herself permission tell her Money Story and release her emotion, allowing how she felt about her life, her finances and her past to spill out. That permission allowed her to open the floodgates, and she did. We were both shocked about how much she had been holding. As the floodwaters released and shifted into a more rhythmic tide through several sessions, she was gradually able to get to her financial bookkeeping in her personal and professional life. She laid her hands on her empowerment energy and value energy in relationship with money and got a footing to facilitate her financial logistics.

For this immigration attorney, exhuming past Money Story and releasing the financial geology meant she could then, literally, lay her hands on her money life.

Spot Check

Sometimes, doing your Money Story excavation after the heavy lifting of installing your Somatic Money Presence Practice might feel like starting all over again. I assure you, it's not. The amazing work you're doing with your Big Dig is giving you extra leverage, extra connection points, extra empowerment and value in your money relationship. What I love most about Money Story excavation is that the layers keep giving in really wonderful moments of, "Aha!"

For tracking your progress, on the short side, this excavation process can take **two weeks. I'd easily give it a month.** Then, let it ride with you and become part of your life.

Money Story excavation usually pops in and out of our lives when we're in the trenches of working on Money Triggers. It's when we're releasing triggers (old Money Story data) out of our bodies that the old stories rise to the surface. Best not to dwell on them too much. Acknowledge them and say, "Bye, bye!" as you release them, making room to usher in your New Money Story!

Time to re-mention that if you do this work intensely, you're dredging information and energy out of your cellular code. Please make sure you check in with your self-care practices, especially hydration, rest, exercise and good nutrition.

CHAPTER NINE

Money Languaging

What Are You Really Saying About Your Money?

Not long after my Spontaneous Financial Intervention in the autumn of 2011, that you read about in the first chapter of this book, I found myself walking around my home feeling a soul itch in my body. The day was a gorgeous, blue-sky, autumn Colorado day outside, yet I felt turned inward, ready to stay inside. For me, this feeling usually precedes a major epiphany and the rolling thunder of a soul shift. I wandered around the house unable to engage projects. "What is this?" I thought. I felt an under-current of twitching. "What am I feeling underneath the layers?" Twitch, twitch. "Something is here. I feel it." Twitch, twitch, twitch.

After half a day of feeling like I had a synapse running loose through my body, like nuts and bolts rolling around in the basement of my soul, the exfoliation of epiphany rumbled through my entire being. I heard it in me. I heard the words I'd been saying to myself for so many years echoing, "I don't have any money!" Then, the words let loose in me like a word storm. "I don't have any money!" ricocheted around and through me from all angles, like echoes in a canyon. The amplification of this lightning bolt awareness astonished me with its layers, and the intent of it specifically said to me, "If I don't get this money relationship message, I am ignorantly blind to it."

The epiphany of this I-don't-have-any-money sentence stopped me cold. I gradually became aware I'd been saying this phrase to myself internally, without audibly voicing it, hundreds, if not thousands of times a day for years. My throat tightened, tears welled up in my eyes, my stomach dropped. It came to me that I'd been financially abusing myself all this time with: The years of tight income. The terror of feeling like I couldn't ever make enough. The panic when I tried to balance my checkbook. The terror of money. Much of it was coming from this singular phrase, repeated *how* many millions of times in my life and in my ancestors' lives before me?

In those moments, I understood the stunning reality that I'd programmed money out of myself, chasing it away from my starving financial self like a madwoman chasing crows away, swatting at them with an imaginary broom. I said to myself as I wrapped my arms around me, "I can't treat myself like this anymore. I have to stop saying these words now!" The friend of compassion showed up.

I sat in that big cavern of energy where the echoes of old words dissipated, and I asked myself, in an effort of change, "What is the opposite of "I don't have any money?"" Of course, the obvious answer is, "I have money." But the crazy thing is, it took me a while to get there. Even though "I have money" is a regular phrase I use now, while I was in that old space, it was terribly hard for me to imagine that there could be a phrase other than, "I don't have any money." That chasm between the two helped me understand how entrenched, how saturated the old wording was within my bones and my being. I knew I didn't want and couldn't hold onto the old wording anymore but getting to a new place with new words – it was a stretch. I was so used to financially abusing myself with subconscious wording and knocking myself down, that it was hard to stand up and consider something new.

Gradually, I energetically unfolded my psyche, let it stretch and let it breathe out from underneath the emotional beating. When I did, the obvious was waiting for me: "I have money." Trying those three words on for size was difficult. They felt foreign in me. Unsafe. I wanted to resist them, but I didn't. Could I actually say that I have money when there was only $12 in my bank account and more bills were flowing in? Could I say, "I have money" and feel it in my body and soul, even though the reality of it did not feel true? The old, rational, fearful aspects of myself struggled to hold on, ready to pick up the broom and continue swatting at the newness. I left the broom on the ground and entertained the idea that "Well, they are just words. I truly don't have anything financially more to lose here. Why not? Let's start saying, "I have money" as deep and as often as I can."

So, I did. I let loose waves of "I have money" during my day, letting the words and feeling saturate me. Sometimes it felt uncomfortable, like clothes that didn't fit. Sometimes I was scared that it wasn't true and I was giving myself a pipe dream. Sometimes it felt like empty promises.

The phrase began taking root in my body, in my soul. It felt more comfortable. It began to pick up steam and feel real. Then, the surprise happened. The change in my body and being began to reflect in my bank account. When I sat down with my checkbook to pay bills and balance my money, I started feeling those words as I worked with my money. Regularly, I felt and heard myself internally say, "I have money" as I paid a utility bill, and the balance shifted to a remaining $20. And a week later, as I paid a telephone bill, and felt and said the words, a remaining balance of $30 was there. And so it went, that by the time I finished the month, a balance of $100 was still in my account, unplanned.

When that happened, I thought, "Oh, this is more real than not." Something magical was happening. The words I said ran through my body, creating a vibrational feeling. I also practiced them at my money desk, and they were beginning to create something more real than not. What was this shift?

Between my Spontaneous Financial Intervention, unlocking old code, and this very conscious word choice with money that I practiced every day, by the end of that first autumn, I began to see a difference of several hundred dollars adding up in my bank account. It was my first financial cushion room in years. A year later, it had added up into a $4,000 income jump with a $500 to $800 base in my bank account. That was a substantial financial improvement for me at the time and it all came from new money languaging backed with presence practice and Money Story excavations.

That's when I knew that words count, quite literally, when it comes to money. The emotion and vibration we feel through our bodies turn into direct programming in our money lives, and they count right into the bank account.

So, I have one question for you? What are the internal words you are saying to yourself daily about your money? What words in your life are powerfully subtracting money out of your bank account or into your bank account? What words and phrases are creating the very financial conundrums in your life that you're struggling with right now? It's time to go word spelunking into the cave of your soul to Big Dig those words to the surface! Who knows? You could only be three to four words away from a powerful financial shift in your life!

That Word You Keep Repeating? Yeah. It's Programming Your Money.

Let's begin with this: *words are powerful.* The teeny phonetic symbols of letters put together to form symbolic vibration of words in print and sound are saturated with meaningful experience that we exchange with one another. That meaning impacts, imprints and also exudes through our bodies and souls. So, the words you use, and especially the ones you use subconsciously through your body to define and describe your money life, are some of the most powerful dialects of your living exchanges. Again: *words are powerful.*

And then there's this — words are mutable through meaning. How we use words, depending on our experiences, changes over time. How we blend words together creates new hues and tones of meaning. We use and receive words to construct, destroy, wound and heal. We use words in the redemption of our soul-claiming processes by naming and describing our lives – one of our most powerful tools. Words are leveraged power and value, structure and flow, with mutable meaning in motion.

For money languaging, this means that you have money words buried in the depths of your somatic genealogy, carrying the impact of certain meanings, and telling your body and psyche how to respond with your money partners, agreements and exchanges. In terms of Somatic Money, your daily conscious and subconscious money words deliver your money agreements in positive or constructive ways, neutral ways and negative or destructive ways. So, if you exhume your money words, name them and give them the power of mutability, you have just claimed a *powerful tool in your financial life: the power to name and change your money life through the power of words.* These are letters, words, symbols and meanings of vibrations, all encoded in your cells, linked to the symbols of numbers, ready for mutability. Change the financial letters in your soul, change the numbers of your money life.

How do you do this? We begin by showing you how to catch the money words you're constantly repeating on the tip of your tongue. Those words are programming your money life, even when you don't know you're doing it.

What Am I Saying About My Money?
One of the fun aspects of money work is catching what you're truly saying to yourself about your money. It's fun because it's a treasure hunt, literally putting financial power, value and money in your pocket. The more you catch your money-word bloopers, the Freudian slips of the tongue illuminating how you truly feel financially, the more opportunities you have to update what you want to say to reprogram or change and improve your money life. And the more you update your money language to truly reflect your money relationship, instead of financial-word default (financial pun intended), the more potential you have to shift. Think of it like this — transforming your money language is about fine-tuning your Money Story ship,

changing the inner-workings of your ship's engine and rudder, and even amplifying its speed!

How does transforming your money language work? Here are a few steps:

1. **Catch the unconscious slips of your tongue,** both verbally and non-verbally, locating the words in your lexicon that show the true color of how you think and feel about your money. For help, you might glean your money words from your Big Dig excavation that reveal what you believe about your financial identity and empowerment. Or, you could glean your money words from your work in Part Two, especially from your triggered money zones. Be sure to scan the words of how you describe your Compelling Money Issues. In other words, go to your financial hot spots and your unconscious money words will be gleaming there, waiting for you.

2. **Consciously use your Somatic Money Presence Practice to illuminate** the impact your wording is having in your body and money programming. Be sure to slow down, breathe, tune in with awareness and feel how those words are vibrating in your body, providing insight into how you feel about the money wording with your financial life.

3. **Consciously select new wording, new programming,** that you can easily and regularly verbalize into a new money state. Somatically check those words to make sure they're an integral fit.

This practice is simple! Yet, I'm sure, after reading my story above and reviewing these simple steps, you can see the catch. The catch is locating words, thoughts and feelings that were once hidden under the radar in your psyche and revealing them in your conscious awareness. The trick is to cajole your money words from their subterranean spaces in your body. In preparation, you need to lay the fertile ground of your foundation by revisiting your sense of self-honesty.

Self-honesty in excavating money language is paramount. That means emotional by-passing, sugar-coating and free passes will get in the way. Moxy up! Self-honesty works. Our words get stuck in unseen places when we are unwilling to see our true nature with all its light and shadow. How ready, willing and able are you to truly be honest with yourself about your money relationship? So honest that you'll embrace whatever rises to the surface, no matter how uncomfortable? So self-honest that you're willing to cut through the emotional gaslighting in which we're all expected to participate? That's the kind of self-honesty you must employ to cajole your money words from deep spaces.

In doing so, you'll be locating and transforming the money language you're using today that is rooted in a few bygone eras. This is the sometimes raw and honest semantics of peeling back the layers. In doing so, you give yourself the choice to re-language your financial words into a powerful and fresh new money state that better matches your true creation.

As you do this work, your ally is your intention. My coaching clients who don't know how to excavate subconscious places, I encourage "holding the intent of allowing words, messages and phrases to surface on their own in obvious ways." Then, over the course of days, or even hours, wording that was hidden is revealed. This especially works if used consistently.

The key foundational pieces of self-honesty, unmasking and intent will help cajole your hidden money words to the surface. Here are a few practical ideas to help the process:

1. **Review the Somatic Money journal** that I know you're keeping (wink, wink) and word-mine it for your financial words. Skim through what you've written about your money relationship, your presence practice and your Money Stories in your Big Dig. You're looking for catchphrases

and specific words that you repeat. Also, you're looking for the words or phrases that stand out and leap off the page with energy. These are the ones that say, "Me, me! I'm the language holding programming space with your money that's ready to change!"

2. **Have a trusted friend or professional listen.** If you don't think you can do it on your own and you need interaction, select a trusted friend or professional, set up a specific sacred space where you won't be interrupted, and tell your person a pertinent Money Story or your Compelling Money Issue for review. Their instructions are to neutrally listen and watch for the seeming benign words or phrases you use repeatedly that are loaded with emotion or energy that describe your money relationship. You may be oblivious to these words, as they are obvious to others. If you need the interaction, but don't want to do this with another person, perhaps record yourself on your phone and listen to your recording. If you don't want to record it, write the Money Story down in your journal and review it with a highlighter.

3. **Simply listen to yourself (concerning money) as you interact** with others during your day. What are the words and phrases you're regularly using to describe who you are and what you're doing in relationship with your primary partner, your friends, your work colleagues and your family?

4. **Listen to your inner dialogue** of what you're constantly saying to yourself, and how you talk to yourself throughout your day. You'll be surprised at what you find!

5. **Review the family money "tapes"** or the money tapes of your closest friend circle. What words get used when you all talk smack in a social setting? What is the primary money lan-

guage your family members used or use? Are you still using those same words and phrases? Are you using them in helpful and supportive ways, or blocked and destructive ways?

Out of this list, select the ones that work for you and practice as needed. These are the money language excavation tools that will bring your current money language, the programming of your financial life, to the surface. It will bring it to life!

Keep Going. Change Those Words!

Once you've hunted for the treasure chest of your unconscious money words and brought them to the light of day, you'll find that one word or phrase is usually the center, anchoring down other words and phrases, much like spokes connected to the center of a wheel. With your handful of money words or phrases, I'd like you to locate the power-core of the one word or phrase that might be anchoring all the others. That one word or phrase is where you want to begin.

If you haven't already done it, please work with your Somatic Money Presence Practice and check in with where that word or phrase is located and anchored in your body. Where do you feel it most? One spot or region? Or networked throughout your body? As you do your check, also notice how the word or phrase makes you feel. How is it resonating, creating certain energy or emotion in your body? Again, a great book to reference emotions and energies in connection with your body is Inna Segal's *The Secret Language of Your Body*. This book will help you clarify your somatic experiences with specific energetics and emotion relating to where words are lodged in your body.

As a side note, if you locate money words or phrases rising up that you like, and that are good and powerful in your life, keep them!

Now that you know the word or phrase, somatic location and experience, it's time for you to consciously choose how you want to change it. Remember, words and their programming in our cells are mutable! Choosing new words to describe your inner money relationship will change your money life. To do this, you can either take a baby step with your money language and shift in degrees, or you can rip off the Band-Aid and change your words 180 degrees like I did. Here are multiple examples for languaging changes. I begin with the unhealthy and move to constructive suggestions. It looks like this:

- **Feminine Money Transformation:** I'm **sick** of my money relationship. **Blech**! To: I'm experiencing my money relationship with **better energy and emotion**. To: I **embrace** my money relationship with **warmth, love and even joy**. To: **Money flows to me and feels good.**

- **Money Empowerment Transformation:** I feel so **helpless** and **frustrated** with my money! To: I'm getting into my **driver's seat** with my money relationship. **I run the show**. To: I'm **empowered** with my money relationship. To: **Money works for me.**

- **Money Value Transformation:** No matter what I do financially, I feel so **under-valued**. To: I am **seen and heard** in **value** in my life. To: I'm getting better at **asking** for what I truly need in my life. To: **I am valued and loved**, especially with my money relationship. To: **I am seen and heard with money.**

- **Masculine Money Transformation:** I just **don't understand** how my money works. To: I am getting present with my money to allow myself to financially **learn**. To: Hey! I **learned one new thing** about how my money works today! Or, I am **competent** with my money. To: **Money supports me.**

See?! Track your data! And then make conscious mutable changes that you can see, hear and feel in your body with your money relationship. If you're tired of your old language and how it makes you feel, and you're ready to leap off your cliff with a whole new word or phrase, go for it – much like I did with "I have money now!" Let the new words or phrases emerge and erupt out of your new space. If you're not a leaper, you may test the waters, create a new word or phrase in the direction you want to go, and try it on for size. That's fantastic too. Remember, no matter what new words or phrases you decide to hold internally and verbalize externally, they're not written in stone. You may change them again. That's the beauty of such a mutable process.

Wording Pitfalls to Name and Change.

The Universe treats our money language like programming; what we financially say is what we get. That means "garbage programming in, garbage programming out." Or, it can also mean, "stellar program in, fantastic results." This is especially true when we allow the negative cultural money words to be so tightly woven into our daily dialogue without the sunlight of constructive financial language to shine through. It's time we loosen ourselves from the hold of old money words so the new ones may work. These are wording habits to ferret out and consciously replace with beautiful new threads of money hope:

- **Keep your money language simple for power.** We tend to get complex, even fancy, in our renaming of new money language. Please don't fall into this trap because it's confusing for the body and psyche. The body and psyche like simple and symbolic road signs. That's what they latch onto. Instead of getting fancy, you're looking for empowered, constructive and positive replacement words that are just as simple and powerful as the dysfunctional ones you found in the first place. Just make sure your new words have better coding. Also, keep your phrases in first person (I am), present tense (here, now) and active language (verbs). Like: "I have money!" or "I win!" or "I receive!" or "I am here!" or "Now" or "Let's do this!" You get the idea.

- **Would, Could and Should** are words the Universe cannot and does not hear. They're impotent and soaked in low value. These words are insulated fillers getting in the way of real clarity, decision, intent and action. The word "should" is a word of guilt, heaping baggage on yourself and others. The words "could" and "would" are words of confused intent, lack of decision or action. Shifting these words to "I am" and "It is" and "We are" phrases, paired with words like "important," are much more powerful.

- When you use words like **Little** and **Small** and **Whatever** to describe your life, your activities and your money, that is exactly what you're going to receive. Please use words that are **Large and Great and Big and Infinite**. The small words make you shrink, hide and disappear. The larger words help you step up to the plate of life!

- If you are weaving the words **Try** and **Trying** through your dialect and never feel like you're getting ahead, there's a reason. The word "try" is a battery drainer that leaks energy (and money) everywhere. Stop that leak. Change your words to **"I am doing this"** and **"It is working"** and **"We're getting this done."** Moving from "try" to words that are more definitive means you move from a lack of commitment to commitment.

- **The Universe and our psyches do not track negative instruction,** only the core phrase. This means a phrase like, "Don't fall out of the tree" becomes "fall out of the tree." You're better off re-languaging the phrase as "Stay in the tree" or "Hang on securely." Speak or language to the active outcome that is most important to you.

There are also a set of cultural money phrases that are worth eliminating from your financial lexicon or entirely changing. As you excavated your Money Story in your Big Dig and financial identity work, and here, as you unearth unconscious money words and phrases, I'm sure you've run across some oldies but *not*-goodies that seeded in our culture like unhelpful weeds. I'm sure you're also noticing the obscure, yet emotionally laden language of your daily money responses. These phrases are filled with disempowered, guilt-filled, fear-filled, deep judgments about money life that create financially weighted, disempowered, hostage money situations. Be on the lookout if your money life or your family's money life includes phrases like the ones listed below. Keep in mind, I cultivated this list from my Caucasian community. Depending upon your cultural ethnicity, gender and sexual orientation, these phrases might not resonate with you or you might have completely different cultural money phrases. My hope is this list ignites a few ideas so you may find what you're ready to change:

- Money is a necessary evil.

- I'm afraid I won't have enough.

- Robbing Peter to pay Paul.

- Beggars can't be choosers.

- We can't do that because of the money.

- Don't stare a gift horse in the mouth.

- A bird in the hand is better than two in the bush.

- A penny/dollar saved is a penny/dollar earned.

- More trouble than it's worth.

- Survival of the fittest.

- Poor as church mice.

- Money burning a hole in your pocket.

- Money flowing through your hands like water.

- Shit rolls downhill.

- I'm behind the eight ball.

- Passing the buck.

- The deck is stacked against me.

- You have to pay to play.

- It's a dog-eat-dog world out there.

These are just a handful of popular and daily money phrases that will help jog your memory as you locate the money phrases used in your family and friend groups. Next, please take a look at how I helped several clients unpack the money language in their business picture.

Client Money Story - "My sales territory is killing me. "
During one of my client sessions, my client was describing her sales territory. Her work put her on the road frequently and the winter travel months were grueling as they stretched across several western states with steep mountain passes. During her descriptions, she said once, "My territory is killing me." And she said it again and then she said it again. The first time, the hairs on the back of my neck stood up. The second time, the red flag waved. The third time, I caught her.

I asked, "Are you aware that you're saying, "My sales territory is killing me?'" She paused and said, "No." Which surprised me, because I thought she was hearing herself. She wasn't!

So, I said, "Well, you've said that phrase three times now. When you listen to the session audio, you can count them." And then I requested, "Could you PLEASE stop saying that phrase? Because it is not helping you in this situation."

What I reflected back was shocking to her since she had no idea she'd been saying her territory was killing her. She was concerned about how many times she'd been repeating it to herself and saying it out loud to others. She did not want it to become a self-fulfilling prophecy.

We took the work a step further and I asked her to track, into her body, the money words about her sales territory killing her. We needed to locate where these words were anchored in her body, what part of herself was saying them and why. Through the excavation, we learned "my sales territory is killing me" was connected to concerns about male authority figures, being able to speak up in her authentic power, without being "killed." After voicing this, she noticed she wanted to take command of her situation.

After we completed the energy work connected to the words and her body, I suggested an optional follow-up: when or if she was ready, to visit with her male boss about her sales territory. We finished the session and said our goodbyes.

I was surprised to receive an email from her about a week later, describing that not only had she spoken to her boss and redefined her work and territories, she also had traded in her automobile for an SUV that was much safer for winter driving. She'd been worried about her car for months. So, to stand in her power and be heard by a male authority figure who loved her sales ideas, and then to upgrade her car – all in one week – was a huge success. This all resulted from capturing one unconscious money phrase!

Client Money Story - "Shit rolls downhill."

Several years ago, I was on the phone with a consultee who continually negatively described, using this phrase of "shit rolling downhill," about the management in her department of a women's clothing retail position. The conversation rolled in a rhythm of "Drama drama drama, shit rolls downhill. And this this this, and that that that, and shit rolls downhill." The phrase, "shit rolling downhill," was a mantra she sprinkled into all her work descriptions.

Finally, after listening to her stories, I caught her and asked if she was hearing what she was saying to herself. When I shared the line about "shit rolls downhill," she was semi-conscious that she was using the phrase, but not aware of the frequency.

I asked her to unpack that phrase and share with me what she meant. When she slowed down and gave it thought, she realized it was deeply connected to feeling like she had no power and that she was always at the receiving end of low vibrational results in her company. I asked her if she wanted to consciously embody being a victim and perpetually play out this role. When she said, "No, absolutely not," we worked on changing the words. The new words embodied consciously responding to work situations with empowerment and consciously releasing drama that wasn't hers. She changed her phrase to: "I am consciously responding to work situations in my power and releasing what isn't mine."

<u>Spot Check</u>

You're in the home stretch now! Keep going! Even though Money Languaging and Money Intent might seem like small end-of-project topics, they are mighty. Plus, they're fun. I've had clients turn their money lives around with these two focal areas. Please stay diligent because you're almost there and you have this!

As far as tracking your progress, both Money Languaging and Money Intent, **take about two weeks each on the short side or a month to complete** on the long side.

Happy treasure hunting for those words, phrases and hidden moments of intent that impact your money world.

CHAPTER TEN

Aligned Money Intent

Unmask Your Real Money Truth

Imagine, it's powder-puff football season, as in the female version of football. If you're a guy, feel free to adjust this to the football game of your gender. And imagine the football is your money game. Imagine you're one of the players, and you're on the field with your teammates surrounded by a stadium filled with people. Coaches, players and referees watch from the sidelines. You're lined up with the other players on the line of scrimmage, and everyone is anticipating the next play. You've got your eye on the ball because you know that's your money game. You hear the count, see the snap, watch the quarterback catch the ball and drop back for a pass and fumble!

Imagine, in slow motion, that you pick up the dropped ball, your money ball, and you turn and start running towards your team's end zone for a financial score. You get a few steps down the field headed in the direction you want to go, but then, SURPRISE, all the players, even your own teammates, pick you up and carry you in the opposite direction. No matter how much you yell and struggle, there isn't anything you can do to stop it. To your surprise, both teams drop you and your money ball in the financial end zone where you don't want to be.

Although this scenario is comically extreme, I shared it with you to represent the schism between your assumed and surface-level money intent and the real money intent of your life happening deep in the DNA coding of your body. No matter how much you think, desire, repeat mantras and plan for your money to go one direction on the surface, it's always going to move in the general direction of the intent anchored deeply in your body, in the programming of your DNA.

I did not stumble upon this clarity about the difference between conscious money intent (what we plan for our money) and real money intent (what actually drives our money) until well into my Somatic Money coaching practice. During the consultation stage of working with one of my clients, I located one of the most profound instances of the difference between the two intents of money. The woman I was working with was in the healthcare industry on the Colorado Front Range. During her initial consultation, an Ascended Master dropped in and directly asked me to ask her, "What is the money manifestation mantra that you're using right now?"

When I shared the question with her, she paused for a moment and then shared her money mantra with me. She said that she'd been using the money mantra, "I am free with my money," very regularly. She meant it as in, "I have plenty of money, so I feel free." But that was not the reality happening in her body. What she intended and what occurred every time she said the phrase were two different things. The moment she said the mantra to me, I saw energy fly out of her body. I asked her to repeat the phrase so I could track the energy dynamic again. She repeated, "I am free with my money." And I saw more energy leave her body. Every time she repeated this phrase, she was literally losing bits and pieces of herself!

I understood her intent and method, but it scared me that her practice was draining energy out of her body instead of attracting money in. Without realizing it, she was telling her energy to leave her body, and her finances were reflecting this loss through financial chaos, money leakage and increased debt. She was creating the opposite of what she intended.

I described the dynamic she was creating in her life, and I asked her to discontinue that phrase and replace it with a new one: "I am in my body and powerful with my money." When we completed the consultation and began coaching, she reported back to me that in the thirty days she'd been using the new phrase, she felt more solid, not as wispy, and she experienced several positive money events.

Keys to Unveiling Tricky Intent.

In comparing the difference between Money Story, language and intent, the real money intent of our lives is subtle, yet powerful, making it deceivingly difficult to put a finger on its pulse. When it comes to excavation, real money intent is the vigorous vapor, the steam rising through your money life that determines the direction of your money engine. While money language is about sifting through the financial vocabulary of your money words to consciously locate your steerage. Which makes Money Story a palpable, visceral experience giving you the solidity of your money relationship.

Here is the tricky paradox of real money intent: while it holds such power in our financial lives, it literally slips through our fingers if we try to clench its fog. So, if we try to chase down our real money intent to locate it, we're chasing down the diaphanous wings of a dream world that vaporizes. If we try to control it, we're clamping down on ghosts. If we try to conjure it, we're materializing figments that vaporize like mists of rain in the desert.

If you want to locate your real money intent, it's more about being in still and soft awareness while allowing it to land around you like butterflies coming to rest on a nearby butterfly bush. Like deer softly treading from your forest into your meadow where you're seated and watching them in sheer delight, this phenomenon of voluptuous magical peace. Like the hummingbird journeying a thousand miles to hover inches in front of your nose as you meditate. Locating your real money intent has more to do with becoming as deeply still and aware as possible, allowing it to land around you, revealing itself. This is the allowing of it revealing itself to you, without you forcing it with an ounce of agenda. This momentary window of revealing shows you the real truth.

If that sounds like a near impossibility to crack this paradoxical nut - it can be - unless you use the tool of intent itself! By using fire upon fire to stop the burn, using intent upon hidden intent coaxes out your true financial butterflies, deer and hummingbirds. Yes, if you hear Buddha laughing, this has to do with calling bluff on the cosmic joke of the Universe. Because usually, when you allow yourself to become still enough in your inner world, no matter what you're doing, that's when the hidden reveals itself — and it's usually a large self-joke about your life that makes you painfully giggle.

The trick is spending time in that place where everything internally lives in stillness, in slow motion, while the world whizzes by you. It's working with your tool of soft intent with refrains of "inner-self, higher-self, show me what I'm *really* doing here. What am I *really* doing with this project? What have I *truly* agreed to in this situation? Who am I? What role am I *really* playing in this partnership?" As you're gently listening and watching for the veil to open, that's when it happens. That's when the tool of intent momentarily reveals.

Then, locating real intent elicits your own inner jokes and painful laughter of, "Oh, dear, *that's* what I'm *really* doing?" When it happens, it's an ironic relief, a deep automatic self-forgiveness that releases the weight of having to try so humanly hard in life, even financially.

While challenges with money usually trigger in us a deep survival response with the corresponding urge to work our fingers to the bone, to work ourselves out of our financial messes, this is the paradoxical beauty of the quest for real money intent: it's not about hard work. In fact, I believe you'll find that the quest for real money intent is the exact opposite, by letting go of working so hard and softening the heavy hand of agenda.

Getting from where you are to this place I'm describing, no matter how simple it sounds, isn't necessarily easy. So, over the course of my coaching, I've located several bridge tools to help you train yourself out of working so hard, trying so hard, so that you may coax your real money intent out of hiding. These slow-down, breathe, get-in-your-body, smell-the-roses questions will help you reveal the diaphanous wings of your real money intent. You may even treat these as slow-motion journeys in your meditation space:

- Slow down, breathe and become present with your core awareness and ask yourself, "If money is my friend, which it is, what is it really trying to tell me? What does it want me to know?"

- Slow down, breathe, and become present with your core awareness and ask yourself, "If my money is animated, which it is, what animal totem is it? Or if I anthropomorphized my money, what would it be? And what is this anthropomorphized animation telling me?"

- Slow down, breathe, and become present with your core awareness and ask yourself, "If money animated as my inner child, and I held my child's hand and took him/her for a walk down to the river, what would my inner money child tell me about my financial life?"

These exercises and questions will help you still and soften yourself to the aspect of your Feminine Money EQ, allowing you to catch the difference between what you *think* you're doing with your money (mind space) and what is actually *happening* through your psyche (your EQ body space).

Illuminating Money Intent by Cutting Through the Mask.

Now that we've landed these insights, I want to point out a significant pitfall that might be keeping you from your real money intent: masking. Although this segment about masking overlaps our previous work, there are several new aspects worth mentioning. These concepts involve *how* we work with our popular consciousness tools in relationship to money intent. For context, I believe money mantras, visioning, abundance and manifestation practices to co-create the life you want to live are good tools. Yet, any good consciousness tool can easily be turned into a mask, a crutch or a weapon if we're not careful.

Here, with your work to uncover true intent, surface-level masking obscures what is actually happening in your body at the deep level of your DNA programming with money agreements. It looks something like this: "While I say this mantra or do this vision or identify my manifestation on the surface, something else entirely is happening in my body." This is the dichotomy of wanting to run one way on the football field with your money football, while all team members from both teams pick you up and carry you in the opposite direction. Your money football is your surface-level intent, and your body, carried by the teams in the opposite direction, is real money intent.

How is it possible to create a powerful and healthy money mantra, visioning, abundance or manifestation practice without it being booby-trapped? How do you create powerful and constructive alignments between your practice and what's happening in your body? The answer is inside the question. It's through your Somatic Money Presence Practice.

Try this: when you say or practice your money mantra, vision, abundance or manifestation practice, check and notice how it makes you feel in your body? And I'm not talking about a body check where you thoughtfully check in as far down as your throat chakra or heart chakra (which most people believe is a somatic check). No, I'm talking a depth charge reality check into your solar plexus, second chakra, root chakra and even legs to find out what is really happening inside of you with your energy medicine money tool of choice. This might also mean pulling off any rose-colored glasses that sugarcoat with the "everything is positive" vibe so that you may experience your transparent self-honesty as you do your check into your illuminated self and your shadow world self. That's the kind of check I'm talking about.

What will happen if you lean into this practice? You'll begin to locate the schism between what you intend, what you're truly creating and why your money football might be going in the opposite direction than you want.

What Are the True Intentions Inside Your Money Practice?

Now that you've had a chance to review the concept of aligned money intent, a sample story and a few key insider tips, it's time to check in with your money intentions and unpack the layers. Let's walk through a handful of steps together:

1. *Is Your Current Intentional Money Practice Conscious or Unconscious?* Please become aware of the type of financial intentional practice that you already have. This will fall into one of two categories: either you're consciously practicing your money intent, or you're running your money intent by unconscious default.

2. *Specifically Identify Your Overall Money Intentions.* Whether your intentional money practice is conscious or unconscious, it's time to identify what you're doing. If you have a conscious money intentional practice, it could include money mantras, visioning, manifesting, Law of Attraction or abundance work. Please specifically identify what that is. If your intentional money practice is unconscious, now is an excellent time for you to shed light in the direction of your real money intent. As you look at your money relationship, what are your intentions? To be healthy with your money or not? To set yourself up for success or not? To be constructive with your money or not? What is the conversation you are having with yourself just below the surface about your money that is directing which way your money football and money body is going?

3. ***Do Your Somatic Money Check.*** Now that you're identifying what you're doing with your money intent, it's time to
use your Somatic Money Presence Practice for deeper body
dives. Please slow down, breathe and become present with
your core awareness. As you do, allow yourself to be present
with your current intentional money practice, whatever it is
(no judgments, please). Notice how you're responding in your
body. Do you feel better or worse? Do you feel more weight,
fear, constriction or nauseousness in your body with your intentional practice? Or do you feel better, lifted, empowered,
sound, happier, focused? Let your body show you what your
intentions are truly doing *because how your body responsively
feels with any specific intent then programs your true money
relationship through you.*

4. ***Upgrading Your Aligned Money Intent.*** As you work with
unpacking the layers of your true money intentions, you may
use these key items to dial in your practice. As you upgrade
to your aligned money intent, please make sure you're working with these elements. You'll find they are similar to the
languaging work we did in the previous chapter:

- Please define your intent as a single intent. No elabo-
rate descriptions that look like layers of pancakes. This is
confusing for the body. It doesn't know what to focus on.

- Speak in the first person with present tense and active
language.

- Remove shoulds, coulds and woulds.

- Lean into the direction you want to go and confirm it
with constructive and positive language.

Here are examples displaying the types of aligned money intentional language to work with:

- I am powerful in my money body.

- Money comes to me.

- I say "YES" to money.

- Money is my friend.

- It's my money turn now.

- My money is filled with joy.

- There is always more than enough money in my bank account.

- My money is good for me and you.

- My money life always works out better than I expected.

- I always have a financial cushion room.

Notice how these intentional money mantras or money programs are short, sweet and pack a bit of oomph?! You totally have permission to own your money intentions with greater empowerment and higher value. The clarity question here is: "When you say your money mantra or program to yourself, does it have enough power for you to believe it?" You don't have to wallow in half-money intentions anymore. So, please locate a money intention that works for you, either from this list or create your own in the spirit of this practice. Once you do, check in with your Somatic Money Presence Practice and see how your body responds. Again, do you feel suppressed, constricted, weighted, fearful? Or do you feel lifted, expanded, light or empowered? Regularly checking in with your intention, how you phrase it with words and what you feel in your body. This will gradually help you dial in your aligned money intent.

Client Money Story - How Clarifying a Money Intention Gave an Entrepreneur Leverage

One of the most profound money mantra intentional shifts I witnessed took place in Portland, Oregon. I was providing a money workshop for a consciousness group, and we mini-workshopped money intentions in group space. One of the participating entrepreneurs volunteered to share her money intention. As she spoke, her money intention reeled out in sentences with long layers, requesting everything she wanted in her money life. As she read her money intention aloud, I watched as energies wrapped around her throat and energetically choked her.

When she was done speaking her mantra, I asked her how she felt and how she felt about her breathing. She mentioned that yes, her breath felt short and her throat felt tight. I confirmed that the mantra and intention she'd just read was not giving her a financial toehold; it was actually restricting her very breath and taking the life out of her. She was surprised. So were all of us, myself included.

I asked her to return to the script of her money mantra, and out of all the words identify specific phrasing that was real and true for her. I asked her to look for anything that packed more of an energy punch, anything that glimmered.

She reviewed her notes and in the quiet of the room, suddenly blurted out, "My money truth is mine!" We all watched her stand straighter as she spoke her words. We watched power surge through her body. We heard her voice speak up from softness into an empowered voice. We witnessed her literally transforming through her new phrase, her new intention. She owned it.

CHAPTER ELEVEN

A New Money Paradigm

*The Three Dimensional (3D)
to Five Dimensional (5D) Money Shift*

I'm sure many of you can tell that through the course of this book I've been regularly inviting you across the traditional money threshold into the non-traditional one that provides ways of embracing money relationship beyond what we've always known. I'm introducing you to concepts and practices, combined in new ways, that help you understand your sense of money relationship as more. I'm taking you from what we currently know about three dimensional (3D), linear, low vibrational money, and blowing the bookends off to walk you into a vaster landscape of five dimensional (5D), multi-option money. Let's talk about what this means.

For a long time on planet Earth (centuries), we've been treating money and experiencing money in a limited fashion (linear survivalism). This treatment has included money perspectives that only fit into a 3D box of depth, width and height, meaning that 3D money is literal and linear with a "what you see is what you get" attitude. 3D money is also based in the ideology of the Gregorian calendar and the twelve-month billing cycle, giving us even more of a feeling that money only runs in a straight line and is limited to certain time periods. The wording that comes with this is, "Financially, there is only so much" and we must work inside this restricted space. This structure of 3D money creates an energy of limitation, fear-based, survival-based, scarcity-based money relationship with the heavy baggage of dread that there is no way out. This financial description and experience can be described as living in the energy of a financial prison planet mentality, where only a few hold the financial keys and many tend to suffer. Though this model is outdated, it's been held in place for so long that many believe, in their body and soul, that this is the only true money reality. But you and I both know this is not true, or I wouldn't be writing this book to you, and you would not be reading it. Hear me loud and clear when I say:

We are transforming the 3D financial prison planet energy and attitude into the new financial realities of 5D money.

Let's talk about what 5D money is, because I'm training you to knock on the door of your 5D money and have that door opened for you. We know from quantum physicists that at least twelve dimensional realities exist, even though our five senses can ascertain only three of them (width, depth, height). It's our sixth sense of intuition, psychic ability and gut instinct that knocks on the door of 4D, 5D and 6D and sees the deep, rich treasures in those dimensions. Currently, we are leaving a 3D reality basis on our planet, through an Ascension process of embodying higher vibrations, and moving into a more heart-based, higher consciousness 4D and especially 5D connections. Given that this shift is occurring, it makes sense that our finances, our money, is going to reflect this vibrational shift. Thus, we're shifting out of low vibrational, survival-level 3D money into the higher and greater vibrations of 5D consciousness-based money.

So, what does shifting from 3D money to 5D money look like? As you let go of the lower vibrational, limited, fear-based and scarcity-based baggage of 3D money (exactly why you're doing the

Somatic Money Presence Practice, resilience building, Heroine's and Hero's Journey, creating sacred money space, excavating Money Story, languaging and intent, to purge these old programs), you'll begin to notice that you can be with your money in higher vibrational, more open, more empowered ways in 5D. This shift into embodying higher frequency and greater potential with your money energy naturally gives the sensations of more and better financial options than what we're able to perceive before. It's about choice. 5D money is about creating better financial options in our lives through higher vibration, higher consciousness and more potentials – literally upgrading our lives into multi-dimensional money through deeper body work.

The processes you're practicing through this book are already giving you greater access to your 5D money:

- Through your **Somatic Money Presence Practice**, especially your breathwork and embodiment, you are **reducing your biological triggers** so that you're not responding out of financial fear. You're responding from an expanded and higher vibrational space of better energy, emotion and options for better money choices. That's 5D money leverage.

- Through **slowing down, embracing your vulnerability and building your resilience**, you're giving yourself an opportunity to peel back the layers of your money life, untangle the mess and find the juice. This process alleviates low vibrational energy and moves you into the trajectory of higher vibrational energy with greater 5D money potentials.

- Through your **Heroine's and Hero's Journey, you are unpacking and unmasking your shadow closet** and reconnecting precious energetic and emotional lines in your vulnerable psyche, putting you in touch with your authentically empowered self. The richness of this fertile ground is filled with 5D potential.

- Through **integrating your logical money skills (Masculine Money IQ) with your conscious money practices (Feminine Money EQ)**, while giving yourself the **safe and sacred money space** that you deserve, you are blending your feminine and masculine in greater co-creational ways. This is your up-level to the 5D money process.

- Through **excavating your Money Story, money language and money intent,** you are lifting the veil of ages of low vibrational 3D energy from your money picture, giving you access to your 5D financial sovereign birthright.

- Through **calling in your Money Guides,** richly vibrating your money space with light and bringing your conscious money tools to your money space, you are explosively opening the gateway to your 5D money picture.

This is the landscape where you leverage out of a tough, tired, hard-fought, tight, baggage-laden 3D money space into a 5D money space of clarity, empowerment, value, flow, creation, leverage and ease of money picture. All of these concepts, stories, ideas and processes are meant to encourage you to consider a new financial reality for yourself. That means no matter where you are along your money journey, I'm asking you to entertain the impossible. The magical. The amazing. This is where you and I, person-by-person, begin to break the shackles of 3D money and open to the far greater, richer and larger potentials of 5D money.

Resources

Developing Breathwork, Presence Practice and/or Meditation

Developing your presence practice foundation, which hopefully includes some kind of breathwork and/or meditation practice is a very personal process. It's something that is never over and always evolving as you grow. Given this, there is no need to be concerned about a right or wrong way to do this, only your best way. Your presence practice and/or meditations might run the gamut from planting your ass in your meditation space and going as deeply into your inner pool of connected quiet as possible, to walking meditations that help you anchor into your root as you walk through the great outdoors. Your breathwork might engage simple, focused breathwork exercises that bring you into your center through your day, or you might work into complex breathing programs helping you develop your breath. You might find your inner Zen through Yoga, Tai Chi, Chi Gong, Pilates or some combination of these. The point is, begin with what you are drawn to first, commit to your practice, allow yourself to deepen and explore your practice, letting it grow from there. Here are a few ideas that might help, delivered from my own collection and suggestions from my audience:

For The Science on Meditation and Awareness

- **Dr. Dan Seigel's** work in the science of awareness, including his book *Aware*, at https://www.drdansiegel.com/.

- **Daniel Goleman and Richard Davidson** explore and scientifically show the benefits of meditation in their book, *Altered Traits*.

- **Alan Fogel's** *Body Sense: The Science and Practice of Embodied Self-Awareness*.

Varying Breathwork, Awareness and Meditation Tools

- **Rebekkah LaDyne's** *The Mind-Body Stress Reset: Somatic Practices to Reduce Overwhelm and Increase Well-Being*.

- **Eckhart Tolle's** *The Power of Now*.

- There are plenty of breathwork books to select from. The one I'm drawn to is *Science of Breath – A Practical Guide* by **Rama and Rudolph Ballantine**.

- If you want video support, type in "breathwork meditation" to your browser, scroll down to videos and there is a vast collection of instructors of all ages, cultures and genders. Find the instructor who resonates with you. Through my audience, The **Wim Hof Breathing Method** came up multiple times.

- Audio that can help you journey with breath into your deeper self, through your chakras, is helpful. Try: **Jonathan Goldman's** chakra and meditation music, **Barry Goldstein's** meditation music, especially his *Ambiology* series.

- Audio meditation mantras with **Deva Premal and/or Snatam Kaur** are wonderful.

- **Insighttimer.com** has more relaxation and meditation audios than you'll ever need.

- For Yoga, Tai Chi, Chi Gong and Pilates, your best bet is to check into local classes in your area provided by local instructors. There is nothing like a commitment to the class experience for greater learning. If this is not available to you, connect with online video resources.

Presence Practice Geared for Those in PTSD/Trauma Recovery

- **Roland Bal's** work with Trauma Care that specializes in meditation and presence practices for those experiencing PTSD and are in recovery from trauma. www.rolandbal.com.

- **David Treleaven's** Trauma-Sensitive Mindfulness Training at www.davidtreleaven.com.

- **Tanya Zajdel's** work on rewiring the nervous system to heal after trauma at www.tanyazajdel.com.

I suggest that you chose one resource to begin with. Sink into that practice on a regular basis. When you're ready, shift, expand and explore. Keep it basic and simple, allowing your practice to unfold as needed.

Self-Care for All the Stages You'll Experience with Somatic Money.

The shifts you're making in your body and soul with your Somatic Money life will impact your cellular code. Yes, you heard that right. The processes we're creating here are not topical. They will potentially cause deep change that informs your DNA coding about transformation where the root of your money patterning, your Money Stories that inform your money life, is held. That means your body will need the supportive attention of energy management and self-care. So, you're going to need a self-care toolkit to support you on the days when you feel the draw-down. Make sure you have this list nearby to remind you of support resources:

1. **Hydrate.** Support your cellular code with water. As you progress through stages of the work in this book, the cellular code in your body is going through a significant shift, and one of the best supports is lubrication with H2O. Water keeps things moving and flushes out toxins from your body.

2. **Clearing with Sage or Aromatherapy.** Through the rest of your work in this book and beyond, you need bundles of sage on hand for clearing. As your deeper light field releases old energy and information, you'll want to energetically clear it from yourself and your surrounding space. Sage is a perfect way to do this. I prefer California White Sage that you can order from Amazon or get at your local holistic shop. Whenever you do deep excavation and shift work with your money relationship, be sure to sage. (Light the sage on fire with a dish underneath to catch the embers. Blow the flame out. Fan the resulting smoke around you, asking and picturing that "Any and all low vibrational energies go, go in the light of God, go in love.") It's a good idea to do this with the windows open. Make sure you completely extinguish the sage when you're done. If you are sensitive to smoke, you may use aromatherapy as a clearing agent. The mints, citrus, eucalyptus, tea trees and aromatherapy of this ilk are great for clearing.

3. **Leafy Greens.** One of your best supports for this work is high-octane nutrients, so the energy resupplied to your body is of high quality. I also like to have spirulina and chlorella powder on hand to mix with my drinks/shakes when I need a particular boost of green.

4. **Salt Baths or the Ocean.** If you've done a deep immersion at any point in this book, especially money recoding work that begins with your Money Story excavation, then you need to experience an immersion in a salt bath or the ocean. Salt is purifying and will clear the physical and energetic toxins from your body. (Be sure to hydrate when you do this.) Epsom salt baths or dips in the ocean are great ways to clear. I like working with Bokek Dead Sea Salt.

5. **White Light Clearing.** Always, as you're doing your clearing work, picture yourself completely immersed in white light. White light is protective, healing and it automatically asks DNA coding to rearrange to the highest and best configuration.

6. **Rest.** Never underestimate the value of a good night's sleep for a reset, or downtime with rest and recuperation. Sometimes, it's not a good idea to push through. Rest gives your cellular code a chance to release, reshuffle the deck and reset so that you may start anew.

7. **Angels, Guides and Ascended Masters.** Be sure to call in your Spirit Team to help you with support, guidance and protection, even in your self-care. They always know exactly what you need.

Also, do not underestimate the amount of shift you're going through, even if you say to yourself, "I don't feel anything." I've had clients do this work and tell me they don't feel anything, while I've energetically witnessed a massive change in their light field! Then, when they did not heed my self-care instructions, they became ill with a cold or flu-like symptoms as their body labored under the weight to release old, low vibrational energy and clear it from their body and energy field. Please make it a habit that anytime you do this work and feel any kind of shift, you support your body with some or all of the clearing practices I listed. Help your body by alleviating the old energy, the toxins out of your system that you do not need. Garbage out, good stuff in!

Trauma and Financial Trauma Mitigation Resources
These are some of the top suggested resources to begin with.

For Trauma Mitigation:

- **Gabor Mate's** science of compassion work at https://drgabormate.com/ and especially his videos on YouTube.

- **Stephen Porges** with the polyvagal nerve for trauma mitigation at https://www.stephenporges.com/ and especially his videos on YouTube.

- **Peter Levine** trauma mitigation work is extensively listed at about three websites and also on YouTube.

- **Mark Wolynn's** work with Family Constellations at https://www.markwolynn.com/ to help locate, alleviate and heal trauma within family lines. Also, YouTube videos.

- **Diane Poole Heller's** work with intergenerational trauma at https://dianepooleheller.com/. Of note is her Sounds True series *Healing Your Attachment Wounds*. Also, YouTube videos.

- **Rhonda V. Magee** at https://www.rhondavmagee.com/ presenting her work *The Inner Work of Racial Justice – Healing Ourselves and Transforming Our Communities Through Mindfulness*. Also, YouTube videos.

- **Thomas Hubl's** work with collective trauma (trauma experienced by groups of people) at https://thomashuebl.com/. Also, YouTube.

- **Alberto Villoldo's** soul retrieval work, especially with *Mending the Future and Healing the Past with Soul Retrieval.*

- **Tsultrim Allione's** *Cutting Through Fear* which is a Tibetan Buddhist meditation tradition to dissolve our greatest fears and attachments in life.

For Financial Trauma Mitigation:

- **Lindsay Lawless's** book *Heal Money Trauma and Create Sustainable Wealth.*

- The team at **The Trauma of Money** at www.thetraumaofmoney.com/.

- A Christian text by **Aprill Harmon** called *Money Wounds – A 28-Day Devotional to Healing Your Money Trauma.*

- Danielle Alexandria's article, *Money and Trauma: The Biggest Missing Piece of the Financial Puzzle,* September 30, 2019 on STNCE website at https://www.stnce.ca/finance/ask-an-expert/money-and-trauma/.

- *Six Trauma-Informed Financial Healing Strategies* at the website Center for Financial Social Work: https://financialsocial-work.com/downloads/six-trauma-informed-financial-heal-ing-strategies.

- *Are You Struggling with Financial PTSD: An Interview with Dr. Galen Buckwalter* at Gwyneth Paltrow's website Goop: https://goop.com/wellness/career-money/are-you-struggling-with-financial-ptsd/.

Bibliography and Notes

Preface

We kick off with:
- IQ reference is from psychology site, 123 Test at https://www.123test.com/history-of-IQ-test/.

- EQ reference is from Goleman, Daniel, *Emotional Intelligence, Why It Can Matter More Than IQ*, New York, New York, Bantom Dell, 2006.

I refer to similarly related soft-sided breakthrough money relationship books of our time as:
- Lynne Twist's, *The Soul of Money*, published by W.W. Norton & Company in New York, New York in 2003.

- Bari Tessler's, *The Art of Money*, published by Parallax Press in Berkeley, California in 2016.

- Kessel and Sherman's *The Money and Spirit Workshop*, published by Sounds True in Boulder, Colorado in 2011.

- Financial advisor and advocate, Suze Orman connects money psychology with life issues at www.suzeorman.com.

- Esther and Jerry Hicks' *Law of Attraction*, published by Hay House in Carlsbad, California in 2006.

- Dr. Joe Vitale and Dr. Hew Len's *Zero Limits,* published by John Wiley & Sons, Inc, in Hoboken, New Jersey in 2007.

Introduction

- I refer to the Somatic Money personality types based on Elaine Aron's model in *The Highly Sensitive Person-How to Thrive When the World Overwhelms You*, published by Broadway Books, in New York, New York, in 1996.

- I love physicist, Fred Wolff's energy and how he frames this idea about "living in the mystery" as quoted from the movie *What the Bleep Do We Know?* released in 2004 by Roadside Attractions and Samuel Goldwyn Films.

Chapter One – Spontaneous Financial Intervention

- I reference my own experience as similar to the story found in the movie *Groundhog Day* released in 1993, screenplay by Danny Rubin and distributed by Columbia Pictures.

Chapter Two – The Map

- The great B.B. King and his blues music as the sounds that your money relationship might be singing from your money relationship closet. His music is found at http://www.bbking.com/.

- Maurice Sendak's children's story, *Where the Wild Things Are,* as the power child and the monsters that might be in your money relationship closet. This book was published by Harper Collins Publishers in New York, New York in 1963.

- Dorothy, Toto, Tin Man, the Scarecrow, and the Lion make a cameo and stay for the rest of the book to represent Heroine's

Journey. From *The Wizard of Oz*, as written by L. Frank Baum in *The Wonderful Wizard of Oz* and adapted to movie screen by Metro-Goldwyn-Mayer Films in 1939.

- America Chavez makes a cameo, representing as an LGBTQ Latina heroine, a fictional superhero. Her character currently stars in her own ongoing series, *America*, written by Gabby Rivera as published by Marvel Comics. The series started in 2017.

- The patterning of Hero's Journey as found in several of Joseph Campbell's works including *The Hero with a Thousand Faces* published by New World Library in Novato, California in 2008.

- Also referenced is *Hero's Journey* published by New World Library in Novato, California in 1990.

- Also referenced is Joseph Campbell's *The Power of Myth* video series with Bill Moyers in 1988 on PBS.

- The feminine answering patterning to *Hero's Journey* is Maureen Murdock's *The Heroine's Journey, Woman's Quest for Wholeness*, published by Shambhala Press in Boulder, Colorado in 1990.

Examples of Heroine's and Hero's Journey stories as represented by:
- *The Wizard of Oz*, already referenced.

- And also, George Lucas' 1977 *Star* Wars released by Lucasfilm.

- Along with J.K. Rowling *Harry Potter* series, published between 1997 and 2007 by Bloomsbury Publishing in the United Kingdom.

- *Black Panther* is a 2018 Marvel Studio based on a Marvel Comics character of the same name.

- And *Captain Marvel* is a 2019 Marvel Studios film based on the Marvel comic character written by Carol Danvers.

- Creating and locating your money relationship map as symbolically represented through the *Where's Waldo* character as created by Martin Handford in his book series between 1987 to the present and published through Walker Books in the United Kingdom.

- The toxic power triangle in money relationship regularly shows up in body-based financial healing work. The Karpman Drama Triangle, developed by Stephen Karpman in 1968, was based off of Eric Berne's transactions analysis model from the 1960's: https://en.wikipedia.org/wiki/Karpman_drama_triangle.

Chapter Three – Somatic Money Presence Practice

- I mention how Eckart Tolle's thorough work of anchoring us in our present moment through his practice of *The Power of Now – A Guide to Spiritual Enlightenment* is a sound basis for practicing in your money relationship exchange space. The book was published in 2004 by New World Library in Novato, California.

- I show how the intrinsic nature of the second chakra relates to the elements of money relationship, as referenced in Anodea Judith's *Wheels of Life*. Published in 1987 by Llewellyn Publications in St. Paul, Minnesota.

Chapter Four – The Biology of Money and Triggers

- Referenced at chapter beginning, you may find George

Brauneis' gentling wild mustang work at his Eagles and Wild Horses Ranch through his Facebook page by the same name.

- *I Love Lucy*, the popular 1950's television show through CBS, starring Lucile Ball and Desi Arnaz, as a name of significance for the horse Lucifer as she transformed to Lucy.

- Mark Rashid's illuminating depictions of the horse and human relationship through the eyes of gentling work gave me deep inspiration in *Horse's Never Lie*, published in 1993 by Skyhorse publishing in New York, New York.

- This Healthline article as reference to confirm the biological fight, flight, freeze trigger: *Fight, Flight, Freeze: What This Response Means* by Kirsten Nunez as reviewed by Timothy J. Legg, Ph.D., CRNP on February 21, 2020 in website Healthline. Posted at: https://www.healthline.com/health/mental-health/fight-flight-freeze#in-the-body.

I compiled several financial trauma articles that corroborate with the financial trauma findings in Somatic Money:
- Statistical numbers from the National Sexual Violence Resource Center with report statistics from their 2015 data brief about sexual assault numbers. https://www.nsvrc.org/statistics#:~:text=The%20self%2Dreported%20incidence%20of,the%20United%20States%20in%202018.

- National Public Radio reports in a 2018 survey that over eighty percent of women in the United States have experienced sexual harassment.https://www.npr.org/sections/thetwo-way/2018/02/21/587671849/a-new-survey-finds-eighty-per-cent-of-women-have-experienced-sexual-harassment.

- Brianna Weist's article *Financial Trauma Is a Reality for One Third of Millenials* published on April 4, 2019 in Forbes https://www.forbes.com/sites/briannawiest/2019/04/04/financial-trauma-is-a-reality-for-one-third-of-millennials-this-expert-explains-how-to-recover/#5f470b37130c.

- Jody Allard's article *I spent my life in debt. Now I know childhood trauma was to blame* appears in The Guardian on June 27, 2016 at https://www.theguardian.com/commentisfree/2016/jun/27/life-in-debt-childhood-trauma-was-to-blame.

- Lindsay Dodgson's article *Using money as a weapon is financial abuse – and it's the ultimate form of manipulative control* appears in Business Insider on June 28, 2018 as she quotes Shannon Thomas' work from her book *Exposing Financial Abuse.* https://www.businessinsider.com/what-is-financial-abuse-2018-6.

- A biological article to confirm the functions of the adrenal glands by Robert M. Sargis MD, in his April 8, 2015 piece titled *An Overview of the Adrenal Glands*, posted on EndocrineWeb at https://www.endocrineweb.com/endocrinology/overview-adrenal-glands.

- When you want to look up meanings about your body and what it is saying to you, please check: Inna Segal's *The Secret Language of Your Body*, Atria Paperback of Simon and Schuster, New York, NY, 2010.

- I reference Candace Pert's *Molecules of Emotion – Why You Feel the Way You Feel* as the basis information showing the significant biological connector between our financial thoughts and the emotions we feel through our bodies. Published in 1997 by Simon and Schuster in New York, New York.

- I clarify the importance of breath as it relates to the sympathetic and parasympathetic nervous systems. Confirmed through article by Rachel Nall and reviewed by Han Seunggu MD, in the April 23, 2020 article *Your Parasympathetic Nervous System Explained* on Healthline's website at https://www.healthline.com/health/parasympathetic-nervous-system.

- Edith Zimmerman, in her May 9, 2019 article, on the website The Cut, discusses the connective root of our well-being through the vagus nerve: *I Now Suspect the Vagus Nerve Is the Key to Well-Being* at: https://www.thecut.com/2019/05/i-now-suspect-the-vagus-nerve-is-the-key-to-well-being.html.

- As I mentioned in the text, the go-to references to learn more about your psoas muscle, how trauma is stored in our root through the psoas, and exercises you can do to release and mitigate stored trauma may be found here: -Jo-Ann Staugaard-Jones' book called *The Vital Psoas Muscle* as published in 2012 by Lotus Publishing in Berkeley, California. -Also, Liz Koch's *Stalking Wild Psoas*, published by North Atlantic Books in 2019 in Berkeley, California.

Chapter Five – Vulnerability and Money

You can't say "vulnerability" without referencing Brene Brown and her incredible work as a vulnerability researcher and trainer:
- In Brown's June 2010 breakout TED Talk named *The Power of Vulnerability* at https://www.ted.com/talks/brene_brown_the_power_of_vulnerability?language=en.

- Also, Brown's presentation at Oprah Winfrey's Super Soul Sunday with *Anatomy of Trust* https://brenebrown.com/videos/anatomy-trust-video/ as referenced in Rising Strong, published in 2015 by Random House in New York, New York.

- And Brown's *Daring Greatly*, published in 2012 by Avery Books in New York, New York.

About Hero's Journey and Shadow Work:

- The patterning in Joseph Campbell's *Hero's Journey* is a key piece of the shadow world journey we all do with our money relationship. Reference to the *Hero's Journey* is sprinkled through this entire book. Published by New World Library in Novato, California in 1990.

- The feminine answering patterning to *Hero's Journey* is Maureen Murdock's *The Heroine's Journey, Woman's Quest for Wholeness*, published by Shambhala Press in Boulder, Colorado in 1990.

- The steps in Joseph Campbell's *Hero's Journey* is significantly outlined here with reference support from Reg Harris' 2017 pictorial of Hero's Journey and https://www.yourheroicjourney.com/.

- I reference *Power of Myth* as part of Joseph Campbell's *Hero's Journey* during interview conversations with Bill Moyer's on this 1988 video series.

- As a reference and resource to shadow work: Debbie Ford's *Dark Side of the Light Chasers – Reclaiming Your Power, Creativity, Brilliance and Dreams*, published by The Berkeley Publishing Group, New York, New York in 1988.

Chapter Six – Financial Masking

- As a way to imprint and confirm the good things that happen to you in your money relationship journey: the movie *happythankyoumoreplease* that was written and directed by Josh Radnor, produced by Tom Sawyer Entertainment in 2010.

Chapter Eight – Money Story

- I open the chapter referencing The Iroquois Native American Indian belief and tradition of seven generations found at multiple reference sites. Of most interest: City Year: https://www.cityyear.org/cleveland/stories/the-corps/seven-generations/ Indigenous Corporate Training: https://www.ictinc.ca/blog/seventh-generation-principle.

- How we inherit the experiences of our family lineages is scientifically described in detail through Dan Hurley's Thursday, June 25, 2015 article in Discover Magazine entitled *Grandma's Experiences Leave a Mark on Your Genes* at https://www.discovermagazine.com/health/grandmas-experiences-leave-a-mark-on-your-genes.

- I took the terminology of The Big Dig from Boston's massive road project in the late 1990's, early 2000's. Your Big Dig will financially reroute you, hopefully saving you time, money and energy. Please reference: https://en.wikipedia.org/wiki/Big_Dig.

- To assist in excavating money story from the sacred ancient sites of your past lifetimes, I refer to Graham Hancock and Santha Faiia's *Heaven's Mirror – Quest for the Lost Civilization,* Three Rivers Press, New York, 1998.

- For brushing up on shadow work, please look into Debbie Ford's *Dark Side of The Light Chasers*, Riverhead Books, New York, NY, 2010.

- The toxic power triangle in money relationship regularly shows up in body-based financial healing work. The Karpman Drama Triangle, developed by Stephen Karpman in 1968, was based off of Eric Berne's transactions analysis model from the 1960's: https://en.wikipedia.org/wiki/Karpman_drama_triangle.

Dana Stovern, Somatic Money founder and coach, brings revolution-ary body-based money relationship work to life by encouraging her clients and audiences to explore authentic money relationships with unique tools for deeper personal value. Somatic Money is Stovern's necessity of invention birthed from tragic loss, triggering her need for better life answers. She now successfully coaches professionals and business owners from across the country with innovative Somat-ic Money practices, concepts and tools. For Somatic Money classes, coaching inquiries, speaking inquiries and to learn more about Dana and Somatic Money, you may go to www.somaticmoney.com

Made in United States
Troutdale, OR
12/11/2023

15652430R00206